CAMBRIDGE TEXT?
HISTORY OF PHIL(

———

FRIEDRICH NIETZSCHE
Writings from the Late Notebooks

CAMBRIDGE TEXTS IN THE HISTORY OF PHILOSOPHY

Series editors

KARL AMERIKS

Professor of Philosophy at the University of Notre Dame

DESMOND M. CLARKE

Professor of Philosophy at University College Cork

The main objective of Cambridge Texts in the History of Philosophy is to expand the range, variety, and quality of texts in the history of philosophy which are available in English. The series includes texts by familiar names (such as Descartes and Kant) and also by less well-known authors. Wherever possible, texts are published in complete and unabridged form, and translations are specially commissioned for the series. Each volume contains a critical introduction together with a guide to further reading and any necessary glossaries and textual apparatus. The volumes are designed for student use at undergraduate and postgraduate level and will be of interest not only to students of philosophy, but also to a wider audience of readers in the history of science, the history of theology and the history of ideas.

For a list of titles published in the series, please see end of book.

FRIEDRICH NIETZSCHE

Writings from the Late Notebooks

EDITED BY

RÜDIGER BITTNER

University of Bielefeld

TRANSLATED BY

KATE STURGE

Aston University

CAMBRIDGE
UNIVERSITY PRESS

PUBLISHED BY THE PRESS SYNDICATE OF THE UNIVERSITY OF CAMBRIDGE
The Pitt Building, Trumpington Street, Cambridge CB2 1RP, United Kingdom

CAMBRIDGE UNIVERSITY PRESS
The Edinburgh Building, Cambridge, CB2 2RU, UK
40 West 20th Street, New York, NY 10011-4211, USA
477 Williamstown Road, Port Melbourne, VIC 3207, Australia
Ruiz de Alarcón 13, 28014 Madrid, Spain
Dock House, The Waterfront, Cape Town 8001, South Africa

http://www.cambridge.org

First published 2003

Printed in the United Kingdom at the University Press, Cambridge

Typeface Ehrhardt 11/13 pt   *System* LATEX 2ε   [TB]

A catalogue record for this book is available from the British Library

ISBN 0 521 80405 1 hardback
ISBN 0 521 00887 5 paperback

Contents

Contents

Acknowledgements

I wish to thank Raymond Geuss, Marie-Luise Haase and Michael Kohlenbach for helpful advice in planning the present volume, and Thorsten Engert, Steffanie Panke and Gitta Schmidt for their support in preparing the manuscript. I am especially grateful to Kate Sturge, who revised the wording of the Introduction, and to Thomas Baumeister and again Raymond Geuss, who gave the Introduction a critical reading.

Rüdiger Bittner

Abbreviations

KGW *Friedrich Nietzsche, Sämtliche Werke, Kritische Gesamtausgabe,*
     ed. G. Colli and M. Montinari (Berlin: de Gruyter, 1967–77)
AC   *The Antichrist* (*Der Antichrist*, 1895)
BGE *Beyond Good and Evil* (*Jenseits von Gut und Böse*, 1886)
D   *Daybreak* (*Morgenröte*, 1881) (also translated as *Dawn* and as
     Dawn of Day)
EH   *Ecce Homo* (*Ecce homo*, 1908)
GM   *On the Genealogy of Morality* (*Zur Genealogie der Moral*, 1887)
GS   *The Gay Science* (*Die fröhliche Wissenschaft*, 1882)
TI   *Twilight of the Idols* (*Götzen-Dämmerung*, 1889)
Z   *Thus Spoke Zarathustra* (*Also sprach Zarathustra*, 1883–85)

Introduction

Nietzsche is a writer whose work stands visibly unfinished. Others by and large completed what they had to say, but in Nietzsche's case the gap between the task he envisaged and the writing he carried out grew wider, not smaller, during his active life – and dramatically so in its last few years. Thus, the texts collected in the present volume may be taken to mark Nietzsche's frontier: this is how far he came. In what follows I will look at the history of these texts, their origin and the way they were handed down to us, as well as the way the present selection has been made. Secondly, I will indicate some of the basic lines of argumentation and some of the philosophical import of these texts.

The texts

All through his life as a writer, Nietzsche recorded his thoughts in note-books or on sheets of paper he carried with him. In this way he could keep writing virtually anywhere, and indeed he made a point of this habit (see TI Maxims 34). While the notebooks and papers contain some material of a merely occasional nature, such as travelling plans or recipes, by far the largest part deals with substantive issues. Nietzsche normally saved these notes, using them as a basis for the manuscripts of his published works, and so a large number of them were preserved. How many are missing is hard to gauge from what we have, but it would seem that a representative portion of Nietzsche's total production has survived. With a few exceptions, all these papers are now kept in the Goethe-Schiller Archive in Weimar.

The relation between Nietzsche's handwritten notes and his publications changed over his lifetime. While the published works never exhausted the content of the notes, it was only from 1885, after the completion of *Thus Spoke Zarathustra*, that the disparity between what Nietzsche wrote down in his notebooks and what he brought to a definitive form for publication grew radical. In fact, Nietzsche sensed he was becoming alienated from the medium he had hitherto relied on. 'My philosophy, if that is what I am entitled to call what torments me down to the roots of my nature, is no longer communicable, at least not in print', he wrote to Franz Overbeck on 2 July 1885. Writing down ideas in his notebooks, in contrast, seemed 'less impossible'. The notebooks became the field where Nietzsche was still able if not to communicate, then at least to express, his ideas. This is why Nietzsche's unpublished manuscript material from the last years of his productive life has been deemed worth publishing by all his editors, from the very first down to the present one.

For all his doubts about communicating his thoughts in print, Nietzsche pursued publication plans in these late years rather more vigorously than he had before. *Beyond Good and Evil* was completed in the spring of 1886 and published in the summer of that year, and *On the Genealogy of Morality* followed a year later. However, *Beyond Good and Evil* was called in the subtitle 'Prelude to a Philosophy of the Future', and Nietzsche saw *On the Genealogy of Morality* as an accompaniment to the earlier book, complementing and clarifying it, as he indicated in a note following the title page in the original edition of GM. Thus *On the Genealogy of Morality* was a supplement to *Beyond Good and Evil*, which itself was a prelude – and the philosophy of the future that these writings aimed to prepare was to be presented in a major new work. As he told his readers in GM III § 27, Nietzsche at this time intended to call it 'The Will to Power. Attempt at a Re-valuation of all Values'.

'The Will to Power' is the largest and most ambitious literary project of Nietzsche's last years, indeed of his whole life; and while it is by no means the only project he considered pursuing during those years, it is the one he worked on most consistently. Thus, he did bring it to an advanced stage of preparation. In note number 12[1], dating from early 1888 (not reprinted here), he put together a list of 374 texts, in most cases deciding which of the planned work's four books they were to go into and dividing the four books into twelve chapters. Completion of the project must have seemed within his reach at this point. Nietzsche was not really satisfied, though, with the emerging book. On 13 February 1888, telling Peter Gast that the first draft of his 'Attempt at a Re-valuation' was finished, he added: 'All in all, it was a torment. Also, I do not yet in any way have the courage for it. Ten years from now I will do it better.' He kept considering alternative ways of organising the material, until early September 1888 brought a change of plans. As shown by fragments 9[3–6], again not reprinted here, he decided to publish an extract of his philosophy that would consist of a number of finished texts previously intended for 'The Will to Power'. A major work remained on his agenda, but from now on it was always called 'Re-valuation of all Values' rather than 'The Will to Power', and was organised in a notably different way from the arrangements previously considered for 'The Will to Power'. Only a short time later, however, he divided the material into two books, one the extract proper, which eventually became *Twilight of the Idols*, and the other *The Antichrist*, which Nietzsche at the time regarded as the first book of the planned 'Re-valuation'. In other words, Nietzsche gave up his plans for a book called *The Will to Power* in the autumn of 1888.[1]

Even so, the history of the project 'The Will to Power' is important for the present purposes. For one thing, many of Nietzsche's notes from the years 1885–89 were at some time intended to form part of the book of that name. A further reason is that in 1901 Nietzsche's first editors, his sister Elisabeth Förster-Nietzsche and his friend Peter Gast, published a selection of notes from his notebooks under the title *Der Wille zur Macht* ('The Will to Power'), suggesting that this book was the execution of a plan which Nietzsche had only been prevented from completing by his illness. A much larger selection followed in 1906, and especially in this version the collection was extremely successful: it became the standard source on the late Nietzsche's thought, in spite of the fact that doubts about its philological reliability had been raised quite early on. In English, Walter Kaufmann and R. J. Hollingdale's 1967 translation of *Der Wille zur Macht* as *The Will to Power* acquired a similarly dominant position.

The Will to Power is a dubious text for several reasons. Firstly and most importantly, the evidence shows that Nietzsche abandoned the project 'The Will to Power' early in September 1888, so that publishing a book of

---

[1] The preceding is an abbreviated version of Mazzino Montinari's account, to be found in the German paperback edition of Nietzsche's collected works, an edition closely based on the KGW: *Friedrich Nietzsche, Sämtliche Werke, Kritische Studienausgabe*, ed. G. Colli and M. Montinari (Munich: Deutscher Taschenbuch Verlag / Berlin: de Gruyter, 1988), vol. 14, pp. 383–400.

this title under his name falsifies his intentions. Secondly, if we waive this objection and suppose that 'The Will to Power' remained Nietzsche's dominant concern right to the end of his writing life, it is in any case arbitrary to arrange the material, as the editors of *The Will to Power* did, in the order Nietzsche sketched in the fragment 7[64] of 1886/1887 (not reprinted here). A number of such projected tables of contents can be found in the notebooks of these years, so why choose this one in particular? It may be replied that the order sketched in 7[64] is also the basis for the list of 374 texts in fragment 12[1], mentioned above. Yet if that is the reason for using the order of 7[64], it would seem natural also to follow the detailed plan set out in 12[1], and that is not what Förster-Nietzsche and Gast did. They excluded roughly a quarter of the texts Nietzsche at that time intended to include in 'The Will to Power', some of these going instead into volumes 13 or 14 of the *Grossoktav* edition produced by the Nietzsche Archive under the direction of Elisabeth Förster-Nietzsche, but most being suppressed entirely; and a good proportion of the texts that were included suffered various changes at the hands of the editors, such as division into separate fragments or the omission of parts of the text.

An attempt was made in the 1930s to remedy this situation by publishing a critical edition, but the enterprise came to a halt after the first five volumes, which covered only the years from 1854 to 1869. It is only now, thanks to the new critical edition by Giorgio Colli and Mazzino Montinari (the 'KGW'), that we have complete and reliable German texts of all of Nietzsche's philosophical writings. The present selection of texts is based on this new edition. It invites English-speaking readers to benefit as well from the massive improvement in the availability of the texts from Nietzsche's literary estate, or *Nachlass*, an improvement owed above all to the efforts of Mazzino Montinari.

Given that the KGW is the sole source of the texts I have included here, it may be useful to indicate how it arranges the material. The whole edition is divided into eight parts, the seventh containing the *Nachlass* material from July 1882 to autumn 1885 and the eighth that from autumn 1885 to January 1889. For the sake of convenience, let us call any notebook, single sheet of paper or collection of sheets that Nietzsche used for his notes a 'manuscript'; the KGW presents the texts from the late *Nachlass* in chronological order throughout, both as regards the sequence of entire manuscripts and the sequence of texts within each manuscript. While manuscripts are normally easy to tell apart, fragments within a manuscript may not be. Sometimes Nietzsche numbered fragments or indicated in other ways where one fragment ends and another begins. Sometimes this emerges from such evidence as the position of text on the page, the style of the handwriting, or similar clues, but sometimes the matter really is not clear. The division of the text into fragments was made by the KGW editors, taking such evidence into account wherever it existed.

The KGW numbers manuscripts chronologically within each part and, in turn, numbers the texts within each manuscript chronologically. The present volume offers a selection of texts dating from between April 1885 and January 1889, which are taken from the latter part of the seventh and the whole of the eighth part of the KGW. Manuscripts numbered 34 and higher are taken from the seventh part, those numbered 1–18 from the eighth. The manuscript number is followed in each case by the chronological fragment number in square brackets. The reason for drawing the starting line at the seventh part, manuscript 34 is the fact that this manuscript marks the beginning of the post-*Zarathustra* phase, which differs markedly, both in substance and in style, from Nietzsche's previous writing; and as I have mentioned, it is the post-*Zarathustra* Nietzsche whose philosophical projects, no longer finding adequate expression in his published writing, have to be gathered from the notebooks.

Let me repeat that this volume offers a *selection* of texts dating from 1885 to 1889. In contrast to Förster-Nietzsche and Gast, I do not pretend that the collection presented here forms a whole, let alone a whole fulfilling Nietzsche's true intentions at any point in his life. As far as we can tell, Nietzsche had no clear, settled and detailed intentions that might be followed in forming a book out of this material. What we have are fragments, and it is of fragments that the present selection consists. It should also be noted that this is a small selection: speaking very approximately, this volume may contain something in the order of a third of Nietzsche's handwritten material from the period.

Individual fragments, in contrast, have not been used selectively. They always appear here in their entirety, with two kinds of exception. The first is that Nietzsche's own occasional numbering of his texts has been deleted throughout, to avoid confusion with the editors' numbering. The second kind of exception concerns notebook 7, of 1886–87. In this manuscript Nietzsche later, in the autumn of 1888, assembled several of his texts under chapter headings derived from the plan for 'The Will to Power' set out in 18[17], and the editors of the KGW decided to treat as one fragment all the texts that Nietzsche placed in one chapter. Given how disparate some of those texts are, this does not seem convincing. I thus felt free to take apart these overly large 'fragments' and include separately some of the texts they contained.

The texts are given here, as in the KGW, in chronological order. The KGW's numbering of the fragments has been retained, since the literature now always refers to Nietzsche's *Nachlass* texts by these numbers. Of course, the selectivity of the present collection means that here the numbers do not form a continuous sequence, only an ordered one.

Turning now to the material considerations guiding the present selection, the chief criterion for including a text here was its philosophical import – and not its historical or, more particularly, biographical interest. My aim was not to offer information about the development of Nietzsche's thought in this period or about the changes in his plans for a major work. Instead, the present collection is intended to serve those readers wishing to know what Nietzsche has to say on a number of topics and also whether what he says is true. Their interest may focus not really on Nietzsche himself but rather on his thoughts.

Hence, none of the many title pages that Nietzsche envisaged for future books has been included. Neither have projected tables of contents, lists of aphorisms and the like. For the same reason, earlier versions of texts eventually published in Nietzsche's books of these years have not been admitted, except where it seemed that the differences between the earlier and final versions could be illuminating. Nietzsche's excerpts from other authors, filling much of manuscript 11, for example, were excluded – again, except where Nietzsche's noting a passage from another author would appear to shed special light on his own thought. To be sure, I may have violated this rule unwittingly: probably not all of Nietzsche's quotes have been identified as such (and those identified have not all been traced to their sources).

For similar reasons, Nietzsche's reflections on himself and his life, not very numerous anyway, have been left aside. Exceptions to this rule are a number of notes which, on the face of it, seem merely to deal with particulars of Nietzsche's life, but in fact also provide a glimpse of some Nietzschean concern or assumption that is philosophically revealing (the very first note in the present selection, 34[3], is a case in point).

Men, women excluded sine for N not philosophical

Following the criterion of philosophical import also meant entirely neglecting a number of themes to which Nietzsche devoted some attention in his writing, like that of men and women, or of 'peoples and fatherlands', as *Beyond Good and Evil* phrases it. To the best of my understanding, Nietzsche had nothing of interest to say on either of these matters – nothing of philosophical interest, that is. His views on women and on Germans, say, suffer from reckless generalising; to be more precise they are chauvinist. As such they may yield some interest for the historian of ideas, showing how deep these prejudices go in the late nineteenth century, even in an individual of so critical a cast of mind as Nietzsche. For someone interested in the topics themselves, Nietzsche's writings offer no enlightenment.

chau-vinist !!

This raises the question of which topics the late Nietzsche does have enlightening things to say about. I shall try to answer that question in the remainder of the Introduction, in broad strokes of course, indicating a number of threads running through the material collected here and showing their philosophical importance. I shall suggest, moreover, that these threads have a common starting-point and that there is a central task Nietzsche is pursuing in his late writings.

The task

naturalism

The task Nietzsche sets himself is to work out a comprehensive and credible naturalism. In BGE § 230 Nietzsche declares that we, 'free, *very free* spirits', have chosen the task of 'translating man back into nature'. The metaphor bears closer attention. Translating back is what you might do if the text you have is a translation, but a bad one: you might try to retrieve the original from the distorted version in your hands. Translating back is not a kind of translating. It does not aim to preserve as much as possible of the text we have before us, as translations do, but instead to recover what that text has failed to preserve. It is an 'untranslating', by analogy, say, to 'untying'. Without the metaphor, then, Nietzsche is saying that traditional conceptions give a distorted picture of what man is, indeed a rosy and flattering one, as he goes on to suggest; and the free spirits' chosen undertaking is to bring to light what was misrepresented in those conceptions. As an Enlightenment writer, Nietzsche both intends and hopes to cast off the misconceptions we have inherited. As a critical

N's point

↑ !! N's task

writer, he does not presume to do this simply on the strength of deciding to; he does not pretend to say immediately what, viewed without distortions, man is. Bringing that to light means having to take the detour through traditional misconceptions. It means untranslating them.

Looked at this way, the polemical attitude implicit in many of the texts collected here becomes intelligible. It is not that Nietzsche frequently attacks particular figures. Rather, he seems to be constantly up in arms against enemies none the less enraging for remaining unnamed. Nowhere in these pages do we find a writer at peace, which Nietzsche often pretended to be and sometimes, perhaps unwittingly, actually was. This is not because Nietzsche had a warrior nature, as he claimed in *Ecce Homo* (Why I am so wise § 7). What we know suggests that he did not, and the passage from *Ecce Homo* is embarrassing to read not because of its arrogance, but because of its blindness. The polemical character of the writings presented in this collection has less to do with Nietzsche in particular than with the situation he faces: error can no longer be traced to a specific source, for instance the fraudulent despots and hypocritical priests of the classic Enlightenment scenario, and thus can no longer be rebutted in a polemical *hors d'oeuvre* which then gives way to an unperturbed statement of the truth. Instead, error is now in the air, and any conception of ourselves we are offered is likely to be one of the high-flown interpretations that, according to BGE § 230, tradition scribbled and painted over the original text of man as nature. What we are can only be recovered by fighting those interpretations.

However, the objective of our fight can be gathered, negatively, from the promises of the seductive voices in BGE § 230 to which Nietzsche asks us to turn a deaf ear: 'You are more! You are higher! You are of a different origin!' Accordingly, the naturalisers must be telling us: you are nothing more, nothing higher, not of a different origin – which, in turn, leaves us wondering: nothing more and higher than what, of an origin no different from what? This is precisely what the naturalisation project will have to determine: the contours of natural man which, once found, will permit us to dismiss as a mere product of human vanity any richer conception of ourselves. Nietzsche's project, then, is reductive. What he envisages is a human self-understanding in radically more modest terms than those traditionally employed. 'Reduction' is to be taken here not in one of the technical meanings current in chemistry and in philosophy of science, but in the ordinary sense where people are told to reduce their

weight: naturalisers invite us to cut back to the lowest level the conceptual
expenses incurred in understanding ourselves.

Nietzsche is convinced that this basic conceptual level – poor but adequate, indeed singularly illuminating, for understanding ourselves – is that of the concepts we use to describe living things. To naturalise something is to understand it in terms of life. This is one reason why his reductive stance differs from that of contemporary reductionists – differs so much, indeed, that many will baulk at hearing him called a reductionist at all. Actually, there should be no quarrel here. Reduction in the general sense was certainly his enterprise. When, in that passage from BGE § 230, he describes the task at hand as that of mastering 'the many conceited and high-flown interpretations and secondary meanings scribbled and painted to this day over the eternal basic text of man as nature', the word 'high-flown' (*schwärmerisch*) leaves no doubt that philosophers are going to see their conceptual wings clipped. Nietzsche's aim was not reduction in the stronger and more specific sense current today, reduction of the kind that eliminates mental terms in favour of physical ones or, more relevantly, concepts of life processes in favour of those of mechanical or electrical processes. He saw no reason to think that mechanical processes could account for life.

Quite the contrary, he saw reason to think that there is no such thing as a merely mechanical process. Pursuing 'the human analogy consistently to the end', he held that the concept of force needs supplementing with an inner side, and that motion is a mere symptom of inner events.[2] A mechanistic reduction was thus a case of putting the cart before the horse. There is nothing deeper for our understanding to turn to than processes of life. It would be misleading to express this by saying that Nietzsche's naturalism is biologistic. After all, he found plenty to disagree with in the biology of his day, even if the notes from his last years, especially, show him deeply indebted to the ideas of biologists. It would be better to say that Nietzsche's naturalism is the commitment to a philosophy that is, from beginning to end, a philosophy of life. ' "Being" –', he notes in 2[172], 'we have no other idea of this than "*living*".'

In this way, Nietzsche's chosen task of translating man back into nature becomes more specific, as the task of understanding some of the basic phenomena of human existence in terms of life. This task can only be

---

[2] See 36[31]; also 34[247], 1[28], 2[69].

completed in a responsible way on the basis of a viable understanding of life. Hence Nietzsche writes: 'here a new, more definite version of the concept "life" is needed' (2[190]).

That passage continues: 'My formula for it is: life is will to power.'[3] While in the late notes other famous notions from Nietzsche's earlier writings loom much less large than before, the will to power is their central theme. The book that Nietzsche intended to write in this period would certainly have borne the right title.

Will to power

The first difficulty that might strike readers here is the phrasing: why 'will *to* power' and not 'of' or 'for'? In fact, 'will to power' does mean 'will for power': a will to power is a will such that the thing willed is power.[4] The expression 'will to power' was presumably modelled on Schopenhauer's 'will to life', to which Nietzsche's concept was meant to be the counterpart.[5]

The term 'will to power' may have recommended itself for a less respectable reason as well. As GM III § 28, for example, shows, Nietzsche had a tendency to regard the meaning of something, in the sense used in phrases like 'the meaning of human existence', as something one would refer to in answering the question 'To what end such and such?', in this case 'To what end human existence?' The expression 'will to power', then, unlike the other expressions that would have been possible, had the advantage of seeming to banish the threat of meaninglessness: this will is not in vain, because it is a will to something, namely to power. The reasoning is doubly fallacious: meaning and purpose may or may not coincide and, above all, purpose and content are two different things. Still, it may have been this reasoning which made the phrasing attractive.

---

3 Similarly, BGE § 13. The connection between the idea of translating man back into nature (BGE § 230) and the doctrine of will to power is confirmed, if somewhat laconically, by 2[131]: 'Homo natura. The "will to power".'

4 For evidence see GM II § 12 and, in the present collection, fragments 14[79], 14[121], 14[174]. Also revealing is the earlier note IV 23[63], dating from 1876/77 and thus not included here, where Nietzsche uses 'will to power' without terminological weight. There it clearly means a person's state of willing power.

5 Z II, Of Self-Overcoming, makes this evident. For Schopenhauer, see Arthur Schopenhauer, *Die Welt als Wille und Vorstellung*, 3rd edn (Leipzig: Brockhaus, 1859), § 54.

different
claims

A further question is what precisely is asserted in the doctrine of will to power, for Nietzsche puts forward different claims in different passages. One is the claim in GM II § 12:

1) GM

> that all that happens in the organic world is an *overpowering*, a *becoming master*.

The natural way to read this would be as saying that however different the things happening in the organic world otherwise are, they share this character of being overpowerings. The cat's purring, my making breakfast, Michael's falling asleep, they all are overpowerings. This, however, can hardly be what Nietzsche has in mind, for two reasons. For one thing, he would in effect be applying a distinction between how things appear and how they are – precisely the distinction he attacks so forcefully in other passages. He must be applying that distinction, for there seems to be no other way to make sense of the statement that this event is a cat's purring together with the statement that this event is an overpowering, unless we add such riders as 'on the face of it', 'appears to be' on the one hand, and 'really', 'essentially' on the other.

not

The second reason not to follow GM II § 12's exposition here is that in this reading, the doctrine of will to power would not satisfy Nietzsche's intention in turning from a mechanistic understanding of events to one put in terms of life; and, remember, will to power was to be 'the new, more definite version of the concept "life" '. As he says in 36[31], Nietzsche turned to life, and thus to will to power, as a way of supplementing with an inner side, even 'an inner world', the 'force' spoken of by the physicists. However, what happens in the organic world does not acquire an inner side simply by virtue of being an overpowering. An overpowering is as much an outer event as the cat's purring is.

2)

2[103]

Zarathustra, in the speech on self-overcoming, propounded a different version of the doctrine of will to power:

3) Z

> Where I found a living thing, there I found will to power.

However, he evidently puts it this way in order to give himself a smoother argument for his claim that even those who serve and obey are inspired by a will to power. For the larger theoretical purposes that Nietzsche pursues in other passages, this version is certainly too weak. If the will to power is

4

only something to be found, possibly alongside other things, in everything living, we cannot reach anything like the famous line in 38[12]:

This world is the will to power – and nothing besides!

A more promising thought comes from 14[121]:

> That there is considerable enlightenment to be gained by positing power in place of the individual 'happiness' each living thing is supposed to be striving for: 'It strives for power, for an augmentation of power'.[6]

The interesting suggestion here is that will to power should be understood not, as in GM II § 12, as a uniform *character*, but as a uniform kind of *source* of whatever happens in the organic world. Aristotle taught that in all their actions, humans strive for one highest goal, which is happiness; and while he denied that non-human animals are capable of happiness, both Schopenhauer and the Utilitarians suggested that they pursue happiness as we do, though they find it in different things. Substituting in this statement 'power' or 'increase of power' for 'happiness', and extending the range of creatures who share the striving from all animals to everything that lives, we arrive at Nietzsche's doctrine of the will to power. In this reading, then, the doctrine maintains that any living thing does whatever it does for the sake of gaining power or of augmenting the power it already has.

This reading does supplement the physicists' notion of force with an inner world, as required in 36[31]. It is not that the living only do things of a certain sort. Rather, they do things – a great variety of things – with an intention of a certain sort; and if anything can be called inner, it is an intention like this. Moreover, at least some of Nietzsche's sweeping statements on the will to power become, if not derivable, at least intelligible with this reading. 'Life is will to power', we read earlier (2[190]), but this statement is certainly not true: something's being alive and its striving for more power remain two different things, and would do even if they were always found together. Still, 'life is will to power' is an understandable overstatement of the claim that, in everything they do, living things strive for more power. Finally, this reading is strongly supported by one of Nietzsche's published statements of his doctrine, BGE § 36. This passage

---

[6] See also 11[111].

considers the possibility that 'all organic functions can be derived from this will to power'; if they could, it continues, we would be entitled to hold that 'all effective force is nothing other than: will to power'. Like the present reading, then, BGE § 36 takes will to power to be not a shared character, but a shared kind of source, of what happens in the organic world.

It might now be asked what grounds Nietzsche believed he had for moving, within BGE § 36, from the statement that 'all organic functions' spring from the will to power to the statement that 'all effective force' does so. Similarly, in 14[121], having said that living things strive for power or for more power, he goes on to claim

> That all driving force is will to power, that there is no physical, dynamic or psychological force apart from this.

Again, in GM II § 12 the domain of the will to power is abruptly extended from 'all that happens in the organic world' to 'all that happens'. What could seem to justify these swift transitions? Nietzsche had no qualms here because, as mentioned earlier, he rejected the very idea of a merely mechanical event:

> one must understand all motion [...] as mere symptoms of inner events (36[31]).

Thus all motion, organic or not, has an inner side; and once it is established that in the organic world this inner side is will to power, it may seem a small step to claim that it is will to power in all that happens. The difference between the organic and the inorganic world is superficial, since it does not touch on the inner sources of things happening. The somewhat cavalier fashion in which Nietzsche proceeds here may be explained by the fact that in this point he is following his 'great teacher Schopenhauer' (GM Preface 5), who was quite as swift to claim that 'it is one and the same will that manifests itself both in the forces of inorganic and the forms of organic nature.'[7] As far as its scope is concerned, Nietzsche's 'will to power' simply takes over the place of Schopenhauer's 'will'.

The great defect of the present reading is that, understood this way, the doctrine of will to power has no chance of being true. Take the animals we know best, humans: there seem to be no good grounds whatsoever for

---

7 Schopenhauer, *Die Welt*, vol. I, § 27, p. 170; see also § 23, pp. 140–41.

saying that power is what they strive for in everything they do, even if it should be true to say that whenever they succeed in what they do they feel better or indeed more powerful. True, neither is it happiness they are striving for in whatever they do. Nietzsche is certainly right to say that 'Man does *not* strive for happiness' (TI Maxims 12). Our experience shows that humans do not strive for any one thing at all; instead, different people, and the same people at different times, and indeed the same people at the same time, strive for different things. To say that these different things only represent various amounts of power seems arbitrary, for why should ice-cream be, or represent, power? The reply is sometimes made that it is never the ice-cream, but one's showing oneself to be master over the ice-cream, that is sought for.[8] In fact, though, this is not our experience. What we find ourselves pursuing is the thing, not the fact of having subdued it. Nor would it be easy to explain along these lines why the demand for ice-cream tends to go up on hot days: after all, the pleasures of mastery should be independent of the temperature. Indeed, in the case of some things we strive for, it makes little sense to speak of 'mastering' them at all. If, say, relief from the constant stress in your office is what you are after, then even when you have achieved it this will not count as having subdued it; and thus neither did you strive to subdue it before you had achieved it.

While it is a defect that the present reading makes the doctrine of will to power come out false, it is not a decisive one: I see no reading intelligible in itself and reasonably true to the texts that does better. The will to power as a theory is really sunk, just as the book of that title is – and perhaps the book sank because the theory did. The theory is Nietzsche's belated attempt to be a 'philosopher' of the sort he simultaneously denounces. It is a piece of mummification, of Egypticism, to use his own terms in TI Reason 1. It is no less 'mummifying' to cut down the variety of things striven for by humans – and by living things in general – to that one thing, power, than to arrest the diversity of shapes a thing may exhibit over time, as the philosophers do. To be sure, Nietzsche's will to power is not a single thing, and is present only in the manifold willings to power; to indicate this, Nietzsche often uses phrases like 'points of will' (11[73]), 'dynamic quanta' (14[79]) or 'quanta of will' (14[82]). Still, the claim that all the willings originating change are willings for *power* displays a

---

[8] In 9[151] Nietzsche may be read as taking this line himself.

why WP
philosophical

generalisation, a simplification, a making uniform as ruthless as any that Nietzsche criticised.

This may explain why Nietzsche, at times proclaiming the thesis that life is will to power as an established truth,[9] is curiously coy about it at other times, as in BGE § 36, where the doctrine is insistently presented as a mere hypothesis. It is quite likely that Nietzsche actually was divided about his idea, on the one hand too eagerly hoping to have found the philosophical solution to all the riddles of the world (38[12]) not to persuade himself again and again that he had indeed done so; on the other hand too critical to believe that things are really as simple as that idea makes them.

hypo-thesis
in § BGE

The reason Nietzsche's idea of the will to power is so philosophically significant, then, is not that it describes the world's 'intelligible character' (BGE § 36) or 'the innermost essence of being' (14[80]) – in fact it does no such thing. It is significant because it served Nietzsche as the conceptual basis, albeit a much too narrow conceptual basis, for his attempt to reinterpret human existence in terms of life. It served him as the grammar of the target language when he tried to 'translate man back into nature' (BGE § 230). That Nietzschean attempt, in turn, is philosophically significant not because it was the first or even the only one of its kind at the time, for in fact it belongs to the broad movement towards a 'philosophy of life' dominant in Continental Europe in the late nineteenth and early twentieth centuries. It is significant because of its radicality. And while 'will to power' was too narrow a translation manual, what he did in using it is not only a remarkable feat, but also philosophically illuminating. For while not 'all driving force is will to power' (14[121]), some certainly is; and more importantly, the translating back that Nietzsche did on the basis of the concept of will to power provides a model for similar attempts to be undertaken today, on a less restricted conceptual basis. This implies that the task is not yet completed, and that it remains a task for philosophy.

not

as grammar
tool
Phil. of Life

Coming to know

Turning now to Nietzsche's reinterpretation of basic phenomena of human existence in terms of life, I shall limit myself to two topics. One is cognition, the other religion and morality; I will leave aside such themes as art and history for reasons of space. In fact, even if Nietzsche considered

---

[9] Notably in Z II, Of Self-Overcoming, but also in, for instance, 14[82] and 14[121].

'will to power' the central concept in understanding living things, he did not cast all his reinterpretations of cognition, or of morality and religion, in terms of this doctrine. 'Will to power' was to be his 'philosophy', in the dubious sense of the word touched upon earlier; but he did not allow his philosophy to regiment all of his thought. In this respect he was right about himself when he claimed to mistrust and avoid system-builders (TI Maxims 26).

However, cognition is based on will to power in 2[90]:

> On the understanding of *logic::: the will to sameness is the will to power.*
>
> – the belief that something is thus and thus, the essence of *judgement*, is the consequence of a will that as far as possible it *shall* be the same.[10]

Knowledge involves judgement, for Nietzsche as for the philosophical tradition; and judgement, he tells us here, involves believing that something is thus and thus. But according to this passage, such believing is based on willing things to be such and such. Since this willing is a kind of will to power, knowledge is based on will to power.

Why, though, does Nietzsche speak of sameness here, as in fact he does quite often in this context, if what he means is inherence, that is, the relation between a property and a thing having that property? It is inherence that he means, for otherwise the inserted phrase 'the essence of judgement' would make no sense.[11] As we can use 'is' both to indicate identity and to indicate inherence, Nietzsche probably confused the two. The claim he is putting forward here is actually that *believing* things to be thus and thus rests on *willing* things as far as possible to be thus and thus. The material question now is why this should be so. Why should it not be possible simply to consider things to be such and such, with no willing involved?

Nietzsche notes in 7[54]:

> Knowledge as such impossible within becoming; so how is knowledge possible? As error about itself, as will to power, as will to deception.[12]

The verdict here 'knowledge as such impossible' is not based on the traditional epistemological scruple that we can never justify our beliefs

---

[10] See also 1[125].   [11] This reading is also supported by 4[8].
[12] 36[23] presents a similar line of thought.

against all reasonable doubts, but on metaphysical worries. In a world of becoming, Nietzsche says, knowledge does not find a foothold. It is not that everything changes so fast that knowledge cannot keep pace with what happens. It can: we do describe things moving, despite Zeno's paradoxes. The idea is that in a world of becoming, there are no knowables.[13] For in a world of becoming there is no being.[14] The sense in which there is no being is not that there is no reality underlying or encompassing things, but simply that things fail to be *thus and thus*. The very idea of something being thus and thus, of being some way, is inadmissible.

Given that being, in the humble predicative sense of the word, is not to be found in the world, how do we come to speak of it all the time? Nietzsche's answer is that we put it in. We 'made' the world 'to be' (9[91]); not in the sense of calling it into existence, certainly (although Nietzsche occasionally does use the vocabulary of creating), but in the sense of imprinting upon it the schema of things being some way (9[97]).

We put being into the world, and we did it 'for practical, useful, perspectival reasons' (11[73]). We need a world of this kind. We could not live in a world of sheer becoming, so we posit being, to preserve ourselves.[15] The being of things, posited rather than found, is only '*a perspectival illusion*' (9[41]), however – it is prompted only by our needs. Still, it is the illusion that provides the basis for any truth. Hence Nietzsche's intentionally shocking claim:

> *Truth is the kind of error* without which a particular kind of living creature could not live. The value for life is what ultimately decides.[16]

In accordance with the programmatic statement in BGE § 230, then, Nietzsche does understand cognition in terms of life. His argument runs as follows. Knowledge involves believing that something is thus and thus. Such believing is always false, since this is a world of becoming, and in such a world there is no being thus and thus. Hence we do not find such being, but posit it; and we do this because we could not live without it. We thus know only because we live and try to keep on living – without that, cognition would not encounter anything knowable.

[13] This, I take it, is the point Nietzsche is expressing, not very happily, when he says that 'the world is false', for example in 9[91].
[14] See 14[93] on this point.
[15] This line of reasoning also appears in 34[49], 34[247], 36[23] and 14[93].
[16] 34[253]. A similar line of thought appears in BGE § 4 and, much earlier, in the eighth paragraph of the essay 'On Truth and Lying in a Non-Moral Sense' (1873).

Several things call for comment here, of which I shall take up three. First, this understanding of cognition in terms of life does not amount to a pragmatic theory of truth, as various writers have suggested. A pragmatic theory of truth holds that a statement is true just in case it fulfils certain needs or desires; for example, just in case it enhances one's feeling of power. While there are passages that support the ascription of such a view to Nietzsche,[17] it does seem to be incompatible with other passages, for example his insistence, in 11[108], that 'the truth is ugly'. Materially speaking, Nietzsche would seem to be on the right track with the latter statement, and not with the former: perhaps *the* truth is not ugly, but certainly some truths are. The argument I outlined in the previous paragraph shows where the pragmatic interpretation goes wrong. The pragmatic line of interpretation requires any putative piece of knowledge to furnish proof of some service rendered. But in the present line of argument, it is not individual statements which earn their status by being useful. Instead, it is the form of knowability, that is, things being some way, which, once projected onto the world, satisfies a basic need we have.

For all his polemic against Kant, in this respect Nietzsche continues the tradition of transcendental philosophy. Kant's concern was to understand the objectivity of judgements in general, not to establish standards of justification for particular judgements. Similarly, when Nietzsche writes

> We are 'knowers' to the extent that we are able to satisfy our needs (34[46])

he is not suggesting that we satisfy our needs statement by statement. His point is that in general we hold the position of knowers who confront knowables because we need to do so. Just as in Kant the objectivity of judgements is partly our own doing, so in Nietzsche we ourselves posit the needed being of things. Kant and Nietzsche differ in the kind of danger that is being warded off: in Kant's view a world without the form of objectivity would be unintelligible for us, while in Nietzsche's a world without being would be unliveable for us. Nietzsche has thus granted life the position that understanding used to hold, but on the new basis transcendental conditions of knowledge are provided, just as before.

Secondly, this understanding of cognition in terms of life does not feature the will to power, even though, as we saw above, life was supposed

[17] For example 34[264] and 9[91].

to be essentially will to power. Instead, Nietzsche's argument turns on our seeking to preserve ourselves, which is a different thing.[18] He does not, then, abide by the strategy of parsimony of principles that led him (or so he claims in BGE §§ 13 and 36) to make will to power the sole moving force among living things. And there are good reasons for him to abandon it. It is not credible that by sheer exuberance of force we should have turned a world of becoming into a world of things being some way, that the 'narrower, abridged and simplified world' (9[41]) we have set up should have been born from an urge to show our strength – the urge characteristic of will to power, according to BGE § 13. The origin of a world made to be is not ecstatic overflowing (14[89]) but need.

Yet this need is life's need, just as it is life which expresses itself in ecstatic overflowing. This is to say that Nietzsche's concept of life is ambivalent, and so is the attempted interpretation of basic phenomena of human existence in terms of life. The fullness of life manifests itself in boundless unbelief and 'freedom of the mind' (9[39]), in denying anything to be this way rather than another (9[41]). On the other hand, in 9[91] 'life is founded on the presupposition of a belief in things lasting and regularly recurring', and 'logicising, rationalising, systematising' are taken 'as life's resources'.[19] Nietzsche failed to make up his mind as to which kind of life he meant,[20] thus leaving his project of reinterpretation indeterminate.

Thirdly, the central premise of Nietzsche's argument is not justified, and neither is it self-evident. This premise has it that ours is a world of becoming which 'could not, in the strict sense, be "grasped", be "known"' (36[23]) and into which things' being some way could only be 'inserted' (11[73]). People generally assume the opposite. They suppose that snow comes as white, and that we have not had to trim things into such shapes for the sake of preserving ourselves. Now, Nietzsche knows that people think this way, and indeed his argument explains why they do so. Yet why could they not just be right, which would also explain it, and more simply?

Nietzsche never said why not. He did, though, indicate what kind of suspicion such a line of thought would prompt – that of wishful thinking.

---

[18] See BGE § 13, also 14[82].

[19] A similar line of thought already appears in GS § 111 and in BGE § 24.

[20] This duality of conceptions of life is related to the opposition of Dionysos and Apollo in Nietzsche's early *The Birth of Tragedy*, which is taken up in the late notes, e.g., 2[106]. In a curious way it returns in Nietzsche's self-characterisation in 7[23].

It is just too good to be true that what we encounter should be things with properties.[21] Nietzsche, in contrast, often saw himself as a sceptic, wary above all of falling for 'fat and good-natured desirabilities' (BGE § 39), and things' being some way seemed to be one of those. In this passage of *Beyond Good and Evil*, he goes on to remind us that the same holds for the negative case. Just as the desirable need not obtain, neither is the harmful and dangerous precluded from obtaining. He does not, however, go on to remind himself that the opposite statement is also true. No, the desirable is not bound to hold nor the undesirable to be absent; but neither is the undesirable bound to hold and the desirable to be absent. Desirabilities are, literally, neither here nor there. In never even entertaining the thought that this might be a world of things being some way, and thus a world ready for cognition, Nietzsche was bracing himself for an epistemological worst case scenario. Now, however, without the need for such a heroic stance, we no longer need to imagine that beyond our garden of things being some way there are tigers roaming, chaos reigning or, more philosophically, a world of sheer becoming.[22] In fact, it would seem to be in the spirit of naturalism, in the sense explained above, to reject such notions. If man as nature is the basic text we are trying to restore, it is more likely that the world is already humanly intelligible, and is not only made to be so by us. Where else but at the world's knee should we have acquired our understanding of what we encounter?

Living well

Nietzsche's project of 'translating man back into nature' required a reinterpretation of the phenomena of religion and morality. Indeed, perhaps there was nothing it required more urgently. The supernatural stands at the centre of the dominant religious tradition of the West, Christianity, and ever since Christianity acquired its dominant position, morality too has been understood as independent from, if not opposed to, the course of nature. In religion and morality Nietzsche very properly saw the chief fortress to attack under the banner of 'man as nature'. And that is what he did: to no topic, probably, did he devote more attention in his late notes

---

[21] That this is Nietzsche's view is suggested by passages like GS § 109; BGE §§ 2, 5, 25, 34, 39; 7[54].

[22] For the tiger see 'On Truth and Lying in a Non-Moral Sense', third paragraph; for chaos GS § 109.

than this one. Likewise, most of his published writings of the period deal, largely or exclusively, with religion and morality, as their titles show: 'Beyond Good and Evil', 'On the Genealogy of Morality', 'Twilight of the Idols', 'The Antichrist'.

In fact, given this series of works published or, in the case of *The Antichrist*, intended for publication by Nietzsche himself, one might wonder why the unpublished notes on these topics still deserve consideration: did he not exploit them to the full in the published books? The fact is that he did not. The published writings, probably for purposes of exposition, draw their lines starkly, while the notes admit of contingencies and alternatives, thereby producing a subtler and indeed more credible picture. An instance of this is relevant at this point. I have been speaking of 'religion and morality' as if these formed one topic, and the published Nietzsche often writes this way, for instance passing smoothly, in the arguments of *Genealogy* II and III, over the difference between them. It is the unpublished Nietzsche who reminds us that 'in itself, a religion has nothing to do with morality' (2[197]). Thus, the link between religion and morality, taken for granted in the published writings, is really accidental, something resulting from the peculiarity of Christianity (and Islam) in being

> *essentially* moral religions, ones that prescribe how we *ought* to live and gain a hearing for their demands with rewards and punishments. (2[197])

It would therefore be a mistake to read *Genealogy* and *The Antichrist* as presenting a philosophy of religion. In joining morality and religion as intimately as they do, they show themselves to be concerned above all with Christianity. True, the notes do not cast their net substantially wider: reflections on religion in general are rare, and Christianity is the focus throughout. Yet by distinguishing between the special case of Christianity as a moral religion and religion as such, the notes, despite their critique of Christianity, open the space for a positive conception of religion – positive, that is, with respect to life. Nietzsche never filled that space. He did, though, frequently use terms like 'God' and, especially, 'divine' without the dismissive tone one would expect in a critic of religion, often even with glowing enthusiasm.[23] Indeed, he can occasionally be found defending the truly divine against its Christian detractors.[24]

---

[23] See, for instance, 2[107], 14[11], 14[89]; see also GM II § 23.   [24] See 10[90], 11[95], 11[122].

A distinction similar to that between Christianity and religion also needs to be drawn in the case of Nietzsche's critique of morality, a point that does appear in the published writings, but becomes especially clear in the notes. Contrary to what many passages, published and unpublished, suggest,[25] the target of Nietzsche's critique is actually not morality, it is *a* morality. Consider 10[86]: here we have, on the one hand, 'the modest virtues' of 'little people' exalted by Jesus and Paul, and on the other 'the more valuable qualities of virtue and of man' which became discredited in the process. What Nietzsche is calling into question here is one morality, that of the little people, in contrast to another, the one with the more valuable qualities. He is evidently not calling into question morality *tout court* or 'all morality' (GM Preface 6).

On the contrary, he insists that we do need some morality.[26] His argument runs like this. A morality is an ordering of human traits and actions by the relation 'better than'. Such orderings tell people what is likely to preserve them, to make them grow or make them decline. Knowing that, however, is itself a part of your strength, less by saving you from mistakes than by giving an interpretation of yourself and the world that answers to your needs and aspirations. A morality allows you to make practical sense of the world: you know where *your* hopes and *your* dangers lie, and that consciousness makes your life a better one. Thus you need a morality, since you grow by knowing what you are and where you are heading.[27]

Actually, the need for morality is normally a social rather than an individual need:

> Up to now a morality has been, above all, the expression of a conservative will to breed the same species. (35[20])

As the context indicates, 'species' does not here mean a kind of animal, but a community of humans. So in the human case, breeding works with

---

[25] This applies notably to the title of GM, which should read *On the Genealogy of a Morality*. The title of BGE may also mislead, as Nietzsche admits by expressly insisting that 'Beyond Good and Evil' does not mean 'Beyond Good and Bad' (GM I § 17). See also passages in 5[98], 10[45], 10[192].

[26] 35[17], 10[68]; also 10[194]; perhaps 7[42] can be read this way as well.

[27] Ascribing this argument to Nietzsche is based on 35[5], 35[17], 40[69], 9[66], 9[77], 11[73]; GS §§ 268, 271, and also the splendid GS § 289.

social rather than biological units; and a morality is, or at any rate has been, a human community's self-interpretation and self-justification for the sake of its own preservation and growth.[28]

In this way Nietzsche completes the programme 'man as nature' for the case of morality. A morality is not a voice from on high, nor do its demands hold an authority independent of what is happening in the lives of the individuals addressed. Instead, it grows from the way they live[29] and in turn supports and enhances their lives. A morality is therefore a good thing for people to have – and why else should they have troubled to set one up in the first place?

Taking 'morality' in this sense, then, Nietzsche is no immoralist, contrary to his own declaration in *Ecce Homo* (EH Untimely 2). Not only does he recognise the existence and effectiveness of moralities (D § 103), he also justifies them by showing how they serve life. He is an immoralist only in the sense of rejecting the morality that he sees as dominant in his time and cultural area. He often calls this morality simply 'morality', thus falling prey to a short-sightedness similar to the one he deplores in 'most moral philosophers', who 'only present the order of rank that rules *now*' (35[5]). Still, the target of his critique cannot be misunderstood. Anyone who asks 'whether "good" is really "good" ' (1[53]) is evidently not discarding the vocabulary of 'good' and 'bad', but inquiring whether it is properly used in current judgements.

If Nietzsche's enterprise is the critique of a dominant morality, one wonders what that morality exactly is. Which valuations belong to it, and which belong to a neighbouring one in time or in space? The late Nietzsche nowhere gives a satisfying answer to this question. At times he describes the object of his critique as 'the morality of compassion' (GM Preface § 5–6), but this is simply to suppose that Schopenhauer is right in basing the current morality on compassion, whereas this is in fact a matter of dispute, as Nietzsche himself points out (GM Preface § 5). At other points he speaks of 'a *critique of Christian morality*' (2[127]), but that will not do, either. Christianity has been too many different things in different

---

[28] This accords with Zarathustra's teaching in the speech 'Of the Thousand and One Goals', Z I. The idea already appears, in a rudimentary version, in D § 165.

[29] See 14[76]. Hence, in his reflections in 10[135] and [181] on the social conditions of Christianity, surprising as they may first appear, Nietzsche is staying true to his basic line of argument: a morality is a natural thing, so it can be understood by tracing it back to 'the *soil* from which it grew' (14[76]), which is largely a social soil.

times and places for us to know what is part of Christian morality and what is not. In the end, Nietzsche does not give us a criterion, and we have to content ourselves with the vague concept of 'the morality dominant in his time and culture' – which presumably is also the morality dominant in our time and culture.

One wonders, secondly, what Nietzsche's objection is. He tried different lines, of which the following might be called the 'official' one in view of its prominence in both published and unpublished writings. Our morality is hostile to life,[30] as is evident especially in how it treats noble and powerful human beings: it discourages and eventually destroys them or, worse still, leads them to destroy themselves.[31] As the naturalist reminds us, we are primarily living creatures; because it is hostile to life, our morality is thus the negation of our very being. Hence we should try to liberate ourselves from it.

Yet it is difficult to understand how there can be such a thing as a morality hostile to life. If we had received our morality from above, it might easily clash with how we live. In Nietzsche's view, however, our morality arises from the way we live – so how can it turn against it? Nietzsche is certainly aware of the problem.[32] The solution he proposes in GM III § 13 is this: our morality has its origin in the protective and healing instinct of a degenerating life. The idea seems to be that the reason we have a morality which denies us great and noble humanity is either to prevent us from getting too excited or to shake us out of being too lethargic, both dangers stemming from our degeneration. This will hardly solve the problem of the clash. For one thing, the question arises of what it is we actually need in our state of degeneration: protection or self-inflicted wounds. But the main difficulty is that in the case Nietzsche sketches, our morality would not be hostile to life after all. It would help life, if by painful means, and so there would be no reason to get rid of it – on the contrary. True, people might complain about our morality, but this would only show they did not understand: in fact our morality is good for us.

---

[30] See GM III § 11, also I § 11; and fragments 5[98], 9[86].
[31] A memorable accusation of this kind is put forward in 11[55]. True, it is directed at Christianity, not at morality, but that matters little given that similar, if less impressive, language is used for current morality as well, as in 10[192], 14[5].
[32] GM III § 13, and perhaps 10[192] as well. 7[15] and 11[227] make a similar point.

historical

Another line of thought that comes to the fore in some of the notes appears more promising. Its key feature is the introduction of a historical dimension. Our morality did grow from the way we live, but now it no longer fits; we have outgrown it. Hence, our morality is not our enemy. The shoes a child wore last year are not hostile to her feet now, though they would harm her if she kept wearing them. Our morality is not something we should fight but something we should discard, for life has moved beyond it. Nietzsche writes:

> Deepest gratitude for what morality has achieved so far: but *now* it's *only a pressure* that would prove disastrous![33]

What we need to do now is

> extricate ourselves from the lazy routine of old valuations which degrade us in the best and strongest things we have achieved. (9[66])

In Nietzsche's view, the best and strongest thing we have achieved is the fact that we no longer need a communal morality. Not only has the morality we now call 'ours' had its day, but we no longer need any other morality to become 'ours'. We can now go it alone, as individuals – we will not be without morality, but the morality we have will be a matter of '*individual legislation*' (35[20]). In this way, Nietzsche rejoins the autonomy tradition of modern moral philosophy, as witness also the 'autonomous individual' of GM II § 2. To be sure, his is not a Kantian autonomy: Nietzsche's individuals do not undertake to legislate for all rational beings. Yet they do legislate, for themselves, and thus do not act erratically but according to their own self-given form.[34]

Perhaps life has moved even beyond what Nietzsche envisaged, and the moralist was not radical enough. After the demise of what we now call *our* morality, will we each still need a morality of our own? Will we still need to justify and glorify ourselves, as is claimed in 35[17], if only in terms of our individual valuations? In the end, it might appear childish to insist on being in the right and on being a glorious individual. To do so might appear especially strange in human beings 'translated back into nature'. One might expect such human beings just to do their human things, rather

---

[33] 5[58]. See also GM II § 2 and 5[61], 10[23], 15[74]. The past tense in 35[20], quoted above, is relevant too.
[34] A precursor of this idea is GS § 290.

than subject themselves to any form, self-given or not. Nietzsche at times seems to support this idea himself, for example when he envisions humans who do not even want praise (9[27]); or when he writes in 6[18]:

> We no longer eat a particular dish for moral reasons; one day we will no longer 'do good' for moral reasons either.

Chronology

1844 Born in Röcken, a small village in the Prussian province of
      Saxony, on 15 October.
1846 Birth of his sister Elisabeth.
1848 Birth of his brother Joseph.
1849 His father, a Lutheran minister, dies at age thirty-six of
      'softening of the brain'.
1850 Brother dies; family moves to Naumburg to live with father's
      mother and her sisters.
1858 Begins studies at Pforta, Germany's most famous school for
      education in the classics.
1864 Graduates from Pforta with a thesis in Latin on the Greek poet
      Theognis; enters the University of Bonn as a theology student.
1865 Transfers from Bonn, following the classical philologist Friedrich
      Ritschl to Leipzig where he registers as a philology student;
      reads Schopenhauer's *The World as Will and Representation*.
1866 Reads Friedrich Lange's *History of Materialism*.
1868 Meets Richard Wagner.
1869 On Ritschl's recommendation is appointed professor of classical
      philology at Basle at the age of twenty-four before completing his
      doctorate (which is then conferred without a dissertation);
      begins frequent visits to the Wagner residence at Tribschen.
1870 Serves as a medical orderly in the Franco-Prussian war; contracts
      a serious illness and so serves only two months. Writes 'The
      Dionysiac World View'.

1872   Publishes his first book, *The Birth of Tragedy*; its dedicatory preface to Richard Wagner claims for art the role of 'the highest task and truly metaphysical activity of his life'; devastating reviews follow.

1873   Publishes 'David Strauss, the Confessor and the Writer', the first of his *Untimely Meditations*; begins taking books on natural science out of the Basle library, whereas he had previously confined himself largely to books on philological matters. Writes 'On Truth and Lying in a Non-Moral Sense'.

1874   Publishes two more *Meditations*, 'The Uses and Disadvantages of History for Life' and 'Schopenhauer as Educator'.

1876   Publishes the fourth *Meditation*, 'Richard Wagner in Bayreuth', which already bears subtle signs of his movement away from Wagner.

1878   Publishes *Human, All Too Human* (dedicated to the memory of Voltaire); it praises science over art as the high culture and thus marks a decisive turn away from Wagner.

1879   Terrible health problems force him to resign his chair at Basle (with a small pension); publishes 'Assorted Opinions and Maxims', the first part of vol. II of *Human, All Too Human*; begins living alone in Swiss and Italian boarding-houses.

1880   Publishes 'The Wanderer and His Shadow', which becomes the second part of vol. II of *Human, All Too Human*.

1881   Publishes *Daybreak*.

1882   Publishes *Idylls of Messina* (eight poems) in a monthly magazine; publishes *The Gay Science* (first edition); friendship with Paul Ree and Lou Andreas-Salomé ends badly, leaving Nietzsche devastated.

1883   Publishes the first two parts of *Thus Spoke Zarathustra*; learns of Wagner's death just after mailing part one to the publisher.

1884   Publishes the third part of *Thus Spoke Zarathustra*.

1885   Publishes the fourth part of *Zarathustra* for private circulation only.

1886   Publishes *Beyond Good and Evil*; writes prefaces for new releases of: *The Birth of Tragedy, Human, All Too Human* vols. I and II, and *Daybreak*.

1887   Publishes expanded edition of *The Gay Science* with a new preface, a fifth book, and an appendix of poems; publishes *Hymn to Life*, a musical work for chorus and orchestra; publishes *On the Genealogy of Morality*.

1888   Publishes *The Case of Wagner*, composes a collection of poems, *Dionysian Dithyrambs*, and four short books: *Twilight of Idols, The Antichrist, Ecce Homo*, and *Nietzsche contra Wagner*.

1889   Collapses physically and mentally in Turin on 3 January; writes a few lucid notes but never recovers sanity; is briefly institutionalised; spends remainder of his life as an invalid, living with his mother and then his sister, who also gains control of his literary estate.

1900   Dies in Weimar on 25 August.

Further reading

Nietzsche's notes of his last productive years should, first and foremost, be studied together with the books he completed during that period. *Beyond Good and Evil* (1886), a comprehensive expression of his late thought in aphoristic form, is available in English in Marion Faber's fluent translation (Oxford World's Classics, Oxford University Press, 1998) and in Judith Norman's version, which may not be as readable but stays closer to the original (ed. R.-P. Horstmann and J. Norman, Cambridge Texts in the History of Philosophy, Cambridge University Press, 2001). *On the Genealogy of Morality* (1887), philosophically perhaps Nietzsche's most important book, is available in an excellent, very precise, if at times strained new translation by Maudemarie Clark and Alan J. Swensen (Indianapolis: Hackett, 1998). Alternatively, there is the translation by Carol Diethe in the volume *Nietzsche: 'On the Genealogy of Morality' and Other Writings* (ed. K. Ansell-Pearson, Cambridge University Press, 1994). *Twilight of the Idols* (1889) and *The Antichrist* (1895) are published in one volume in translations by R. J. Hollingdale (Harmondsworth: Penguin, 1968).

The secondary literature on Nietzsche is vast, owing among other things to the fact that so many disciplines take an interest in his work. This may also explain why the Nietzsche literature, far more than research on any other major philosopher, is so deeply divided into different camps. People do not merely disagree – there often hardly seems even to be a bridge from one writer's Nietzsche to the next writer's. Accordingly, any recommendation on secondary reading is bound to be partisan. Mine would be as follows: the best discussion of the late Nietzsche's thought is Maudemarie Clark's *Nietzsche on Truth and Philosophy* (Cambridge

University Press, 1990). Focusing on Nietzsche's views about truth, the book also covers many of the other themes important for the late Nietzsche, and provides in a relatively small space a lucid and well-argued account of them. Richard Schacht's *Nietzsche* in the series 'The Arguments of the Philosophers' (London: Routledge, 1983) is far more extensive and discusses in detail a broad range of Nietzschean topics, especially from the post-*Zarathustra* writings.

Among the more idiosyncratic readings of Nietzsche, three may be singled out as particularly influential, all of them again based primarily on Nietzsche's late writings. Martin Heidegger's *Nietzsche*, originally a series of lectures held in the 1930s, then published in German in 1961 and translated by David Krell (4 volumes, New York: Harper, 1979–86), is chiefly concerned with Nietzsche's position within the broad history of Western metaphysics, as construed by Heidegger. Gilles Deleuze, *Nietzsche and Philosophy*, published in French in 1962 and translated into English by Hugh Tomlinson (New York: Columbia University Press, 1983) takes Nietzsche to be opening up a new kind of philosophy that is anti-dialectic, pluralist and interpretative. Influenced by Deleuze to some extent, Alexander Nehamas, *Nietzsche: Life as Literature* (Cambridge, Mass.: Harvard University Press, 1985) sees Nietzsche's writing as an exercise in self-creation: in writing what he did, Nietzsche made an artwork out of himself, the literary character of a philosopher.

Nietzsche's political philosophy is addressed by Tracy B. Strong, *Friedrich Nietzsche and the Politics of Transfiguration* (Berkeley: University of California Press, 1975) and by Bruce Detwiler, *Nietzsche and the Politics of Aristocratic Radicalism* (University of Chicago Press, 1990). Helpful on Nietzsche's philosophy of art, both early and late, is J. Young's study *Nietzsche's Philosophy of Art* (Cambridge University Press, 1992).

There are a large number of collections of critical essays, mostly assembling authors of a more or less similar outlook. The following three are particularly helpful. John Richardson and Brian Leiter's *Nietzsche* (Oxford Readings in Philosophy, Oxford University Press, 2001) brings together the best of current Nietzsche scholarship, though almost only from the English-speaking world. Richard Schacht's anthology *Nietzsche, Genealogy, Morality* (Berkeley: University of California Press, 1994) concentrates on the book *On the Genealogy of Morality*, treating in detail both the methodological and the substantive issues it raises. *Nietzsche's New Seas*, edited by Michael Gillespie and Tracy B. Strong (University of Chicago Press, 1988), is interested in Nietzsche as simultaneously a philosopher and a poet.

There is no better source on Friedrich Nietzsche the human being than his letters. Giorgio Colli and Mazzino Montinari, the editors of the standard edition of Nietzsche's works, the KGW, also edited the complete Nietzsche correspondence (*Friedrich Nietzsche, Briefwechsel, Kritische Gesamtausgabe*, 24 volumes, Berlin: de Gruyter, 1975–84) and, based on this, a complete paperback edition of Nietzsche's letters (*Friedrich Nietzsche, Sämtliche Briefe, Kritische Studienausgabe*, 8 volumes, Munich: Deutscher Taschenbuch Verlag / Berlin: de Gruyter, 1986). In English, useful collections are Peter Fuss and Henry Shapiro's *Nietzsche: A Self-Portrait from His Letters* (Cambridge, Mass.: Harvard University Press, 1971) and Christopher Middleton's *Selected Letters of Friedrich Nietzsche* (University of Chicago Press, 1969).

Nietzsche's autobiographical essay *Ecce Homo* (trans. R. J. Hollingdale, Harmondsworth: Penguin, 1979) is rather disappointing, at least for biographical interests. The standard biography, in German, is Curt Paul Janz's extensive and detailed *Friedrich Nietzsche* (3 volumes, Munich: Hanser, 1978). In English there is Ronald Hayman's *Nietzsche: A Critical Life* (Oxford University Press, 1980). Very useful is the detailed chronicle, in German, of Nietzsche's life between 1869 and 1889, in volume 15 of the paperback edition of Nietzsche's works, an edition closely based on the KGW (*Friedrich Nietzsche, Sämtliche Werke, Kritische Studienausgabe*, 15 volumes, Munich: Deutscher Taschenbuch Verlag / Berlin: de Gruyter, 1988).

Translator's note

A large part of the present text has been available in English since the 1960s, in Walter Kaufmann's and R. J. Hollingdale's translation *The Will to Power*. Their work has been invaluable in the preparation of the present translation. However, as the Introduction has explained, Kaufmann and Hollingdale had to work with source texts that are problematic in several respects. They are often rearranged or cut down; and a tendency to tidy up stray lines of text and reduce ambiguity also obscures the fragmentary, tentative nature of the language. In this translation, my principle has been to leave open as much as possible of the original's space for interpretation. Unfinished sentences are left unfinished, and ambiguities reproduced wherever possible. Likewise, while it was tempting to replace Nietzsche's strings of commas and dashes with more conventional punctuation, I decided that this would unacceptably break up Nietzsche's lines of thought and over-simplify his syntactically demanding German style. Accordingly, my translation follows the original punctuation except where the different conventions of English would make that positively misleading.

In terminology, I have aimed for consistency on the high-profile words – like 'valuation' for *Wertschätzung* – that run through generations of Nietzsche translations. More than that, though, I wanted to offer the reader some sense of the dense lexical networks to be found in Nietzsche's work, by remaining consistent in the less conspicuous words as well. That is why, for example, *Kraft* is translated by 'force' throughout, not only in the scientific contexts but also at points where 'strength' would have been a more obvious choice. Conversely, I have tried not to collapse

Nietzsche's distinctions between synonyms and different grammatical forms of a word. Thus, Nietzsche uses both *das Tun* and *die Tat* as nouns derived from the verb *tun*, 'to do'. Rather than translating both with the smoother 'deed', I have distinguished each time between 'the doing' and 'the deed'. A more extreme example is Nietzsche's extraordinary, punning exploitation of the etymological relationships between German words. Though such games are often impossible to re-create in translation, I have tried to avoid normalising them quite out of existence. In short, this translation's aim, however unsatisfactorily achieved, has been to maximise closeness to the source fragments without entirely sacrificing the liveliness of Nietzsche's language.

Of the many individual terms worthy of comment, one or two may be mentioned here. The most pervasive is the translation of the German *Mensch* as 'man'. This over-gendering was done reluctantly, for the German term covers all human beings and can be contrasted with *der Mann*. However, the text leaves little doubt that Nietzsche has the male of the species in mind, and neither does 'person' or 'human being' seem appropriate to the text's date or register. It is left to the translation's reader to think in the supplement – the additional meaning present in the German. A further difficult word is *Geist*, which might be translated as 'mind', 'spirit' or 'intellect'. Unlike Kaufmann and Hollingdale, I have generally chosen 'mind', except where a person is intended ('free spirits'); however, the reader may like to keep in view the word's larger hinterland. Less consistency was possible for the verb *wollen*, which in German means both 'to want' and 'to will' and is inextricable from its noun *der Wille*, 'will'. I have translated *wollen* as 'to will' where the active, achieving element was important, but in weaker cases as 'to want'.

Finally, some words on the notation are in order. In general, this translation keeps closely to the form of the texts collected in Colli and Montinari's KGW. None of the fragments translated here has been abridged,[1] and the suspension points . . . thus do not indicate an omission. They are Nietzsche's own 'hesitation' points. As in the KGW, a set of dashes – – – shows an incomplete sentence in the manuscript, [–] an illegible word, and + a gap in the manuscript; single dashes are Nietzsche's own punctuation. Italics indicate his underlining (bold italics his double or treble underlining), and in the rare cases where I have added my own

---

[1] Some of the fragments in notebook 7 are taken from longer collections; see Introduction.

italics, this is explicitly noted. To avoid confusion, foreign words are not set in italics but left as they stand in the text. My hope is that readers will enter into the spirit of Nietzsche's kaleidoscopic German with its rich complement of French, Latin and Italian.

It almost goes without saying that a project like this depended on unstinting help from many quarters. The translation has benefited from the suggestions and inspiration of numerous translators in London and Berlin. Above all, though, I would like to thank Rüdiger Bittner for his expert, meticulous and imaginative comments on successive drafts. Of course, the translation's remaining errors and infelicities are all my own.

Kate Sturge

Notebook 34, April – June 1885

34[3]

In my youth I was unlucky: a very ambiguous man crossed my path. When I recognised him for what he is, namely a great actor who has no authentic relationship to anything (not even to music), I was so sickened and disgusted that I believed all famous people had been actors, otherwise they wouldn't have become famous, and that the chief thing in what I called 'artist' was the *theatrical* force.

34[11]

Our age feeds off, lives off the morality of previous ages.

34[12]

Pascal was offended by the idea that he could be influenced by the weather, by bright and serene skies. Now – the theory of *milieu* is the most comfortable one: *everything* exerts an influence, the result is man himself.

34[30]

Sense-perception happens without our awareness: whatever we become conscious of is a perception that has already been processed.

34[31]

He makes the great release *for himself*, without demanding it from others or even considering it his duty to communicate it to others and impose it on them.

34[36]

The problem of 'belief' is really: *whether instinct has more value than reasoning and why?*

Hidden behind the many disputes about 'knowledge and belief', Utilitarianism and intuitionism, is *this* question of *valuation*.

Socrates had naively placed himself on the side of reason, against instinct. (Yet fundamentally, he had in fact followed all moral instincts, only with the wrong motivation: *as if* motives originated in reason. Likewise Plato, etc.)

Without meaning to, Plato tried to reach the result that reason and instinct *want* the same thing. Likewise, up to the present day: Kant, Schopenhauer, the English.

In belief, the instinct of *obedience to the highest authority*, thus *one* instinct, takes precedence. The categorical imperative is a *wished-for* instinct, where reason and *this* instinct are one.

34[46]

If *I* have anything of a unity within me, it certainly doesn't lie in the conscious 'I' and in feeling, willing, thinking, but somewhere else: in the sustaining, appropriating, expelling, watchful prudence of my whole organism, of which my conscious self is only a tool. Feeling, willing, thinking everywhere show only outcomes, the causes of which are entirely unknown to me: the way these outcomes succeed one another as if one succeeded *out of* its predecessor is probably just an illusion: in truth, the causes may be connected to one another in such a way that the final causes give me the *impression* of being associated, logically or psychologically. *I deny* that one intellectual or psychological phenomenon is the direct *cause* of another intellectual or psychological phenomenon – even if this seems to be so. *The true world of causes is hidden from us*: it is unutterably more complicated. The intellect and the senses are, above all, a *simplifying* apparatus. Yet our *erroneous*, miniaturised, *logicised* world of causes is the one we can live in. We are 'knowers' to the extent that we are able to satisfy our needs.

Studying the body gives some idea of the unutterable complication.

If our intellect did not have some *fixed* forms, living would be impossible. But that doesn't prove anything about the truth of all logical facts.

34[48]

NB. A little more clear-headedness and a little good will, and one can no longer bear, for reasons of taste, to interpret one's experiences to suit 'the honour of God' – I mean, to see everywhere the traces of his caring, warning, punishing, schooling. Just as a good philologist (and indeed any philologically trained scholar) is repulsed by false textual interpretations (e.g., those made by the Protestant preachers in the pulpits – which is why the learned professions no longer go to church –), in the same way, and not as a consequence of great 'virtue', 'honesty', etc., one's taste is offended by the counterfeiting inherent in the religious interpretation of all experiences. –

34[49]

Our pleasure in simplicity, transparency, regularity, brightness, from which in the end a German 'philosopher' could extract something like a categorical imperative of logic and beauty – I admit that a strong *instinct* of this kind exists. It is so strong that it governs among all the activities of our senses, and reduces, regulates, assimilates, etc., for us the abundance of real perceptions (unconscious ones –), *presenting them to our consciousness* only in this trimmed form. This 'logical', this 'artistic' element is our continual occupation. *What* made this force so sovereign? Obviously the fact that without it, for sheer hubbub of impressions, no living being would live.

34[53]

Critique of the instinct of causality

The *belief* that an action happens in consequence of a motive was one gradually and instinctively generalised, in the days when everything that happened was imagined after the pattern of conscious, living beings. 'Everything happens because of a motive: the *causa finalis* is the *causa efficiens*[36]' –

This belief is *erroneous*: purpose, motive are means of making something that happens comprehensible, practicable. The generalisation, too, was erroneous and illogical.

No purpose.
No will.

34[54]

The chronological order reversed

The 'external world' affects us: the effect is telegraphed into our brain, there arranged, given shape and traced back to its cause: then the cause is *projected*, and *only then does the fact enter our consciousness*. That is, the world of appearances *appears* to us as a cause only once 'it' has exerted its effect and the effect has been processed. That is, *we are constantly reversing the order of what happens*. – While '*I*' see, *it* is already seeing something different. Similar to the case of pain.

34[55]

Belief in the senses. Is a fundamental fact of our intellect, which receives from the senses the raw material that it *interprets*. This way of treating the raw material offered by the senses is, considered *morally*, *not* guided by an intention to truth but as if by a will to overpower, assimilate, consume. Our constant functions are absolutely egoistic, machiavellian, unscrupulous, subtle. Commanding and obeying pushed to the extreme, and so that it can obey perfectly, the individual organ has much freedom.

The error in the belief in purposes.
Will – a superfluous assumption.
The chronological order reversed.
Critique of the belief in causality.

---

[36] Aristotle (Phys. II 3) distinguished four ways of speaking of a thing's cause: we may be referring to the matter it consists of, to its essential form, to what made it, or to its purpose. The standard Latin terminology translates the latter two as *causa efficiens* and *causa finalis*.

Belief in the senses as a fundamental fact of what we are.

The central power – must not differ essentially from what it rules.

Properties are not explained by the history of their genesis. They must already be known. *Historical* explanation is the reduction to a sequence we are *used to*: by means of analogy.

34[67]

NB. Our era is sceptical in its most essential instincts: almost all the subtler scholars and artists are sceptics, even if they don't like to admit it to themselves. Pessimism and *No-saying* is only easier for the mind's indolence: our muggy era with its democratic air is above all indolent. Where the mind is more particular it says: 'I don't know' and 'I no longer trust myself or anyone else' and 'I no longer know which way to turn', and 'hope – that's an empty phrase for liars or for demagogic orators and artists'. Scepticism is the expression of a certain *physiological* constitution, one inevitably produced in the great crossing of many races: the many inherited valuations struggle with each other, hinder each other's growth. The force which loses most here is the *will*: therefore great fear of responsibility, because no one can vouch for himself. Hiding behind communities is the order of the day, 'you scratch my back and I'll *cover* yours'. Thus a herd-like species emerges: and anyone with a strong, domineering and audacious will is certain to come to rule in such times.

34[74]

The human horizon. One can think of the philosophers as those who make the most extreme efforts to *try* how far man can *raise* himself (especially Plato): how *far* his strength will reach. But they do this as individuals; perhaps the instinct of the Caesars, the founders of states, etc., was greater – those who think about how far man can be driven in *development* and under 'favourable circumstances'. But they did not sufficiently grasp what 'favourable circumstances' are. Great question: where the plant called 'man' has grown most magnificently up to now. That requires a comparative study of history.

34[81]

To be put at the very top: the *instincts*, too, have *become*; they prove nothing about the super-sensible, not even about the animal, not even about the typically human.

That the mind has become and is still becoming; that among countless ways of inferring and judging, the one now most familiar to us is some-how the most useful to us and has been passed down to us because the individuals who thought that way had better prospects: that this proves nothing about 'true' and 'untrue', – – –

34[87]

We *imagine* that what is commanding and highest resides in our con-sciousness. Ultimately we have a double brain: we encompass in the word 'consciousness' our capacity *itself* to *will, feel and think* something of our own willing, feeling and thinking.

34[88]

NB. Those law-giving and tyrannical spirits capable of *tying fast* the mean-ing of a concept, *holding fast* to it, men with that spiritual force of will, who know how to turn the most fluid thing, the spirit, to stone for long periods and almost to eternalise it, are commanding men in the highest sense. They say: 'I want to be sure that such and such a thing is seen, I want it exactly *this way*, I want it *for this* and only for this.' – Law-giving men of this kind were bound to exert the strongest influence in all ages; all the typical formations of man are owed to them: they are the sculptors – and the rest (the very great majority, in this case –) are, compared to them, only *clay*.

34[89]

The best-established movements of our mind, our regulated gymnastics in, e.g., ideas of time and space, or in the need for 'justification' – this *philosophical* habitus of the human mind is our real potency; thus, in many matters of the mind *we can no longer do otherwise*, which is referred to as 'psychological necessity'. This necessity is one that has *become* – and it is downright childish to believe that *our* space, *our* time, *our* instinct for causality are something that could have meaning even apart from man.

34[92]

One owes the Christian church:

1. the intellectualisation of *cruelty*: the idea of hell, the tortures and inquisitions, the autos-da-fé, after all, represent great progress over the magnificent but semi-imbecilic butchery in the Roman arenas. Much intellect, much hidden design, has entered cruelty. – The church has invented many enjoyments –

2. its 'intolerance' made the European mind *refined* and *supple*. One sees immediately how in our democratic age, with the freedom of the press, thought becomes coarse. The Germans invented gunpowder – hats off to them! But they made up for it: they invented the press. The ancient polis[37] was of just the same disposition. The Roman Empire, in contrast, allowed much freedom of belief and unbelief: more than any empire allows today: immediately, the consequence was an enormous increase in the degeneracy, doltishness and crudeness of the mind. – Leibnitz and Abelard, Montaigne, Descartes and Pascal – how good they look! Seeing the supple audacity of such minds is an enjoyment one owes the church. – The intellectual pressure of the church is essentially the unbending severity with which concepts and valuations are treated as *fixed*, as aeternae.[38] Dante gives us pure enjoyment through this fact: that under an absolute regime one certainly need not be *narrowly restricted*. If there were restrictions, they were stretched across a tremendous space, thanks to Plato; and one could move within them like Bach within the forms of counterpoint, *very freely*. – Baco[39] and Shakespeare seem almost revolting when one has thoroughly learned to savour *this* 'freedom under the law'. Likewise the most recent music in comparison to Bach and Handel.

---

37 The ancient Greek city state.   38 Eternal truths.
39 Francis Bacon (1561–1626), politician and writer, a contemporary of Shakespeare's.

34[108]

I take the democratic movement to be something inevitable: yet something that isn't inexorable but can be delayed. Overall, though, the rule of the herd instinct and of herd valuations, Epicureanism and benevolence increase of a piece: man becomes weak, but good and agreeable.

34[121]

That *my* valuation or condemnation of someone does not give another man the right to value or condemn the same way – unless he is my equal and of equal rank. The opposite way of thinking is that of the newspapers, which believe a valuation of people and things to be something 'in itself' that anyone can make use of as if it were *his own* property. This presupposes that *everyone is of equal rank.* – To be truthful is a distinction

34[123]

That man is a multiplicity of forces which stand in an order of rank, so that there are those which command, but what commands, too, must provide for those which obey everything they need to preserve themselves, and is thus itself *conditioned* by their existence. All these living beings must be related in kind, otherwise they could not serve and obey one another like this: what serves must, in some sense, also be an obeyer, and in more delicate cases the roles must temporarily switch so that what otherwise commands must, this once, obey. The concept of the 'individual' is false. In isolation, these beings do not exist: the centre of gravity is something changeable; the continual *generation* of cells, etc., produces a continual change in the number of these beings. And mere *addition* is no use at all. Our arithmetic is too crude for these relations, and is only an arithmetic of single elements.

34[124]

The logic of our conscious thinking is only a crude and facilitated form of the thinking needed by our organism, indeed by the particular organs of our organism. For example, a thinking-at-the-same-time is needed of which we have hardly an inkling. Or perhaps an artist of language does: reckoning back with the weight and the lightness of syllables, reckoning ahead, and at the same time looking for analogies between the weight of the thought and the phonetic, or physiological, conditions of the larynx: all this happens at the same time – though not *consciously*.

Our feeling of causality is something quite crude and isolated compared to our organism's real feelings of causality. In particular, 'before' and 'after' is a great piece of naivety.

Finally: we first had to acquire everything for *consciousness*: a sense of time, a sense of place, a sense of causality; it having long existed, and far more richly, without consciousness. And what we acquired was a certain simplest, plainest, most reduced form: our *conscious* willing, feeling, thinking is in the service of a much more comprehensive willing feeling thinking. – Really?

We are still growing continually, our sense of time and place, etc., is still developing.

34[125]

Nothing can be predicted, but with a certain heightening of the human type a *new* force may reveal itself of which we have previously known nothing. (Namely a synthesis of opposites?)

34[130]

For many people, abstract thinking is fatiguing work – for me, on good days, it is a feast, an intoxication.

34[131]

Just as there are many things a general doesn't want to know, and must not know if he is to keep hold of his overall view, so in our conscious mind there must be *above all* a drive *to exclude, to chase away*, a selecting drive – which allows only *certain* facts to be presented to it. Consciousness is the hand with which the organism reaches out furthest: it must be a firm hand. Our logic, our sense of time, sense of space are prodigious capacities to abbreviate, for the purpose of commanding. A concept is an invention which nothing corresponds to *wholly* but many things *slightly*: a proposition such as 'two things, being equal to a third thing, are themselves equal' assumes (1) things and (2) equalities – neither exists. Yet with this invented and rigid world of concepts and numbers, man gains a means of seizing by signs, as it were, huge quantities of facts and inscribing them in his memory. This apparatus of signs is man's superiority, precisely because it is at the furthest possible distance from the individual facts. The reduction of experiences to *signs*, and the ever greater quantity of things which can thus be grasped, is man's *highest strength*. Intellectuality as the capacity to be master of a huge number of facts in signs. *This intellectual world, this sign-world, is pure 'illusion and deception'*, as is every 'phenomenal thing' *– and 'moral man' will probably be outraged!* (Just as, in his calculations, Napoleon considered only man's most essential instincts and was entitled to ignore the exceptional ones, e.g., compassion – at the risk of miscalculating now and again.)

34[135]

I have often watched these German idealists, but they haven't watched me – they know nothing of what I know, don't even scent it, they go their sweet strolling way, their hearts are full of different desires from mine: they seek different air, different nourishment, different comfort. They look *upwards*, I look *outwards* – we never see the same thing.

– Dealing with them irks me. They may love cleanliness as far as their body is concerned, but their mind is unwashed, their 'consequently' smells tainted to me, they are indignant where I feel the rise of cheerful curiosity, they haven't cleaned out their ears when I am ready to sing my song.

34[141]

NB. The *emasculating* and perhaps *castrating*[40] effect of so much *praying* is another of those injuries done to the German character since the Reformation. It is always bad taste to ask much instead of giving much: the combination of meek servility and an often arrogant, vulgar importunity with which, e.g., St Augustine wallows before God in his Confessions reminds us that man may not be the only one of the animals to have religious feeling: the dog has a similar 'religious feeling' for man. – Communicating with God in prayer breeds the humiliating mood and attitude which still,

[40] *entmännlichend* and *entmannend*.

even in impious times, asserts its right through heredity: it's well known that the Germans have swooned before princes or party leaders or the assurance of being 'ever your most humble and obedient servant'. Let that now be over.

34[142]

NB. It has never entered my head to 'derive' all the virtues from egoism. First I want it demonstrated that they are 'virtues' and not just passing instincts of self-preservation in particular herds and communities.

34[161]

NB. A proficient craftsman or scholar looks very fine when he takes pride in his art and views life with modesty and satisfaction. In contrast, nothing is more miserable to see than a shoe-maker or schoolmaster who, an expression of suffering on his face, lets it be understood that he was really born for something better. There is nothing better than what is good! And that means having one or another proficiency and creating out of it – that is virtù in the Italian, Renaissance sense.

34[162]

NB. Today, in the age when the state has an absurdly fat belly, all the fields and disciplines have, alongside their real workers, also 'representatives', e.g., alongside the scholars there are the literati, alongside the suffering classes there are the chattering, boastful scoundrels who 'represent' those sufferings, not to mention the professional politicians, who are perfectly comfortable and 'represent' hardship before Parliament with their powerful lungs. Our modern life is extremely *costly* because of the large number of intermediaries; whereas in an ancient city, and, echoing that, still in many a Spanish and Italian city, a man appeared in person and wouldn't have given this kind of modern representative and middle-man the time of day – at best a kick!

34[167]

In every judgement of the senses, the whole pre-history of the organism is at work – 'that is green', for example. *Memory in instinct*, as a kind of abstraction and simplification, comparable to the logical process: the most important element has been underscored again and again, but the weakest features too *remain*. In the organic realm there is no forgetting; though there is a kind of *digestion* of what has been experienced.

34[174]

Good a preliminary stage of evil; a mild dose of evil –

34[179]

That there is a *development* of the whole of humanity is nonsense, nor is it to be wished. The fashioning of man, drawing out a kind of *diversity* from within him, breaking him to pieces when a certain type has passed its zenith – in other words, being creative and destructive – seems to me the highest pleasure that men can have. Certainly, Plato was not really that kind of dullard when he taught that concepts were *fixed* and *eternal*: yet he wanted this to be believed.

34[187]

The development of consciousness as an *apparatus of government*: only accessible to *generalisations*. Even what the eye shows enters consciousness *generalised* and *trimmed*.

34[195]

The philosophers (1) have always had the miraculous capacity for contradictio in adjecto.[41]

(2) their trust in concepts has been as unconditional as their mistrust of the senses: they have not reflected that concepts and words are our inheritance from days when things were very dark and unaspiring in men's heads.

NB. What dawns on the philosophers last of all: they must no longer merely let themselves be given concepts, no longer just clean and clarify them, but first of all must *make* them, *create* them, present them and persuade in their favour. Up to now, one generally trusted in one's

[41] Contradiction in terms (i.e., between the meaning of the noun and its adjective).

concepts as a miraculous *dowry* from some miracle world: but in the end they were the legacies left us by our most distant, stupidest and yet cleverest forebears. This *filial respect* towards *what is to be found in us* is perhaps part *of the moral component* in *knowing*. What's needed first is absolute scepticism towards all received concepts (something *perhaps* possessed by one philosopher – Plato: of course, he *taught the opposite – –*)

34[205]

As regards Richard Wagner: I have not recovered from the disappointment of summer 1876. All at once there was too much imperfection in the work and the man for me – I fled. Later I came to understand that one distances oneself from an artist most thoroughly when one has *seen his ideal*. After such a vision, which was mine in youth (my remaining, short text on Richard Wagner bears witness to it), I had no choice but to bid farewell, dismayed and gnashing my teeth, to what I had suddenly begun to find an 'unbearable reality'. – It does not concern me that he, grown old, transformed himself: almost all Romantics of that kind end up under the sign of the cross – I loved only the Wagner I knew, i.e., an honest atheist and immoralist who invented the figure of Siegfried, a very free man. Since then, from the humble corner of his *Bayreuther Blätter*,[42] he has sufficiently given to understand how highly he values the blood of the Saviour, and – he has been understood. Many Germans, many pure and impure fools[43] of every kind, have since begun to believe in Richard Wagner as their 'saviour'. I find all this distasteful. –

It goes without saying that I don't easily grant anyone the right to make this, my estimation, his own, and the disrespectful mob with which the body of today's society is crawling like lice should not be permitted even to pronounce such a great name as Richard Wagner's, whether to praise or to object.

34[208]

NB. 'The struggle for existence' – that describes an exceptional state. The rule is, rather, the struggle for *power*, for 'more' and 'better' and 'faster' and 'more often'.

[42] The journal of the Wagner circle, published from 1878 on.
[43] Allusion to Wagner's Parsifal, who is referred to as the 'pure fool'.

34[230]

The tempter

There are many different eyes. The sphinx too has eyes: and consequently there are many different 'truths', and consequently there is no truth.

34[241]

NB. How many false *interpretations* of things there have been! Consider what all men who *pray* must think of the association of causes and effects: for no one can persuade us to *strike* from prayer the element of 'entreating'[44] and the belief that there is some *point* in entreating, that an entreaty could be 'answered'. Or that other interpretation, in which a man's destinies are 'sent'[45] to improve, admonish, punish, warn him; or that third interpretation, that right and justice are to be found in the course of things itself, and that behind all causal events lies a kind of criminalistic hidden meaning. – Thus the entire *moral* interpretation of *our actions* might also be merely a prodigious misunderstanding, just as, quite evidently, the moral interpretation of all natural events has been.

34[244]

NB. '*Knowing*' is how we come to feel that we *already know*[46] something: thus, it means *combating a feeling of newness and transforming the apparently new into something old*.

34[247]

Something can be irrefutable; that doesn't make it true.

The whole of the organic world is the threading together of beings with little fabricated worlds around them; by their projecting, as they experience, their strength, their desires, their habits outside themselves, as their *external world*. The capacity to create (fashion, fabricate, invent) is

---

[44] *beten* (to pray) and *bitten* (to ask, request).   [45] *Schicksal* (destiny) and *geschickt* (sent).
[46] *erkennen* (to come to know, cognise) and *wissen* (to know).

their fundamental capacity: naturally, their idea of themselves is likewise only a false, fabricated, simplified one.

'A being with the habit of dreaming according to some kind of rule' – that is a living being. Huge numbers of such habits have finally become so hardened that whole *species* can live upon them. Probably they stand in a favourable relation to the conditions of such beings' existence.

Our world as *illusion, error* – but how is illusion and error possible? (Truth does not signify the antithesis of error but the status of certain errors vis-à-vis others, such as being older, more deeply assimilated, our not knowing how to live without them, and so on.)

The creative element of every organic being: what is it?

– that whatever is some being's 'external world' consists of a sum of valuations; that green, blue, red, hard, soft are inherited *valuations and their emblems.*

– that the valuations must stand in some kind of relation to the conditions of existence, but by no means that of being *true*, or *exact*. The essential thing is precisely their inexactitude, indeterminacy, which gives rise to a kind of *simplification of the external world* – and precisely this sort of intelligence favours survival.

– that it is the will to power which guides the inorganic world as well, or rather, that there *is* no inorganic world. 'Action at a distance' cannot be eliminated: *something draws something else closer, something feels drawn.* This is the fundamental fact: compared to this, the mechanistic notion of pressing and pushing is merely a hypothesis based on *sight* and *touch*, even if it does indeed serve us as a regulative hypothesis for the world of sight!

– that for this will to power to express itself, it must perceive those things which it draws closer; that it *feels* the approach of something it can assimilate.

– the supposed 'natural laws' are formulae for 'power relationships' of – – –

The mechanistic way of thinking is a philosophy of the foreground. It educates us to determine formulae, it provides a great sense of relief

– the various philosophical systems should be regarded as *methods of educating* the mind: they have always *trained up* one of the mind's forces in particular, with their one-sided demand that things be seen thus and not otherwise.

34[250]

That we are *effective* beings, forces, is our fundamental belief. *Free* means: 'not pushed and shoved, without a *feeling of compulsion*'.

NB. Where we encounter a resistance and have to give way to it, we feel *unfree*: where we don't give way to it but compel it to give way to us, we feel *free*. I.e., it is *our feeling of having* **more** *force* that we call 'freedom of will', the consciousness of our force *compelling* in relation to a force which is compelled.

34[253]

Truth is the kind of error without which a particular kind of living creature could not live. The value for life is what ultimately decides. Very vulgar and virtuous people – – –

34[264]

By morality, I understand a system of valuations which is contiguous with a being's conditions of life

Does inquiry involve moral forces and valuations?

The criterion of truth lies in the increase of the feeling of power.

'Thus and thus it shall be' – that stands at the beginning: later, often after long series of generations, it becomes a 'thus it is'. Later it's called 'truth'; at first it was a will to see something thus and thus, to name it thus and thus, a saying Yes to a value-creation of one's own. –

We compare something with what we hold to be true, according to the method we are used to believing in.

Notebook 35, May – July 1885

35[2]

The historical sense: the capacity to divine quickly the order of rank of the valuations by which a people, a society, a man lives – the relationship of these valuations to the conditions of life; the relation between the authority of the values and the authority of the forces that are at work (the presumed relation usually even more than the actual one): being able to *reproduce* all this within oneself constitutes the historical sense.

35[5]

Morality is the doctrine of the order of men's rank, and consequently also of the significance of their actions and works *for* this order of rank: thus, the doctrine of human valuations in respect of everything human. Most moral philosophers only present the order of rank that rules *now*; on the one hand lack of historical sense, on the other they are themselves ruled by the morality which teaches that what is at present is eternally valid. The unconditional importance, the blind self-centredness, with which every morality treats itself wants there not to be *many* moralities, it wants no comparison and no criticism, but rather unconditional belief in itself. It is, thus, in its very essence anti-scientific – and for that reason alone the perfect moralist would have to be *immoral*, beyond good and evil. – But is science then still *possible*? What is the search for truth, truth-fulness, honesty, if not something moral? And without these valuations and the corresponding actions: how would science be possible? Take the conscientiousness out of knowledge and what remains of science?[47] Is scepticism in morality not a contradiction, insofar as it is precisely here that the highest refinement of moral expectations is at work: as soon as the sceptic ceases to consider these finer evaluations of the true to be authoritative, he no longer has reason to doubt and to study: *unless the will to knowledge were to have quite another root than truthfulness.* –

35[15]

Regarding the plan. *Introduction*

1. the organic functions translated back into the fundamental will, the will to power – and as having split off from it.
2. thinking, feeling, willing in everything that lives –
   what is a pleasure other than a stimulation of the feeling of power by an obstacle (more strongly still by rhythmical obstacles and resistances) – leading it to swell? Thus, every pleasure includes pain. – If the pleasure is to become very great, the pain must be very long and the tension of the drawn bow prodigious.
3. the will to power specialising as will to nourishment, to property, to *tools*, to servants –
   obeying and mastering: the body.
   – the stronger will directs the weaker. There is no other causality whatsoever than that of will on will. So far there has been no mechanistic – – –
4. the intellectual functions. Will to shape, to assimilate, etc.

Annex. The philosophers' great misunderstandings.

35[17]

Man, in whatever situation he may find himself, needs a kind of valuation by means of which he justifies, i.e., *self-glorifies*, his actions, intentions and states towards himself and, especially, towards his surroundings. Every natural morality is the expression of one kind of man's satisfaction with himself: and if one needs praise, one also needs a *corresponding* table of values according the highest esteem to those actions of which we are most

---

[47] *Gewissenhaftigkeit* (conscientiousness), *Wissen* (knowledge), *Wissenschaft* (science).

capable, in which our real *strength* expresses itself. Where we are strongest is where we wish to be seen and honoured.

35[19]

One must free oneself from the question, 'What is good? What is compassionate?' and ask instead, 'What is the good *man*, the compassionate man?'

35[20]

Up to now a morality has been, above all, the expression of a conservative will to breed the same species, with the imperative: 'All variation is to be prevented; only the enjoyment of the species must remain.' Here a number of properties are long held *fast* to and *cultivated* while others are sacrificed; all such moralities are *harsh* (in education, in the choice of wives, generally against the rights of the young, etc.), and the result is men whose characteristics are few, but very strong and always the same. These characteristics are related to the bases upon which such commonwealths can hold their own and assert themselves against their enemies.

All at once, the bonds and fetters of such breeding collapse (– for a time there are no enemies left –). The individual now lacks such restraints and grows wild; there is immense ruin alongside magnificent, multifarious, jungle-like upwards growth. For the new men, who now inherit the *most diverse* things, the need arises to make themselves an *individual legislation*, one appropriate to their peculiar conditions and *dangers*. The moral philosophers appear, who are usually representatives of some more common type and, with their discipline, useful to a particular kind of man.

35[24]

1. is the 'philosopher' still *possible* today? Is not the extent of what is known too large? Is it not very unlikely that he will be able to reach an *overview*, the less so the more conscientious he is? Or only *too late*, when his best days are over? Or damaged, coarsened, degenerated, so that his *value judgement* no longer counts? – Otherwise he becomes a '*dilettante*' with a thousand little snail-like feelers, losing that great pathos:[48] respect

---

[48] Pathos here in the sense of grand affect.

for himself – and his good, refined conscience too. In short: he no longer leads, he no longer commands. If he wanted to do so, he would have to become a great actor, a kind of philosophical *Cagliostro*.[49]

2. what does it mean to us today to *live* philosophically, to be wise? Is it not almost a way of *extricating* oneself cleverly from an ugly game? A kind of flight? And someone who lives in that remote and simple way: is it likely that this has let him show his understanding the best way forward? Ought he not to have tried out life personally in a hundred ways, so as to have something to say about its value? In short: we believe that a man must have lived absolutely 'unphilosophically' according to the received ideas, above all not to have lived in timid virtuousness, in order to reach judgements on the great problems from his own *experience*. The man with the widest experience, compressing it into general conclusions: ought he not to be the most powerful? – The wise man has too long been confused with the scholar, and even longer with the religious enthusiast.

35[32]

I fight against all the hypocrisy of scientific attitude:

1. regarding *exposition*, if it doesn't correspond to the *genesis* of thoughts,

2. in the claims to *methods* which at a particular moment in science may not yet even be possible,

3. in the claims to *objectivity*, to cold impersonality, where, as in all valuations, we tell something about ourselves and our inner experiences in a few words. There are ridiculous kinds of vanity, e.g., that of Saint-Beuve,[50] who never overcame his vexation at having had, here and there, real warmth and passion in his For and Against, and would have liked to lie it out of his life.

35[35]

What separates me most deeply from the metaphysicians is: I don't concede that the 'I' is what thinks. Instead, I take the *I itself to be a construction of thinking*, of the same rank as 'matter', 'thing', 'substance', 'individual',

---

[49] Count Alessandro di Cagliostro (actually Giuseppe Balsamo) was an alchemist and impostor who died in prison in 1795.
[50] Charles-Augustin Saint-Beuve (1804–1869), French literary historian and critic.

'purpose', 'number': in other words to be only a *regulative fiction* with the help of which a kind of constancy and thus 'knowability' is inserted into, *invented into*, a world of becoming. Up to now belief in grammar, in the linguistic subject, object, in verbs has subjugated the metaphysicians: I teach the renunciation of this belief. It is only thinking that posits the I: but up to now philosophers have believed, like the 'common people', that in '*I* think' there lay something or other of unmediated certainty and that this 'I' was the given cause of thinking, in analogy with which we 'understood' all other causal relations. However habituated and indispensable this fiction may now be, that in no way disproves its having been invented: something can be a condition of life and *nevertheless be false*.

35[51]

In a world of becoming in which everything is conditional, the assumption of the unconditional, of substance, of being, of a thing, etc., can only be error. But how is error possible?

35[52]

Showing the succession of things ever more clearly is what's named *explanation*: no more than that!

35[55]

'Timeless' to be rejected. At a particular moment of a force, an absolute conditionality of the redistribution of all its forces is given: it cannot stand still. 'Change' is part of the essence, and therefore so is temporality – which, however, just amounts to one more conceptual positing of the necessity of change.

35[69]

NB. The *measure* of a man is how much of the *truth* he can endure without *degenerating*. Likewise, how much *happiness* – – likewise, how much *freedom* and *power*!
    On the order of rank

Notebook 36, June – July 1885

36[2]

Never has more been demanded of living creatures than when dry land emerged. Habituated and adapted to life in the sea, they had to turn around and overturn their bodies and customs and act in every respect differently from what they had been used to before – there has never been a more remarkable change on earth. – Just as then, through collapses, through the earth slowly breaking apart, the sea sank into the ruptures, caves and troughs and gained *depth*, so (to continue the metaphor) what is happening today among men perhaps offers the exact counterpart: man's becoming whole and rounded, a disappearance of the ruptures, caves and troughs, and consequently also – a disappearance of dry land. For a man made rounded and whole by my way of thinking, 'everything is at sea', the sea is everywhere: however, the sea itself has lost depth. – But I was on my way to quite another metaphor and took the wrong turning! I was trying to say that I, like everyone, was born a creature of the land – and yet now I *have to* be a creature of the sea!

36[7]

My 'compassion'. – This is a feeling for which no name satisfies me: I experience it when I see a waste of precious capacities, for example at the sight of Luther – what force, and what insipid provincial problems (at a time when in France, the bold and cheerful scepticism of a Montaigne had already become possible!). Or when I see a man falling behind what he could have become, due to some stupid chance. Or worse, when thinking about mankind's lot – as when, with fear and contempt, I happen to observe the European politics of today, which is certainly also helping to weave the fabric of *all* mankind's future. Yes, what might 'man' become if – –! This is my kind of 'compassion'; even if there's no one suffering whose suffering I would *share*.[51]

36[10]

How long have I been concerned in my own mind to prove the perfect *innocence* of becoming! And what strange paths I've taken in this quest! At one point it seemed to me the right solution to decree that 'existence, as something like a work of art, does not fall under the jurisdiction of morality at all; instead, morality itself belongs to the realm of appearance.' Another time I said: 'Objectively, all notions of guilt are entirely without value, but subjectively all life is necessarily unjust and alogical.' Then again, I wrested from myself the denial of all purposes and felt the unknowability of causal connections. And what was this all for? Was it not to give myself a feeling of complete irresponsibility – to place myself outside all praise and blame, independent of all past and present, in order to run after my own goal in my own way? –

36[15]

If the world had a goal, it could not fail to have been reached by now. If it had an unintended final state, this too could not fail to have been reached. If it were capable at all of standing still and remaining frozen, of 'being', if for just one second in all its becoming it had this capacity for 'being', then in turn all becoming would long since be over and done with, and so would all thinking, all 'mind'. The fact of 'mind' *as a becoming* proves that the world has no goal and no final state and is incapable of being. – But the old habit of thinking about all events in terms of goals, and about the world in terms of a guiding, creating God, is so powerful that the thinker is hard-pressed not to think of the goallessness of the world as, again, an intention. This idea – the idea that the world is intentionally

---

[51] The German word *Mitleid* (compassion, pity) is composed of *mit* (with) + *leiden* (to suffer).

evading a goal and even has the means expressly to prevent itself from being drawn into a cyclical course – is what occurs to all those who would like to impose upon the world the faculty for *eternal novelty*, that is, impose upon a finite, determinate force of unchanging magnitude like 'the world' the miraculous capacity to refashion its shapes and states *infinitely*. They would like the world, if no longer God, to be capable of divine creative force, an infinite force of transformation; they would like the world to *prevent itself* at will from falling back into one of its earlier shapes, to possess not only the intention but also the *means* of *guarding* itself from all repetition. The world is, thus, to *control* every one of its movements at every moment so as to avoid goals, final states, repetitions – and whatever else the consequences of such an unforgivably crazy way of thinking and wishing may be. This is still the old religious way of thinking and wishing, a kind of longing to believe that in *some way or other* the world does, after all, resemble the beloved old, infinite, boundlessly creative God – that in some way or other 'the old God still lives' – that longing of Spinoza's expressed in the words 'deus sive natura'[52] (he even felt 'natura sive deus'). But what, then, is the proposition and belief which most distinctly formulates that critical turn, the present *ascendancy* of the scientific spirit over the religious, god-inventing spirit? Is it not: the world, as force, must not be conceived of as unlimited, for it *can*not be conceived of that way – we forbid ourselves the concept of an *infinite* force, *as being incompatible with the concept of 'force'*. Thus – the world also lacks the capacity for eternal novelty.

36[18]

I take good care not to talk of chemical '*laws*': that has a moral aftertaste. It is rather a matter of the absolute establishment of power relations: the stronger becomes master of the weaker to the extent that the weaker cannot assert its degree of autonomy – here there is no mercy, no forbearance, even less a respect for 'laws'!

36[19]

It is unlikely that our 'knowing' would go any further than what's just necessary for the preservation of life. Morphology shows us how the

[52] 'God – that is, nature'.

senses and nerves, also the brain, develop in proportion to the difficulty of finding food.

36[20]

In the realm of the inorganic, too, for an atom of force only its direct proximity counts: forces at a distance cancel one another out. Here we find the core of perspectivism, and the reason why a living being is 'egoistic' through and through.

36[21]

The weaker pushes its way to the stronger, out of a lack of food; it wants to take shelter, if possible to become *one* with it. Conversely, the stronger repulses the weaker, it doesn't want to perish this way; instead, as it grows it splits into two and more. The greater the urge to unity, the more one may infer weakness; the more there is an urge to variety, differentiation, inner fragmentation, the more force is present.

The drive to come closer and the drive to repulse something – in both the inorganic and the organic world, these are what binds. The whole distinction is a prejudice.

The will to power in every combination of forces – *resisting what's stronger, attacking what's weaker – is more correct.* NB. *Processes as 'beings'.*

36[22]

The connection of the inorganic and the organic must lie in the force of repulsion which every atom of force exerts. Life should be defined as an enduring form of the *process* of *testing force*, where the different combatants grow unequally. In how far obeying also involves resisting; the obeyer by no means gives up its own power. Likewise, in commanding there is a concession that the opponent's absolute power has not been vanquished, not incorporated, dissolved. 'Obeying' and 'commanding' are forms of martial art.

36[23]

The continual transitions do not permit us to speak of the 'individual', etc.; the 'number' of beings is itself in flux. We wouldn't speak of time at all and would know nothing of motion if we didn't, in a crude way, believe we saw something 'at rest' alongside things in motion. Just as little would we speak of cause and effect, and without the erroneous conception of the 'empty space' we would never have arrived at the conception of space itself. The principle of identity has as its background the 'appearance' that things are the same. A world of becoming could not, in the strict sense, be 'grasped', be 'known': only inasmuch as the 'grasping' and 'knowing' intellect finds an already created, crude world, cobbled together out of deceptions but having become solid, inasmuch as this kind of illusion has preserved life – only to that extent is there such a thing as 'knowledge': i.e., a measuring of earlier and more recent errors against one another.

36[27]

Philosophy in the only way I still allow it to stand, as the most general form of history, as an attempt somehow to describe Heraclitean[53] becoming and to abbreviate it into signs (so to speak, to *translate* and mummify it into a kind of illusory *being*[54])

36[30]

It is unfair to Descartes to call his appeal to God's credibility frivolous. Indeed, only if we assume a God who is morally our like can 'truth' and the search for truth be at all something meaningful and promising of success. This God left aside, the question is permitted whether being deceived is not one of the conditions of life.

36[31]

The triumphant concept of 'force', with which our physicists have created God and the world, needs supplementing: it must be ascribed an inner world which I call 'will to power', i.e., an insatiable craving to manifest power; or to employ, exercise power, as a creative drive, etc. The physicists cannot eliminate 'action at a distance' from their principles, nor a force of repulsion (or attraction). There is no help for it: one must understand all motion, all 'appearances', all 'laws' as mere symptoms of inner events, and

---

53 Heraclitus, a Greek philosopher living around 500 BC, held that everything moves.
54 *'being'*: italics added.

use the human analogy consistently to the end. In the case of an animal, all its drives can be traced back to the will to power: likewise all the functions of organic life to this one source.

36[35]

Along the guiding thread of the body. –

Supposing that 'the *soul*' was an attractive and mysterious idea which philosophers, rightly, gave up only with reluctance – perhaps what they're now learning to exchange for it is even more attractive, even more mysterious. The human body, in which the whole most distant and most recent past of all organic becoming regains life and corporeality, through which, over which, beyond which a tremendous, inaudible river seems to flow: the body is a more astonishing idea than the old 'soul'.

36[36]

In every era people have believed better in the body as our most certain being, in short as our ego, than in the mind (or the 'soul' – or the subject, as the language of schoolmen now prefers to term it). It has never occurred to anyone to think of his stomach as an alien stomach, perhaps a divine one; but as for regarding his thoughts as 'inspired', his valuations as 'prompted by a God', his instincts as mysterious activity: for this tendency and taste of man there are testimonies from all the ages of mankind. Even today, particularly among artists, one often enough finds a kind of wonder and deferential unhooking of judgement when the question arises of how they succeeded in making the best throw and from what world the creative thought came to them. When they ask themselves this kind of thing, there's something of innocence and child-like bashfulness about them; they hardly dare to say 'That came from me, it was my hand that cast the die'. – Conversely, even those philosophers and religious men whose logic and piety gave them the most pressing grounds to view their bodily side as a deception, and a deception overcome and put away – even they couldn't avoid acknowledging the stupid reality that the body has not fled. On this matter we find the strangest testimonies, partly in Paul, partly in Vedanta[55] philosophy.

---

[55] The philosophy based on the Upanishads, which are elaborations on the most ancient Hindu sacred texts, the Vedas.

But in the end, what does *strength of belief* signify! It could still be a very stupid belief! – Here one must reflect: –

And in the end, if belief in the body is only the result of an inference: supposing it were a false inference, as the idealists claim: is not the credibility of the mind itself cast into doubt by its being the cause of such false inferences? Supposing multiplicity, and space and time and motion (and whatever else may be the presuppositions of a belief in corporeality) were errors, what mistrust of the mind would be aroused by the thing that induced us to reach such suppositions! Enough: for the time being, belief in the body is still a stronger belief than belief in the mind; and anyone who wants to undermine it will most thoroughly be undermining – belief in the authority of the mind as well!

Notebook 37, June – July 1885

37[4]

Morality and physiology

– We find it ill-considered that precisely human consciousness has for so long been regarded as the highest stage of organic development and as the most astonishing of all earthly things, indeed as their blossoming and goal. In fact, what is more astonishing is the *body*: there is no end to one's admiration for how the human *body* has become possible; how such a prodigious alliance of living beings, each dependent and subservient and yet in a certain sense also commanding and acting out of its own will, can live, grow, and for a while prevail, as a whole – and we can see this does *not* occur due to consciousness! For this 'miracle of miracles', consciousness is just a 'tool' and nothing more – a tool in the same sense that the stomach is a tool. The magnificent binding together of the most diverse life, the ordering and arrangement of the higher and lower activities, the thousand-fold obedience which is not blind, even less mechanical, but a selecting, shrewd, considerate, even resistant obedience – measured by intellectual standards, this whole phenomenon 'body' is as superior to our consciousness, our 'mind', our conscious thinking, feeling, willing, as algebra is superior to the times tables. The 'apparatus of nerves and brain' is *not* constructed this subtly and 'divinely' so as to bring forth thinking, feeling, willing at all. It seems to me, instead, that precisely this thinking, feeling, willing does not itself require an 'apparatus' but that the so-called apparatus, and it alone, is the thing that counts. Rather, such a prodigious synthesis of living beings and intellects as is called 'man' will only be able to live once that subtle system of connections and mediations, and thus lightning-fast communication between all these higher and lower beings, has been created – and created by nothing but living intermediaries: this, however, is a problem of morality, not of mechanics! Nowadays we've forbidden ourselves to spin yarns about 'unity', the 'soul', the 'person': hypotheses like these make one's problem *more difficult*, that much is clear. And for us, even those smallest living beings which constitute our body (more correctly: for whose interaction the thing we call 'body' is the best simile –) are not soul-atoms, but rather something growing, struggling, reproducing and dying off again: so that their number alters unsteadily, and our living, like all living, is at once an incessant dying. There are thus in man as many 'consciousnesses' as – at every moment of his existence – there are beings which constitute his body. The distinguishing feature of that 'consciousness' usually held to be the only one, the intellect, is precisely that it remains protected and closed off from the immeasurable multiplicity in the experiences of these many consciousnesses and that, as a consciousness of a higher rank, as a governing multitude and aristocracy, it is presented only with a *selection* of experiences – experiences, further-more, that have all been simplified, made easy to survey and grasp, thus *falsified* – so that it in turn may carry on this simplification and making graspable, in other words this falsification, and prepare what is commonly called 'a will' – every such act of will requires, so to speak, the appointment of a dictator. However, what presents this selection to our intellect, what has simplified, assimilated, interpreted experiences beforehand, is at any rate not that intellect itself; any more than it is the intellect which *carries out* the will, which takes up a pale, watery and extremely imprecise idea of value and force and translates it into living force, precise measures of value. And just the same kind of operation as is enacted here must keep being enacted on all the deeper levels, in the behaviour of all these higher and lower beings towards one other: this same selection and presentation of experiences, this abstraction and thinking-together, this willing, this translation of always very unspecific willing back into specific activity. Along the guiding thread of the body, as I have said, we learn that our life is possible through an interplay of many intelligences that are very unequal in value, and thus only through a constant, thousand-fold obeying and commanding – speaking in moral terms: through the incessant exercise of many *virtues*. And how could one not speak in moral terms! – – Prattling in this way, I gave myself up dissolutely to my pedagogic drive, for I was overjoyed to have someone who could bear to listen to me. However, it was just then that Ariadne[56] – for this all took place during my first stay on Naxos – could actually bear it no more: 'But, sir,' she said, 'You're talking pigswill German!' – 'German,' I answered untroubled, 'Simply German! Leave aside the pigswill, my goddess! You underestimate the difficulty of saying subtle things in German!' – 'Subtle things!' cried Ariadne, horrified, 'But that was just positivism! Philosophy of the snout! Conceptual muck and mish-mash from a hundred philosophies! Whatever next!' – all the while toying impatiently with the famous thread that once guided her Theseus through the labyrinth. – Thus it came to light that Ariadne was two thousand years behindhand in her philosophical training.

37[8]

Inexorable, hesitating, terrible as fate, the great task and question is approaching: how shall the earth as a whole be governed? And *for what* shall 'man' as a whole – no longer just one people, one race – be raised and bred?

The legislative moralities are the main means of fashioning out of men whatever a creative and profound will desires, assuming that such an artistic will of the highest rank holds power and can assert its creative will over long periods of time, in the shape of laws, religions and customs. Such men of great creativity, the really great men in my understanding, will be sought in vain today and probably for a long time to come: they *are missing*; until, after much disappointment, one finally has to begin to understand why it is that they're missing and that nothing now presents, or will present for a long time to come, a more hostile obstacle to their emergence and development than what in Europe is nowadays straightforwardly called '*morality*', as if there were and must be no other one – that morality of the herd animal, already described, which strives with all its force for a universal green-pasture happiness on earth, namely security, harmlessness, comfort, easy living, and which in the end, 'if all goes

---

[56] In Greek mythology Ariadne was the daughter of Minos, King of Crete. With a thread she helped Theseus escape the labyrinth and they left Crete together. Abandoned by him on the island of Naxos, she became the wife of the god Dionysos. Ariadne was a deeply significant figure for the later Nietzsche (see, e.g., BGE 295, TI Skirmishes 19, EH Z 8, D Ariadne; also the letters to Cosima Wagner, 3 January 1889, and to Jacob Burckhardt, 6 January 1889).

well', also hopes to rid itself of all kinds of shepherds and bellwethers. The two doctrines it preaches most profusely are 'equal rights' and 'sympathy with all that suffers' – and it takes suffering itself to be something that absolutely must be *abolished*. That such 'ideas' can still be fashionable gives one an unpleasant notion of – – – However, anyone who has thought carefully about where and how the human plant has hitherto sprung up most vigorously must suppose that it was under the *reverse* conditions: that the danger of man's situation has to grow huge, his powers of invention and dissimulation to fight their way up through protracted pressure and coercion, his will to live become intensified into an unconditional will to power and overpower, and that danger, harshness, violence, danger in the alleyway and in the heart, inequality of rights, secrecy, stoicism, the arts of temptation, devilry of all kinds, in short the antithesis of everything desirable for the herd, are needed if the human type is to be heightened. A morality with such reverse intentions, which wants to breed men to be high not comfortable and mediocre, a morality whose intention is to breed a ruling caste – the future *masters of the earth* – must, if it is to be taught, introduce itself by starting from the existing moral law and sheltering under its words and forms. That this, however, requires many means of deception and transition to be devised, and that because the lifespan of one man signifies almost nothing compared to the time needed to carry out such lengthy tasks and intentions, above all *a new species* must first be bred, in which the same will, the same instinct is guaranteed to last through many generations: a new species and caste of masters – this is as readily understood as the Etcetera of this thought, long and difficult to express. To prepare a *reversal of values* for a certain strong species of men of the highest spirituality and strength of will, and for this purpose to unleash in them, slowly and cautiously, many instincts previously reined in and calumniated: anyone who thinks about this is one of us, the free spirits – admittedly, a newer kind of 'free spirits' than the ones before, who wished for more or less the opposite. To us belong, it seems to me, especially the European pessimists, the poets and thinkers of an outraged idealism, insofar as their dissatisfaction with the whole of existence also drives them, at least *logically*, to dissatisfaction with present-day man; likewise certain insatiably ambitious artists who fight unscrupulously and unconditionally for the special rights of higher men and against the 'herd animal', and who use the means of seduction offered by art to lull to sleep all herd instincts and herd caution among more exquisite spirits;

thirdly and finally, all those critics and historians by whom the success-fully initiated discovery of the world of antiquity – it is the work of the *new* Columbus, of the German spirit – is courageously *continued* (for we are still at the beginning of this conquest). For certainly, in the world of antiquity a different and more masterful morality ruled from today's; and the man of antiquity, under the educating spell of his morality, was a stronger and more profound man than the man of today – he was the only 'well-formed' man there has been. But the seduction exerted by an-tiquity on well-formed, i.e., strong and enterprising, souls today remains the most subtle and effective of all anti-democratic and anti-Christian seductions, as it was in the days of the Renaissance.

Notebook 38, June – July 1885

38[1]

In the form in which it comes, a thought is a sign with many meanings, requiring interpretation or, more precisely, an arbitrary narrowing and restriction before it finally becomes clear. It arises in me – where from? How? I don't know. It comes, independently of my will, usually circled about and clouded by a crowd of feelings, desires, aversions, and by other thoughts, often enough scarcely distinguishable from a 'willing' or 'feeling'. It is drawn out of this crowd, cleaned, set on its feet, watched as it stands there, moves about, all this at an amazing speed yet without any sense of haste. *Who* does all this I don't know, and I am certainly more observer than author of the process. Then its case is tried, the question posed: 'What does it mean? What is it allowed to mean? Is it right or wrong?' – the help of other thoughts is called on, it is compared. In this way thinking proves to be almost a kind of exercise and act of justice, where there is a judge, an opposing party, even an examination of the witnesses which I am permitted to observe for a while – only a while, to be sure: most of the process, it seems, escapes me. – That every thought first arrives many-meaninged and floating, really only as the occasion for attempts to interpret or for arbitrarily fixing it, that a multitude of persons seem to participate in all thinking – this is not particularly easy to observe: fundamentally, we are trained the opposite way, not to think about thinking as we think. The origin of the thought remains hidden; in all probability it is only the symptom of a much more comprehensive state; the fact that *it*, and not another, is the one to come, that it comes with precisely this

34

greater or lesser luminosity, sometimes sure and imperious, sometimes weak and in need of support, as a whole always exciting, questioning – because every thought acts as a stimulus to consciousness – in all of this, something of our total state expresses itself in sign form. – The same is true of every feeling. It does not mean something in itself: when it comes it first has to be interpreted by us, and *how strange* this interpretation often is! Think of the distress of the entrails, almost 'unconscious' to us, of the tensions of blood pressure in the abdomen, of the pathological states of the nervus sympathicus[57] – and how many things there are of which the sensorium commune[58] gives us hardly a gleam of consciousness! – Faced with such uncertain feelings of displeasure, only the expert anatomist can guess the right type and *location* of their causes, whereas everyone else, in other words almost all men for as long as they have existed, searches not for a physical explanation of this kind of pain but for a psychological and moral one. They *misconstrue* the body's actual ill humours by fetching from their store of unpleasant experiences and fears a reason to feel so bad. Under torture, almost anyone confesses himself guilty; under a pain whose physical cause is unknown, the tortured man subjects himself to an interrogation as long and inquisitorial as it takes to *find* himself or others *guilty*: – like, for example, the Puritan who, as a matter of habit, made a moral interpretation of the ill humour resulting from an unwise lifestyle: as the pangs of his own conscience. –

38[4]

'Truth': in my way of thinking that does not necessarily mean an antithesis of error, but in the most fundamental cases only the relative position of various errors: such as one being older, more profound than another, perhaps even ineradicable, in that an organic being of our species could not live without it; while other errors do not tyrannise us like this as conditions of life but, compared to such 'tyrants', can be discarded and 'refuted'. An assumption may be irrefutable – why should that make it *true*? This proposition may outrage logicians, who posit *their* limits as the limits of things; but I have long since declared war on this optimism of logicians.

---

57 Part of the autonomic nervous system that regulates the workings of the body's internal organs.
58 The seat of sensation in the brain.

38[8]

The will

– Every willing unites a multiplicity of *feelings*: the feeling of the state to be *left*, the feeling of the state to be *reached*, the feeling of this 'leaving and reaching' itself, the feeling of the duration of the process, then lastly an accompanying feeling of the muscles which begins its play through a kind of habit, even without our moving arms or legs, as soon as we 'will'. Feeling, then, in fact many ways of feeling, must be recognised as an ingredient of the will, and so, secondly, must *thinking*. In every act of will, a thought commands – and it would be a great mistake to believe we could separate this thought off from the willing itself, as if willing would then remain behind. Thirdly, the will is not only a complex of feeling and thinking, but above all also an *affect*: that affect of command. What is called freedom of the will is essentially a feeling of superiority over the one who must obey: 'I am free, he must obey' – this consciousness is present in every will, and it's that tense alertness, that clear gaze focused on one thing only, that exclusive valuation: 'this and nothing else is now necessary', that inner certainty of being obeyed, how all this belongs to the state of the one commanding. A man who *wills* – commands a something in himself which obeys, or which he believes will obey. Now, however, notice what is the most essential aspect of 'will', of this so complicated thing for which the common people have a single word. Because in a given case we are simultaneously the commanders and the obeyers, and as obeyers know the feelings of resisting, harassing, pushing, *moving*, which usually begin immediately after the act of will; because, however, in using the synthetic concept 'I' we habitually disregard, *disguise from ourselves* this duality, willing has become encumbered with a whole chain of erroneous conclusions and consequently false valuations of will itself — so that the willer believes in all good faith that his will itself is the actual and sufficient motor for the whole action. And because, in almost every case, willing only happened where some effect of the command – obedience, thus some action – was to be expected, the appearance has translated itself into the feeling that there is a *necessity*[59] of effect. Enough: the willer believes with a fair degree of certainty that will and action are somehow one – he ascribes the success of execution to the will itself, enjoying a growth in that feeling

---

[59] '*necessity*': italics added.

of power which all commanding brings with it. 'Freedom of will': this is the word for that very mixed state of the willer, who commands and at the same time, as the executor of the command, enjoys the triumph of superiority over resistance; who, however, judges that the will itself is what overcomes the resistance. He takes the pleasurable feelings of the successfully executing tool – the ministering will and sub-will – and adds them to his pleasurable feelings as the giver of the command. – This tangled nest of feelings, states and false assumptions, which the common people designate with one word and as one thing, because it is there suddenly and 'at once' and is among the very most frequent, consequently most 'well-known' experiences: *the will*, as I have described it here – who can credit that it has never been described before? That the common people's clumsy prejudice has kept its validity and remained unexamined in every philosophy? That philosophers' opinions have never differed on what 'willing' is, because they all believed that precisely here one had an immediate certainty, a fundamental fact, that precisely here there was no room for opinion? And that all logicians still teach the holy trinity of 'thinking, feeling, willing' as if 'willing' did not include feeling and thinking? – After all this, Schopenhauer's great mistake of taking the will to be the best-known thing in the world, indeed as the genuinely and solely known thing, seems less crazed and arbitrary: he only adopted a tremendous prejudice of all previous philosophers, a prejudice of the common people – adopted it and, as philosophers generally do, *exaggerated* it.

38[10]

Man is a creature that makes shapes and rhythms; he is practised at nothing better and it seems that he takes pleasure in nothing *more* than in *inventing* figures. Only observe how our eye occupies itself as soon as it receives nothing more to see: it *creates* itself something to see. Presumably in the same situation our hearing does just that, too: it *practises*. Without the transformation of the world into figures and rhythms there would be nothing 'the same' for us, thus nothing recurrent, and thus no possibility of experiencing and appropriating, of *feeding*. In all perception, i.e., in the most original appropriation, what is essentially happening is an action, or more precisely: an imposition of shapes upon things – only the superficial talk of 'impressions'. In this way man comes to know his force as a resisting and even more as a determining force – rejecting, selecting, shaping to fit, slotting into his schemata. There is something active about our taking on a stimulus in the first place and taking it on as *that particular* stimulus. It is in the nature of this activity not only to posit shapes, rhythms and successions of shapes, but also to appraise the formation it has created with an eye to incorporation or rejection. Thus arises our world, our whole world: and no supposed 'true reality', no 'in-themselves of things' corresponds to this whole world which we have created, belonging to us alone. Rather it is itself our only reality, and 'knowledge' thus considered proves to be only a *means of feeding*. But we are beings who are difficult to feed and have everywhere enemies and, as it were, indigestibles – that is what has made human knowledge *refined*, and ultimately so proud of its refinement that it doesn't want to hear that it is not a goal but a means, or even a tool of the stomach – if not itself a kind of stomach! – –

38[12]

And do you know what 'the world' is to me? Shall I show you it in my mirror? This world: a monster of force, without beginning, without end, a fixed, iron quantity of force which grows neither larger nor smaller, which doesn't exhaust but only transforms itself, as a whole unchanging in size, an economy without expenditure and losses, but equally without increase, without income, enclosed by 'nothingness' as by a boundary, not something blurred, squandered, not something infinitely extended; instead, as a determinate force set into a determinate space, and not into a space that is anywhere 'empty' but as force everywhere, as a play of forces and force-waves simultaneously one and 'many', accumulating here while diminishing there, an ocean of forces storming and flooding within themselves, eternally changing, eternally rushing back, with tremendous years of recurrence, with an ebb and flood of its forms, shooting out from the simplest into the most multifarious, from the stillest, coldest, most rigid into the most fiery, wild, self-contradictory, and then coming home from abundance to simplicity, from the play of contradiction back to the pleasure of harmony, affirming itself even in this sameness of its courses and years, blessing itself as what must eternally return, as a becoming that knows no satiety, no surfeit, no fatigue – this, my *Dionysian* world of eternal self-creating, of eternal self-destroying, this mystery world of dual delights, this my beyond good and evil, without goal, unless there is a goal in the happiness of the circle, without will, unless a ring feels good will towards itself – do you want a *name* for this world? A *solution* to all its riddles? A *light* for you too, for you, the most secret, strongest, most intrepid, most midnightly? – *This world is the will to power – and nothing besides!* And you yourselves too are this will to power – and nothing besides!

38[13]

When I was younger I worried about what a philosopher really was: for I believed I saw contradictory features in the famous philosophers. Finally I realised that there are two different kinds of philosopher: those who have to hold fast some large body of valuations, that is, of previous assignments and creations of value (logical or moral ones), and then those who are themselves the legislators of valuations. The former try to gain power over the present or past world by summarising and abbreviating it with signs. These inquirers are charged with making all events and all evaluations up to now easy to survey, easy to think through, to grasp, to manage, with subduing the past, abbreviating everything that is long, even time itself – a great and wondrous task. However, the real philosophers *command and legislate*, they say: this is how it *shall* be! and it is they who determine the Where to and the What for of man, making use of the spadework done by the philosophical labourers, those subduers of the past. This second kind of philosopher rarely turns out well; and indeed their situation and danger is tremendous. How often have they intentionally blindfolded themselves to stop having to see the narrow margin that separates them from the abyss, the headlong fall: for instance Plato when he persuaded himself that the good, as he wanted it, was not the good of Plato but the good in itself, the eternal treasure that just happened to have been found on his path by some man called Plato! In much coarser forms this same will to blindness rules among the founders of religion: their 'thou shalt' must on no account sound to their ears like an 'I want' – only as the command of a God do they dare to discharge their task, only as 'divine inspiration' is their legislation on values a *bearable* burden which does *not* crush their conscience. – Once those two means of consolation, Plato's and Mohammed's, have fallen away and no thinker can any longer relieve his conscience with the hypothesis of a 'God' or 'eternal values', the claim of the legislator of new values arises with a new and unprecedented terror.

Now those chosen ones, on whom the presentiment of such a duty begins to dawn, will try and see whether they can't slip out of that duty, as if out of their greatest danger, 'just in time', through some trick or other: for example by telling themselves that the task is already solved, or is insoluble, or that they don't have the shoulders to carry such burdens, or that they are already weighed down with other, more immediate tasks, or even that this new, distant duty is a seduction and a temptation, a diversion from all duties, a sickness, a kind of madness. One or the other of them may in fact succeed in evading it: the trace of such evaders and their bad conscience runs through the whole of history. Mostly, however, such men of fate have been reached by that redeeming hour, that autumn hour of ripeness, where they *had* to do what they did not even 'want' to do – and the deed they had most feared fell easily and undesired from the tree, as a deed without choice, almost as a gift. –

Notebook 39, August – September 1885

39[17]

It may be hoped man will raise himself so high that the things previously highest to him, e.g., the belief in God he has held up to now, appear childlike, childish, and touching: indeed, that he will *do again* what he did with all the myths – turn them into children's stories and fairy-tales.

Notebook 40, August – September 1885

40[9]

There are schematic minds, who hold a complex of thought to be *truer* if it can be inscribed into schemata or tables of categories drawn up beforehand. The self-deceptions in this field are countless: almost all great 'systems' are among them. The *fundamental prejudice* is, though, that it is inherent to the *true being* of things to be ordered, easy to survey, systematic; conversely, that disorder, chaos, the unpredictable can only make its appearance in a world that is false or incompletely known – in short, that it is an error – which is a moral prejudice, drawn from the fact that the truthful, reliable human being is a man of order, of maxims, and all in all tends to be something predictable and pedantic. And yet it cannot be demonstrated at all that the in-themselves of things follows this recipe for the model civil servant.

40[13]

Logic is tied to the condition: *assuming that identical cases exist.* Indeed, in order to think and conclude logically, the fulfilment of this condition *must* first be feigned. That is: the will to *logical truth* cannot realise itself until a fundamental *falsification* of all events has been undertaken. From which it follows that a drive rules here which is capable of both means, firstly of falsifying, then of implementing a single viewpoint: logic does *not* originate in the will to truth.

40[15]

Judgement: this is the belief that 'such and such is the case'. Thus, judgement involves admitting having encountered an identical case: it thus presupposes comparison, with the help of memory. Judgement does *not* create the appearance of an identical case. Instead, it believes it perceives one; it works on the supposition that identical cases even exist. But what is that function, which must be much *older* and have been at work much earlier, that levels out and assimilates cases in themselves dissimilar? What is that second function which, on the basis of the first, etc. 'What arouses the same sensations is the same': but what is it that *makes*[60] sensations the same, 'takes' them as the same? – There could be no judgements at all if a kind of levelling had not first been carried out within the sensations: memory is only possible with a constant underscoring of what has been experienced, has become habit – – *Before* a judgement can be made, *the process of assimilation must already have been completed*: thus, here too there is an intellectual activity which does not enter consciousness, as in the case of pain caused by an injury. Probably, all organic functions have their correspondence in inner events, in assimilation, elimination, growth, etc.

Essential to start from the body and use it as a guiding thread. It is the far richer phenomenon, and can be observed more distinctly. Belief in the body is better established than belief in the mind.

'However strongly something is believed, that is not a criterion of truth.' But what is truth? Perhaps a kind of belief which has become a condition of life? In that case, its strength would indeed be a criterion. E.g., regarding causality.

40[21]

Starting point the *body* and physiology: why? – What we gain is the right idea of the nature of our subject-unity – namely as rulers at the head of a commonwealth, not as 'souls' or 'life forces' – and likewise the right idea of these rulers' dependence on the ruled and on those conditions of order of rank and division of labour which make possible both the individual and the whole. Just as living unities continually arise and die, and eternity is not a quality of the 'subject'; that struggle also expresses itself in obeying

---

[60] '*makes*': italics added.

and commanding, and that a fluid setting of the boundaries of power is a quality of life. A certain *ignorance* in which the ruler is kept regarding the individual functions and even malfunctions of the community – this is among the conditions which make ruling possible. In short, we gain esteem for not-knowing, too, for the rough survey, for simplifying and falsifying, for the perspectival. What's most important, however: that we understand the ruler and his subjects as being *of the same kind*, all feeling, thinking, willing – and that wherever we see or sense movement in the body, we learn to infer a kind of corresponding, subjective, invisible life. Movement is a symbolism for the eye; it indicates that something has been felt, willed, thought. – The danger in all direct questioning of the subject about the subject, and all self-contemplation of the mind, is that it could be useful and important for the subject's activity to misinterpret itself. This is why we ask the body, and reject the testimony of the sharpened senses: we try, so to speak, to see whether the subordinated themselves can't take up communication with us.

40[27]

Just as mathematics and mechanics were long considered sciences with absolute validity, and only now does the suspicion dare show its face that they are nothing more and nothing less than applied logic on the strength of the particular, indemonstrable assumption that 'identical cases' exist – and logic itself is a consistent notation based on that assumption (that identical cases exist) being carried out – in the same way, the *word* too used to be considered the cognition of something, and even now grammatical functions are the things most strongly believed, against which one cannot guard too carefully. Possibly the same kind of man who later thought up Vedanta philosophies thousands of years earlier thought up a philosophical language, perhaps on the basis of imperfect languages, *not*, they believed, as a notation but as cognition of the world itself; yet whenever a 'that is' has been posited, a later and subtler age has revealed it to be no more than a 'that means'. Even now, most philosophers have no *inkling* of the real critique of concepts or (as I once called it) a real 'history of the genesis of thinking'. The *valuations* that surround logic must be revealed and reappraised – e.g., 'the certain is more valuable than the uncertain', 'thinking is our highest function'; likewise the optimism in logic, the sense of victory in every conclusion, in judgement the imperative element, in concept the innocence of the belief in intelligibility.

40[28]

There must have been thinking long before there were eyes: 'lines and shapes' were thus not originally given. Instead, thinking has longest been based on the sense of touch: yet this, if it is *not* supported by the eyes, only teaches degrees of pressure, not shapes. Thus, before we started practising our understanding of the world as moving shapes, there was a time when the world was 'grasped' as changing sensations of pressure of various degrees. There is no doubt that we can think in pictures, in sounds: but we can also think in sensations of pressure. Comparison in respect to their strength and direction and sequence, memory, etc.

40[36]

The mathematical physicists have no use for lump atoms in their science; consequently they construct for themselves a world of force-points which can be reckoned with. Men and all organic creatures have done more or less the same thing: they have arranged, thought, devised the world to fit, until they could make use of it, until it could be 'reckoned' with.

40[38]

The point is to describe correctly the unity in which thinking, willing and feeling, and all affects, are conjoined: it's clear that the intellect is only a *tool*, but a tool in whose hands? Surely the hands of the affects, and these are a multiplicity behind which it is not necessary to posit a unity: it's enough to understand them as regents. – The fact that everywhere organs have taken shape, as morphological development shows, may certainly also serve as a metaphor for the intellectual, so that something 'new' can only be discerned when a single force has been isolated from out of a synthesis of forces.

Thinking itself is an action like this, which *takes apart* what is really one. Everywhere, even in thinking, is the *illusion* that there are multiplicities whose contents can be counted. In reality there is nothing 'added', nothing 'divided', two halves of a thing are not equal to the whole.

40[42]

The assumption of the *single subject* is perhaps unnecessary; perhaps it is just as permissible to assume a multiplicity of subjects on whose interplay and struggle our thinking and our consciousness in general is based? A kind of *aristocracy* of 'cells' in which mastery resides? Certainly an aristocracy of equals which together are used to ruling and know how to command?

My hypotheses:

the subject as multiplicity

pain as intellectual and dependent on the judgement 'harmful': projected

the effect always 'unconscious': the 'cause', an inferred and imagined one, is projected, *follows* in time.

pleasure is a kind of pain.

the only *force* which exists is of the same kind as that of the will: a commanding of other subjects, which thereupon change.

the constant transience and volatility of the subject, 'mortal soul'

number as perspectival form.

40[46]

NB. Our past and distant destiny rules over us, even if we don't yet have eyes for it; for long periods of time we experience only riddles. The choice of men and things, the selection of events, the pushing away of what's most agreeable, often what's most revered – it frightens us, as if chance, arbitrariness were breaking out of us here and there like a volcano: yet it's the higher reason inherent in our future task. Looking forwards, all the events that involve us may seem like just the concurrence of chance and nonsense: looking backwards, I for my part can no longer find anything of either in my life.

40[61]

Regarding the plan

Our intellect, our will, likewise our feelings are dependent on our *valuations*: these correspond to our drives and the conditions of their existence. Our drives can be reduced to *the will to power*.

The will to power is the final fact to which we descend.

$\begin{cases} \text{Our intellect a tool} \\ \text{Our will} \\ \text{Our feelings of unpleasure} \\ \text{Our sensations} \end{cases}$ $\begin{cases} \text{themselves dependent on valuations} \\ \\ \end{cases}$

40[69]

Our mental life, including 'feelings' and sensations, is a tool at the service of a many-headed, variously-minded master: this master is our valuations. Our valuations, however, betray something of what the *conditions of our life* are (the smallest part being the conditions of the individual, a larger part those of the human species, the largest and most extensive the conditions under which *life* is possible at all).

Notebook 41, August – September 1885

41[6]

The highest and most illustrious human joys, in which existence celebrates its own transfiguration, are reached, as is just, only by the rarest and best-formed men: and even by these only after they and their forebears have led long, preparatory lives towards this goal, without even knowing of the goal. Then, within one man an overflowing wealth of the most diverse forces lives amicably alongside the most agile power of a 'free willing' and of lordly decree; then the spirit feels just as comfortable and at home in the senses as the senses feel at home and comfortable in the spirit; and anything which occurs only in the spirit must call forth a subtle, extraordinary happiness and play in the senses. And just the same in reverse! – consider this reversal in the case of Hafiz;[61] even Goethe, if in a weakened echo, gives us an inkling of this process. Probably for such perfect and well-formed men, in the end the most sensual functions are transfigured by a metaphor-intoxication of the highest spirituality: they experience in themselves a kind of *deification of the body* and are as remote as it is possible to be from the ascetic philosophy of the proposition 'God is a spirit': and it becomes clear that the ascetic is 'the ill-formed man' who calls *good* only one something in himself, and precisely that something which judges and condemns – and calls it '*God*'. From that height of joy, where a man feels himself, and completely, to be nature's deified form and self-justification, right down to the joy of healthy peasants and healthy

---

[61] Shams-ud-din Mahommed, great fourteenth-century Persian poet whose *Diwan* was widely translated in Germany in the nineteenth century and inspired Goethe's *West-östlicher Divan*.

animal-like half-humans: to this whole, long, prodigious light and colour scale of *happiness* the Greeks, not without the grateful shudder of the initiate into a mystery, not without much caution and devout reticence – gave the divine name: Dionysos. – As for all more recent men, children of a brittle, multifarious, sick, strange mother, what do they know of the *compass* of Greek happiness, what could they know of it! What right would the slaves of 'modern ideas' have to Dionysian festivals!

41[11]

'Thinking' in the primitive state (pre-organic) is the *effecting of shapes*, as in the crystal. – In *our* thinking the *essential* thing is the fitting of the new material into the old schemata (= Procrustean bed[62]), *making* it alike.

---

[62] Procrustes was a robber who forced his victims to fit a bed by stretching or cutting off their limbs.

Notebook 43, autumn 1885

43[1]

Draft

The first problem is: how deeply the '*will to truth*' goes into things? Gauge the whole value of ignorance within the combination of the means of preserving living things, likewise the value of simplifications *in general* and the value of regulative fictions, e.g., the logical ones; consider, above all, the value of interpretations, and the extent to which not 'it is' but 'it means' – – –

one thus arrives at this solution: the 'will to truth' develops in the service of the 'will to power': to be exact, its real task is to help a certain kind of untruth to victory and permanence, to take a connected whole of falsifications as the basis for preserving a certain kind of living things.

Problem: how deeply the *will to goodness* goes down into the essence of things. Everywhere, in plant and animal, one sees its opposite: indifference or harshness or cruelty. 'Justice', 'punishment'. The development of cruelty.

Solution. Fellow-feeling exists only in social formations (one of which is the human body, whose individual living beings 'feel with' one another), as a consequence of a larger whole *wanting to preserve* itself against another whole, and again because in the total economy of the world, where there is no possibility of perishing and losing, goodness would be a *superfluous* principle.

Problem: how deeply reason inheres in the fundament of things. According to a critique of ends and means (– not a factual relation but always just one that has been interpreted in), the character of wastefulness, of madness is normal within the total economy. 'Intelligence' appears as a special form of unreason, almost as its most malicious caricature.

Problem: how far the 'will to the beautiful' reaches. Reckless development of forms: the most beautiful are merely the strongest: victorious, they establish themselves and take pleasure in their type; reproduction. (Plato's belief that even philosophy is a kind of sublime sexual and reproductive drive.)

The things, then, which we have esteemed most highly until now, as the 'true', 'good', 'reasonable', 'beautiful', turn out to be individual cases of the *reverse* powers – I point my finger at this prodigious *perspectival falsification* which allows the human species to assert itself. It is a condition of the species' life to take pleasure in itself on this account (men find joy in the means of their preservation: and among these means is their not wanting to be deceived, their helping one another, their willingness to understand each other; that, overall, the successful types know how to live at the expense of the failures). In all this the will to power expresses itself, reaching unscrupulously for the means of deception: one can imagine a *malicious enjoyment* that a God might feel at the sight of man admiring himself.

Thus: the will to power.

Consequence: if this idea is *hostile* to us, why do we acquiesce in it? Give us those lovely phantasms! Let's be the swindlers and beautifiers of humanity! Fact of *what* a *philosopher* actually is.

Notebook 44, autumn 1885

44[6]

What is it, then, this struggle of the Christian 'against nature'? We certainly won't let ourselves be deceived by his words and interpretations! It's nature against something that is nature. For many: fear, for some: revulsion, a certain intellectuality for others, love of an ideal without flesh and desire, of an 'epitome of nature' in the case of the highest of them – those want to rival their ideal. It goes without saying that abasement in place of self-esteem, anxious wariness towards the desires, distancing oneself from the usual duties (which, in turn, creates a higher feeling of rank), the excitement of a constant battle over tremendous things, the habit of effusions of feeling – all make up one type: in it the *over-sensitivity* of an atrophying body preponderates, but the nervousness and its inspiration are *interpreted* differently. The *taste* of such natures tends (1) towards sophistry, (2) towards floweriness, (3) towards extreme feelings. – The natural inclinations *do* satisfy themselves, but are interpreted in a new way, e.g., as 'justification before God', 'feeling of redemption through grace' (– every unpreventable *feeling of well-being* is interpreted like this! –), pride, voluptuousness, etc. – General problem: what becomes of the man who reviles to himself what is natural and, in practice, denies it and has it atrophy? In fact, the Christian proves to be a form of self-mastery *that exaggerates*: to tame his desires, he seems to need to annihilate or crucify them. –

The *Epicurean kind of Christian and the Stoic kind* – the former includes François de Sales,[63] the latter Pascal

The victory of Epicurus – but precisely this kind of man is imperfectly understood and *is bound to* be imperfectly understood. The Stoic kind (which has great need of struggle and *consequently* sets the value of the struggler unreasonably high –) always slanders the 'Epicurean'!

44[7]

Greek and Roman antiquity had need of a tyrannical and exaggerating anti-nature morality; so did the Germanic tribes, in a different respect.

Our present kind of man really *lacks* strict order and discipline; but this poses no serious danger, because this kind of man is weaker than those of the past, and on the other hand because the unconscious disciplinarians (like hard work, ambition in getting on, bourgeois respectability) have a very restricting, curbing effect. – But *how* the men of Pascal's day had to be held in check!

Superfluous Christianity: at those points where extreme methods are no longer *needed*! There everything becomes false, and every word, every Christian perspective just hypocrisy and fine words.

---

[63] Francis of Sales (1567–1622), anti-Calvinist Bishop of Geneva who argued that spiritual perfection could be reached in earthly affairs, not only in retreat from the world.

Notebook 1, autumn 1885 – spring 1886

1[7]

– moral feeling is first developed with reference to man (starting with classes!); only later is it transferred to actions and characteristics. The *pathos*[64] *of distance* is at the deepest root of that feeling.

1[10]

– 'punishment' develops within the narrowest space, as a reaction by the powerful, by the master of the house, as an expression of his anger at his command and prohibition being flouted. – *Before* the morality of custom (whose canon wants 'everything conventional to be honoured') comes the morality of the ruling personality (whose canon wants 'the one who commands to be honoured alone'). The pathos[65] of distance, the feeling of difference in rank, lies at the ultimate root of all morality.

1[14]

– A man will misunderstand every action he is not capable of. Always to be misunderstood in one's actions is a sign of distinction. It is then necessary, and no reason to become embittered.

---

[64] See note to 35 [24].   [65] See note to 35 [24].

1[16]

Thoughts are actions

1[18]

The problem of sincerity is quite new. I am amazed: in this matter we consider natures like Bismarck at fault due to negligence, those like Richard Wagner due to a lack of modesty; we would condemn Plato for his pia fraus,[66] Kant for the derivation of his categorical imperative, even though this was surely not the path by which he reached his belief

1[20]

– All our conscious motives are superficial phenomena: behind them stands the struggle of our drives and states, the struggle for dominion.

1[21]

– That this melody sounds beautiful is *not* something taught to children by authority or by lessons, as little as the sense of well-being in looking at a venerable man. *Valuations are innate* (despite Locke![67]), inherited: admittedly, they develop more strongly and beautifully if the people who look after and love us also value the same way as we do. What torture for a child always to posit his good and evil in contradiction to his mother, and to be mocked and despised wherever he reveres!

1[22]

– How manifold is that which we experience as '*moral feeling*': in it there is reverence, dread, a touch as if by something holy and mysterious, in it is the voice of something commanding, something that takes itself more seriously than we do; something that elevates, kindles, or brings calm and profundity. Our moral feeling is a synthesis, a simultaneous resounding of all the lordly and subservient feelings that have shaped the history of our forebears

---

[66] Pious fraud.
[67] The reference is to John Locke's critique of the doctrine of innate ideas in Book I of his 'Essay Concerning Human Understanding', which first appeared in 1689.

1[24]

– Soul and breath and *existence*, esse,[68] equated. What *lives* is being, there is no other being.

1[28]

– all *movements are to be taken as gestures*, as a kind of language through which the forces understand each other. In the inorganic world misunderstanding is absent, and communication seems perfect. It's in the organic world that *error* begins. 'Things', 'substances', qualities, act-'ivities' – these must not be carried across into the inorganic world! They are the specific errors which enable organisms to live. Problem of the possibility of 'error'? The opposition is not between 'false' and 'true' but between the *'abbreviations of signs'* and the signs themselves. What's essential is the evolution of forms which *represent* many movements, the invention of signs for whole species of signs.

– all movements are *signs* of something happening within; and all that happens within expresses itself in such alterations of form. Thinking is not itself what happens within, but likewise just a sign language for the balancing out of the affects' power.

1[30]

A. Psychological *point of departure*:

– our thinking and valuating is only an expression of desires that govern it
– desires become more and more specialised: their unity is *the will to power* (to take the term from the strongest of all drives, which has directed all organic development up to now)
– reduction of all basic organic functions to the will to power
– question whether it is not the moving force in the inorganic world as well? For the mechanistic interpretation of the world still needs a moving force
– 'law of nature': as a formula for the unconditional production of relations and degrees of power

[68] Being.

– mechanical *movement* is only a means of expression for something that happens within
– 'cause and effect'

1[33]

– man's most dreadful and deep-rooted craving, his drive to power – this drive is known as 'freedom' – must be kept within bounds for the longest time. This is why until now the aim of ethics, with its unconscious instincts to educate and discipline, has been to keep the lust for power within bounds: it vilifies the tyrannical individual and underscores, with its glorification of patriotism and charitable aid, the herd's instinct for power.

1[37]

– movements are not '*effected*' by a '*cause*': that would be the old concept of soul again! – they are the will itself, but not wholly and completely!

1[38]

NB. The belief in causality goes back to the belief that I am what effects, to the divorce of the 'soul' from its *activity*. Thus, an age-old superstition!

1[44]

– the offence taken at the doctrine 'of the unfreedom of the will' is that it seems to assert 'you do what you do not voluntarily but unwillingly, i.e., under coercion'. Now, everyone knows how it feels to do something unwillingly. This doctrine thus seems to teach that everything you do, you do unwillingly, that is, *reluctantly*, 'against your will' – and one doesn't concede *that*, because one does many things, in particular many 'moral' things, *gladly*. One thus understands 'unfree will' as meaning 'a will co-erced by an *alien* will', as if the assertion were: 'Everything you do, you do under coercion by somebody else's will'. Obedience to one's own will is not called coercion, for there is pleasure in it. *That you command yourself*, that is 'freedom of will'

1[46]

Religions live for the longest time without being mingled with morality: morality-free. Consider what every religion actually wants – it's palpable even today: one wants religion to provide not only redemption from *distress* but, above all, redemption from the *fear of distress*. All distress is viewed as the consequence of the evil, hostile action of spirits: the distress that afflicts us, while not 'deserved', still prompts us to ask what might have *led* a spirit to be irritated with us. Man trembles before unknown roaming fiends and would like to induce them to a friendlier attitude. So he scrutinises his conduct: and if there's any way of putting certain spirits he knows into a more amiable mood, he wonders *whether* he really has done everything possible to this end. Just as a courtier scrutinises his conduct towards a prince whose ungracious mood he notices – he looks for some oversight, etc., on his part. Originally, 'sin' is what might seriously offend some spirit: some oversight, a – – – : one has something *to make up for*. – Only when a spirit, a divinity, expressly sets up certain moral commandments as ways of pleasing and serving *him* does the element of moral valuation enter 'sin', or rather: only then can the breach of a moral commandment be felt as 'sin', as something that separates one from God, that offends him and leads to danger and distress emanating from him.

1[47]

Prudence, caution and foresight (in contrast to indolence and living in the moment) – nowadays naming those motives is thought almost to *degrade* an action. Yet what it cost to cultivate these qualities! Among the Greeks, *prudence* was still considered a *virtue*!

Likewise sobriety and 'circumspection' in contrast to acting out of violent impulse, to 'naivety' of action.

1[51]

Thinkers of humble or dishonourable descent misunderstand the lust to dominate, even the drive for distinction: they count both as vanity, as if the point were to appear respected, feared or worshipped in the *opinion* of other people.

1[53]

These are discrete tasks:

1. to grasp and ascertain what way of morally appraising men and actions predominates at the present time (and in a limited cultural area)
2. an era's entire moral code is a *symptom*, e.g., as a means of self-admiration or dissatisfaction or hypocrisy: the task is thus not only to ascertain the present *character of morality* but secondly to *interpret and explain this character*, for without that it's ambiguous
3. to explain the emergence of the way of judging that predominates just now
4. to provide a critique of this way of judging, to ask how strong it is, what it aims for, what will *become* of humanity (or of Europe) under its spell. Which forces does it nurture, which does it suppress? Does it make us more healthy, more sick, more courageous, more subtle, more needful of art, etc.?

This already assumes that there is no eternal morality: this may be considered proven, just as there is no eternal kind of judgement about diet. What is new is the critique, the question whether 'good' is really 'good'. And what usefulness may there be in what is now denigrated and disdained? Temporal discrepancies may be of some account.

1[55]

Fundamental question: how deep does morality go? Is it merely part of what is learned for a time? Is it a way we express ourselves?

All deeper men – Luther, Augustine, Paul come to mind – agree that our morality and its events do not coincide with our *conscious will* – in short, that an explanation in terms of having goals *is insufficient*.

1[58]

Starting from each of our fundamental drives there is a different perspectival appraisal of everything that happens and is experienced. Each of these drives feels restrained, or fostered, flattered, in respect to each of the others; each has its own law of development (its up and down, its tempo, etc.) – and one approaches death as the other rises.

Man as a multiplicity of 'wills to power': each one with a multiplicity of means of expression and forms. The individual *supposed* 'passions' (e.g., man is cruel) are merely *fictitious unities*: that which enters consciousness from the different fundamental drives as *of the same kind* becomes, through a synthesising fiction, a 'being' or 'faculty' – a passion. Just as the 'soul' itself is an *expression* of all the phenomena of consciousness which, however, we *interpret as the cause of all these phenomena* ('self-consciousness' is a fiction!).

1[61]

Everything which enters consciousness is the last link in a chain, a closure. It is just an illusion that one thought is the immediate cause of another thought. The events which are actually connected are played out below our consciousness: the series and sequences of feelings, thoughts, etc., that appear are symptoms of what actually happens! – Below every thought lies an affect. *Every thought*, every feeling, every will is *not* born of one particular drive but is a *total state*, a whole surface of the whole consciousness, and results from how the power of *all* the drives that constitute us is fixed at that moment – thus, the power of the drive that dominates just now as well as of the drives obeying or resisting it. The next thought is a sign of how the total power situation has now shifted again.

1[73]

Morality is part of the theory of the affects: how closely do the affects approach the heart of existence?

1[75]

Thoughts are *signs* of a play and struggle of the affects: they are always connected to their hidden roots

1[81]

Just as nowadays we no longer pray and raise our hands to heaven, one day we will no longer need to treat certain drives within us as *enemies* using *slander* and *calumny*, and in the same way our power, which compels us to destroy people and institutions, will one day be able to do so without our falling prey to affects of indignation and disgust: to annihilate undisturbed and with the gaze of a god! Starting with the annihilation of people *who feel contented*! Experimentum crucis.[69]

1[83]

Religious *interpretation* overcome.

Morality belongs to the theory of the affects (only a means of subduing them, while others are to be cultivated.

1[87]

The 'I' (which is *not* the same thing as the unitary government of our being!) is, after all, only a conceptual synthesis – thus there is no acting from 'egoism'

1[90]

NB. Let's honestly admit to our inclinations and disinclinations and resist beautifying them from the palettes of morality. Just as surely as we'll cease to interpret our distress as our 'struggle with God and the devil'! Let's be naturalistic and concede the rights, too, of what we have to combat – whether inside or outside ourselves!

1[91]

The division of labour has almost detached the senses from thinking and judging: while in the past these were *inside* the senses, undivorced. Earlier still, the desires and the senses must have been *one*.

1[92]

All struggle – and everything that happens is a struggle – *takes time*. What we call 'cause' and 'effect' omits the struggle, and as a result does not correspond to what happens. It is then only consistent to deny time in cause and effect.

---

[69] The crucial experiment.

1[97]

On the confusion of cause with symptom
  Pleasure and unpleasure are the oldest symptoms of all *value judgements*: but *not* causes of value judgements!
  Thus: pleasure and unpleasure, like moral and aesthetic judgements, belong to *a single category*.

1[104]

Many of the more subtle want *respite*, peace from their *affects* – they strive for *objectivity*, neutrality, they are content to remain behind as *observers* – and as critical observers with an inquisitive and playful superiority.
  Others want *outward* respite, a life without danger – they would like not to be envied, not to be attacked – and prefer to allow 'everyone his rights' – call it '*justice*' and philanthropy, etc.
  For the chapter: 'The Virtues as Disguise'.

1[105]

The loss involved in all specialisation: the synthetic nature is the *higher* one. Now, all organic life is specialisation; the *inorganic world* behind it is the *greatest synthesis of forces* and therefore the highest and most worthy of reverence. – In it there is no error, no narrowness of perspective.

1[114]

The absolute necessity of everything that happens contains no element of compulsion: to have thoroughly realised and felt that is to have reached a high degree of knowing. Such a belief does not give rise to forgiving and excusing – I strike through a sentence that has turned out badly just as I realise the necessity which made me write it badly, for the noise of a cart disturbed me – thus we strike through actions, possibly people, because they've turned out badly. 'Comprehending everything' – that would mean abolishing all perspectival relations, that would mean comprehending nothing, mistaking the nature of the knower.

1[115]

The interpretative character of everything that happens.
    There is no event in itself. What happens is a group of phenomena *selected* and synthesised by an interpreting being.

1[116]

Fear was elaborated into the *sense of honour*, *envy* into *equity* ('give every-one his due' and even 'equal rights'), the importunity of the lonely and imperilled into loyalty, – – –

1[117]

the sluggishness of the mind that settles down wherever it happens to find itself, the indolence that doesn't want to learn things afresh, the good-humoured submission to a power and the delight in serving, the warm, damp brooding over thoughts, wishes – all German – origin of *loyalty* and *faith*.

1[120]

The same text allows of countless interpretations: there is no 'correct' interpretation.

1[122]

Overcoming the affects? – No, not if it means weakening and annihilating them. *Instead, drawing them into service*, which may include exercising a long tyranny over them (not just as an individual but even earlier, as a community, race, etc.). In the end they are trustingly given back some freedom: they love us like good servants and voluntarily go where our best interests want to go.

1[124]

How does the perspectival sphere and error arise? When, by means of an organic being, not the being *but struggle itself wants to preserve itself, wants to grow and wants to be conscious of itself.*

What we call 'consciousness' and 'mind' is merely a means and a tool with which not a subject but *a struggle wants to preserve itself.*

Man is the testimony to the prodigious forces that can be set in motion by a small being with a multiplicity of content (or by a perennial struggle concentrated on many small beings)

Beings that play with the stars

1[125]

– To change the belief 'it is thus and thus' into the will *'it shall become thus and thus'*.

1[127]

– there have to be those who consecrate all functions, not just eating and drinking: and not just in remembrance of them, or in becoming one with them, *but ever anew and in new ways* shall this world be transfigured.

1[128]

– what is essential about organic being is *a new interpretation of what happens*, the perspectival, inner multiplicity which itself is something happening.

1[130]

– to say that *nothing* is deserved, but to do what is above all praise, indeed above all understanding

1[157]

That moral judgement, when it presents itself in concepts, looks narrow, crude, impoverished, almost ridiculous compared to the subtlety of that same judgement when it presents itself in actions, in selecting, rejecting, shuddering, loving, hesitating, doubting, in every contact between human beings.

1[193]

I love the magnificent exuberance of a young beast of prey that plays gracefully and, as it plays, dismembers.

1[216]

I have never desecrated the holy name of love.

1[222]

Only under great despotism is freedom of conscience useful and possible – a symptom of *atomisation*

1[223]

NB. The last virtue.

We are the squanderers of virtues which our forebears amassed, and thanks to them, to their long self-discipline and thrift, we may for some considerable time to come be able to play the rich and wanton heirs.

1[234]

The extent to which a craft causes bodily and intellectual deformation: likewise the purely scientific attitude, likewise the earning of money, likewise every kind of art – the *specialist* is necessary, but belongs to the *category of tools.*

1[247]

How men fell sick with God, and became estranged from man *himself.*

Notebook 2, autumn 1885 – autumn 1886

2[1]

There's a noble and dangerous carelessness that affords a profound inference and insight: the carelessness of the over-wealthy soul that has never *laboured* at getting friends but only knows hospitality, only ever practises, and knows how to practise, hospitality – heart and home open to anyone who wants to step inside, whether beggar, cripple or king. This is genuine affability: those who have it have a hundred 'friends', but probably no friend.

2[7]

A spirit we can comprehend – we are not the *like* of[70] that spirit: we are superior to it!

2[8]

What is young, still standing on shaky legs, always makes the greatest clamour: it falls over too often. For example 'patriotism' in Europe today, 'love of the fatherland', which is just a child – one mustn't take the squalling little thing too seriously!

---

[70] Allusion to the Earth Spirit's words to Faust: 'Du gleichst dem Geist, den du begreifst, Nicht mir!' (You are like that Spirit which you can grasp, Not me!; Goethe, *Faust I*, 512–13)

2[12]

Inter pares:[71] a phrase that intoxicates – it encompasses so much happiness and unhappiness for someone who's been alone a whole life long; who's encountered no one that belongs to him despite having searched along so many paths; who, in his dealings with others, has always had to be the man of benevolent and cheerful dissimulation, of assimilation sought and often achieved, and who is all too personally familiar with that brave face known as 'affability' – and, to be sure, also sometimes with those dangerous, heart-breaking eruptions of all his concealed wretchedness, all his unsuffocated desire, all the dammed-up rivers of love run wild – the sudden madness of that hour when the lonely man embraces the first to cross his path and treats him as a friend and godsend and most precious gift, only to cast him aside in disgust an hour later – in disgust now at himself, at how sullied, how humiliated, how alienated from himself, how sick of his own company –

2[13]

This is my suspicion, which keeps returning; my concern, which never lies down to sleep; my question, which no one hears or wants to hear; my Sphinx, alongside which is more than one abyss: I believe we are wrong today about the things we Europeans love above all, and a cruel (or not even cruel, just callous and childish) goblin is playing with our hearts and their enthusiasm, as perhaps it's already played with everything else that ever lived and loved – I believe that everything we in Europe today are used to admiring as 'feeling for humanity', as 'morality', 'humaneness', 'sympathy', justice, while it may have a superficial value in weakening and softening certain dangerous and powerful fundamental drives, is nevertheless in the long term nothing other than the diminishment of the whole human type – its irreversible *mediocratisation*, if I may be forgiven a desperate word in a desperate matter. I believe that, for an Epicurean spectator God, the commedia umana[72] would have to consist in men's increasing morality allowing them, in all innocence and vanity, to fancy they can rise from the animal to the rank of the 'gods' and to supernatural missions, whereas in fact they *sink*; that is: by cultivating all the virtues by means of which a herd can flourish, and pushing back those other

[71] Among equals.   [72] The human comedy.

and opposite virtues which give rise to a new, higher, stronger, *master-ful* species, they only develop the herd animal in man and perhaps thus *fix* the animal called 'man' – for up to now man has been the 'unfixed animal'. I believe that the great, advancing and unstoppable *democratic* movement of Europe, that which calls itself 'progress' – and equally its preparation and moral augury, Christianity – fundamentally signifies only the tremendous, instinctive conspiracy of the whole herd against everything that is shepherd, beast of prey, hermit and Caesar, to preserve and elevate all the weak, the oppressed, the mediocre, the hard-done-by, the half-failed; as a long-drawn-out slave revolt, at first secret, then more and more self-confident, against every kind of master, ultimately against the very concept of 'master'; as a battle to the death against every morality which springs from the womb and consciousness of a higher, stronger, as I have said: masterful species of men – from a species that requires slavery in one form or another and under one name or another as its basis and condition. I believe, finally, that up to now every heightening of the human type has been the work of an aristocratic society which believed in a long ladder of order of rank and difference in value between man and man, and which had need of slavery: yes, that without the *pathos*[73] *of distance*, as it arises from the deeply carved differences between the classes, from the ruling caste's constant looking outwards and downwards onto its underlings and tools, and its equally constant practice of commanding, keeping down, keeping away – without this pathos there can be no emergence of that other, more mysterious pathos, that craving for ever greater expansion of distance within the soul itself, the development of ever higher, rarer, remoter, wider, more encompassing states, in short (to use a moral formula in a sense beyond morality), the 'self-overcoming of man'. One question occurs to me again and again, a tempting and wicked question perhaps – let it be whispered in the ear of those who have a right to such questionable questions, the strongest souls of the day, who also have themselves most strongly under control: might it not now, as the 'herd animal' type is increasingly developed in Europe, be high time to try a whole, artificial and conscious *breeding* of the opposite type and its virtues? And would it not in fact be a kind of goal, redemption and justification of the democratic movement itself if someone came along who *made use of* that movement: if, at last, its new and sublime elaboration

---

[73] See note to 35 [24].

of slavery – as which the perfection of European democracy will one day appear – were joined by that higher species of masterful and imperial spirits which now *needed* this new slavery? Needed it for new, previously impossible prospects, for *its* prospects? For *its* tasks?

2[14]

Our four cardinal virtues: courage, compassion, insight and solitude – they would be unbearable to themselves if they hadn't forged an alliance with a cheerful and mischievous vice called 'courtesy'. –

2[15]

Cruelty may be the relief of taut, proud souls, of those who are used to exercising constant harshness against themselves; for them it has become a festival to at last hurt others, see them suffer – all the warrior races are cruel. Cruelty may, conversely, also be a kind of saturnalia of oppressed and weak-willed beings, of slaves, seraglio women, as a little piquancy of power – there is a cruelty of evil souls and a cruelty of base and trifling souls.

2[20]

'Eagles swoop straight down'. A soul's nobility can be recognised not least by the magnificent and proud stupidity with which it *attacks* – 'straight down'.

2[21]

There is also a squandering of our passions and desires: by the modest and petty bourgeois way we satisfy them – which corrupts taste, and, even more, corrupts our respect and veneration for ourselves. Phases of asceticism are the means of *damming* them up – of lending them dangerousness and grand style –

2[24]

– And to repeat once more: the beast in us wants to *be lied to* – morality is a necessary lie.

2[29]

Music does *not* reveal the essence of the world and its 'will', as claimed by Schopenhauer (who was wrong about music as he was about compassion, and for the same reason – he had too little experience of either –): music only reveals our dear musicians! And they don't even know it! – And what a good thing, perhaps, that they don't know it!

2[34]

I loved and admired Richard Wagner more than anyone else, and if he hadn't in the end had the bad taste – or the sad compulsion – to throw in his lot with a type of 'spirits' quite impossible for me, with his disciples the Wagnerians, then I would have had no reason to bid him farewell while he still lived: him, the deepest and most audacious, as well as the most misunderstood of all these hard-to-understand men of today, the encounter with whom has benefited my understanding more than any other encounter. Putting first things first, though, his cause was not to be confused with mine, and it took a good deal of self-overcoming before I learned to separate 'his' and 'mine' thus with the proper cut. That I came to my senses about the extraordinary problem of the actor – a problem perhaps further from me than any other, for a reason difficult to express; that I discovered and recognised the actor at the root of every artist, what is typically artistic: for this I needed my contact with that man, and it seems to me I think more highly, and also worse, of both the actor and the artist than previous philosophers have done. – The improvement of the theatre doesn't concern me much, and even less its becoming a church; the real Wagnerian music is not sufficiently part of me – I could be happy and healthy without it (quod erat demonstrandum et demonstratum[74]). What I found most alien about him was the Teutomania and semi-ecclesiasticism of his final years – – –

2[35]

A new way of thinking – which is always a new way of measuring and pre-supposes the availability of a new yardstick, a new scale of feelings – feels

---

[74] Which was to be proved and has been proved.

itself to contradict all other ways of thinking and, resisting them, continually says 'That is wrong'. Looked at more subtly, such a 'That is wrong' really only means 'I feel nothing of myself in it', 'I don't care about it', 'I don't understand how you can fail to feel with me'

2[57]

From now on conditions will favour more extensive structures of mastery, the like of which have never yet been seen. And there's something even more important: it has become possible for international dynasties to emerge which would set themselves the task of rearing a master race, the future 'masters of the earth' – a new, tremendous aristocracy built upon the harshest self-legislation, in which the will of philosophical men of violence and artist tyrants is made to last for thousands of years: a higher species of men who, thanks to the superiority of their willing, knowing, wealth and influence, would make use of democratic Europe as their most tractable and flexible tool to take the destinies of the earth in hand, to sculpt at 'man' himself as artists.

In short: the time is coming where we will learn to think differently about politics.

2[58]

I believe we lack political passion: we would get by just as creditably under democratic skies as under absolutist ones.

2[68]

Along the guiding thread of the body. When protoplasm divides $\frac{1}{2} + \frac{1}{2}$ does *not* $= 1$, but $= 2$. Thus the belief in the soul as monad becomes untenable.

Self-preservation only as one of the consequences of self-expansion. And 'self'?

2[69]

Mechanical force is known to us only as a *feeling of resistance*: and *pressing* and *pushing* are only palpable *interpretations* of this, not *explanations*.

What is the nature of the coercion that a stronger soul exerts upon a weaker one? – And it would be possible that what seemed to be 'disobedience' to the higher soul actually arose from a failure to understand its will, e.g., a rock cannot be commanded. But – the differentiation of degree and rank must be gradual: *only* the closest relatives can understand each other, and consequently it's here that there can be obedience.

Might it be possible to view all movements as signs of psychological happenings? Natural science as a symptomatology –

It may be wrong to take the fact that the formations of life are very small (e.g., cells) as a reason to search for even smaller units, 'force-points', etc.?

The *preliminary stage of structures of mastery*.

Devotion to the *person* (father, forebear, prince, priest, god) as *facilitating* morality.

2[76]

About the order of rank:

Re: 1. On the physiology of power.

Aristocracy in the body, the majority of the rulers (struggle of the tissues?)

Slavery and division of labour: the higher type only possible by *pressing down* a lower one until it becomes just a function.

Pleasure and pain not opposites. The feeling of power.

Nourishment only a consequence of insatiable appropriation, of the will to power.

Procreation, decay occurring when the ruling cells become powerless to organise what has been appropriated.

It is the *shaping* force that wants to have ever new 'material' (ever more 'force') in stock. The masterpiece of an organism's being constructed out of an egg.

'Mechanistic view': wants nothing but quantities, yet force is to be found in quality; mechanistic theory can thus only describe processes, not explain them.

'Purpose'. The 'sagacity' of plants to be taken as the starting point.

Concept of 'perfecting': *not* only greater complexity but also greater *power* (– need not be merely greater mass –).

Inference regarding human evolution: perfecting consists in producing the most powerful individuals, into whose tools (and tools of the greatest intelligence and flexibility) the greatest numbers of people are transformed.

Artists as the little makers. In contrast, the pedantry of the 'pedagogues'.

Punishment: preservation of a higher type.

Isolation.

False conclusions from history. Just *because* something high miscarried or was misused (such as the aristocracy), this does not mean it is refuted!

2[77]

The appearance of emptiness and fullness, of tautness and slackness, of resting and moving, of like and unlike.

(absolute space	the oldest appearance is
(substance	*made metaphysics*

– these contain the animal-human value measures of *security*.

Our *concepts* are inspired by our *need*.

The positing of antitheses reflects indolence (a distinction that *is enough* for nourishment, security, etc., is considered '*true*')

simplex veritas![75] – The indolent thought.

Our values are *interpreted into* things.

Is there, then, any *meaning* in the in–itself??

Isn't meaning bound to be relative meaning and perspective?

All meaning is will to power (all relative meanings can be resolved into this).

A thing = its qualities; but these equal everything which *matters* to *us* about that thing: a unity under which we collect the relations that *may be of some account* to us. At bottom, the changes we *perceive* in ourselves (not those we do not perceive, e.g., something's electricity). In brief: the 'object' is the sum of the *obstacles* encountered that we have become *conscious* of. A quality thus always expresses something of 'usefulness' or 'harm' to us. E.g., colours – each one corresponds to a degree of pleasure or unpleasure, and each degree of pleasure or unpleasure is the result of appraisals of how 'useful' and 'not useful' it is. – Disgust.

---

[75] The simplicity of truth. Allusion to the traditional philosophical doctrine 'simplex sigillum veri', simplicity is a sign of truth.

2[81]

It is only a matter of force: to have all the century's sickly features, yet to balance them out into a superabundant, sculptural, restorative force. *The strong human being*: description

2[83]

Man believes himself to be cause, doer –

Everything that happens relates as a predicate to some subject

Every judgement contains the whole, full, profound belief in subject and predicate or in cause and effect; and the latter belief (namely the assertion that every effect is a doing and that every doing presupposes a doer) is, in fact, a special case of the former, so that the belief which remains as the fundamental belief is: there are subjects

I notice something and look for a *reason* for it – that originally means: I look for an *intention* in it, and above all for someone who has intentions, for a subject, a doer – in the past, intentions were seen in *all* that happened, all that happened was doing. This is our oldest habit. Do animals share it? Do they, as living creatures, not also rely on interpretations in accordance with *themselves?* – The question '*Why?*' is always a question about the causa finalis,[76] about a 'What for?' We do not have a 'sense of the causa efficiens': here *Hume* is right, and habit (but *not* just that of the individual!) makes us expect that one particular, frequently observed occurrence will follow another, nothing more than that! What gives us the extraordinary strength of our belief in causality is *not* the great habit of the succession of occurrences but our *incapacity* to *interpret* what happens other than as happening out of *intentions*. It is the *belief* that what lives and thinks is the only thing which effects – belief in will, intention – belief that all that happens is doing, that all doing presupposes a doer; it is belief in the 'subject'. Might not this belief in the concept of subject and predicate be a great stupidity?

Question: is intention the cause of something happening? Or is that, too, illusion? Is intention not itself *that which* happens?

---

[76] See note to 34 [53].

'Attraction' and 'repulsion' in the purely mechanical sense is a complete fiction: a phrase. We cannot conceive of an attraction without an intention. – The will to gain power over something or to resist its power and push it away – *that* 'we understand': that would be an interpretation we could make use of.

In short: the psychological compulsion to believe in causality lies in the *unimaginability of things happening without intentions*: which, of course, says nothing about truth or untruth (the justification of such a belief). The belief in causae falls with the belief in τέλη[77] (against Spinoza and his causalism).

2[84]

Judging is our oldest belief, our most habitual holding-to-be-true or holding-to-be-untrue

In judgement our oldest belief is to be found, in all judging there is a holding-to-be-true or holding-to-be-untrue, an asserting or denying, a certainty that something is thus and not otherwise, a belief in having really 'come to know' – *what* is believed true in all judgements?

What are *predicates*? – We have regarded changes in ourselves *not* as such but as an 'in-itself' that is alien to us, that we only 'perceive': and we have posited them *not* as something that happens but as something that is, as a 'quality' – and invented for them a being in which they inhere, *i.e.*, we have posited the *effect as something that effects* and *what effects as something that is*. But even in this formulation, the term 'effect' is still arbitrary: for of those changes that take place in us and of which we firmly believe we are *not* ourselves the causes, we only infer that they must be effects – according to the inference: 'Every change has an author'. – But this inference itself is mythology: it *divorces* what effects *from* the effecting. If I say: 'Lightning flashes', I have posited the flashing once as activity and once as subject, and have thus added on to what happens a being that is not identical with what happens but that *remains*, *is*, and does not '*become*'. – *To posit what happens as effecting*, and *effect as being*: that is the *twofold* error, or *interpretation*, of which we are guilty. Thus, e.g., 'The lightning flashes' – 'to flash' is a state of ourselves; but we don't take it

---

[77] *causae*: efficient causes; τέλη (tele): final causes (see also note to 34 [53]).

to be an effect on us. Instead we say: 'Something flashing' as an 'in-itself' and then look for an author for it – the 'lightning'.

2[86]

What alone can *knowing* be? 'Interpretation', *not* 'explanation'.

2[87]

All unity is *only* unity as *organisation and connected activity*: no different from the way a human community is a unity: thus, the *opposite* of atomistic *anarchy*; and thus a *formation of rule* which *means* 'one' but *is* not one.

One would have to *know* what being *is* in order to *decide* whether this or that is real (e.g., 'the facts of consciousness'); likewise, what *certainty* is, what *knowledge* is, and so on. – But since we *don't* know that, a critique of our capacity to know is nonsensical: how should the tool be able to criticise itself when it can, precisely, only use *itself* for the critique? It can't even define itself!

if all unity is only unity as organisation? but the 'thing' we believe in is only a kind of yeast *invented as an addition to* various predicates. If the thing 'exerts effect', that means: we comprehend *all the other* qualities, those that are also present and as yet latent, as the cause of a single quality now coming to the fore: *i.e., we take the sum of its qualities – x* as *cause of the quality x*: which is *quite* stupid and deranged!
    'The subject' or the 'thing'

2[88]

A force we cannot imagine (like the allegedly purely mechanical force of attraction and repulsion) is an empty phrase and must be refused rights of citizenship in *science* – which wants to *make the world imaginable* to us, nothing more!

Everything that happens out of intentions can be reduced to the *intention of increasing power*.

2[90]

Sameness and similarity.

1. the cruder organ sees much illusory sameness
2. the mind *wills* sameness, *i.e.*, the subsumption of a sensory impression into an existing series: just as the body *assimilates* inorganic matter into itself.

On the understanding of *logic: : : the will to sameness is the will to power.*
– the belief that something is thus and thus, the essence of *judgement*, is the consequence of a will that as far as possible it *shall* be the same.

2[91]

If our 'I' is our only *being*, on the basis of which we make everything *be* or understand it to *be*, fine! Then it becomes very fair to doubt whether there isn't a perspectival *illusion* here – the illusory unity in which, as in a horizon, everything converges. Along the guiding thread of the body we find a tremendous *multiplicity*; it is methodologically permissible to use the more easily studied, the *richer* phenomenon as a guiding thread to understand the poorer one. Finally: assuming that everything is becoming, *knowledge is only possible on the basis of belief in being.*

2[93]

To what extent dialectic and belief in reason still rest upon moral prejudices. For Plato we, as former inhabitants of an intelligible world of the good, are still in possession of a legacy of that age: the divine dialectic, as originating from the good, leads to all good (– thus, as it were, 'back' –). Descartes also had a conception that in a mode of thought that is fundamentally Christian-moral, which believes in a *good* God as the creator of things, it is God's truthfulness that *stands guarantor* for our sensory judgements. Without a religious sanction and guarantee for our senses and reasonableness – where would we find the right to trust existence! That thinking is even a measure of the real – that what cannot be thought *is* not – is the crude non plus ultra of a moralist credulity[78] (trusting in an essential truth-principle at the fundament of things), itself an extravagant

---

[78] *Vertrauens-seligkeit*: Nietzsche's insertion of a hyphen highlights the German compound's two elements: trust + blissfulness or blessedness.

ontradicted at every moment by our experience. The point is
precisely that we can't think anything at all to the extent that it *is* . . .

2[95]

Our perceptions, as we understand them: i.e., the sum of all *those* perceptions the *becoming conscious* of which has been useful and essential to us and
to the whole organic process before us; not, then, all perceptions in general
(e.g., not the electrical ones). That is: we have *senses* only for a certain range
of perceptions – those we have to be concerned with in order to preserve
ourselves. *Consciousness exists to the extent that consciousness is useful.* There
is no doubt that all sensory perceptions are entirely suffused with *value
judgements* (useful or harmful – consequently pleasant or unpleasant). A
particular colour simultaneously expresses a value for us (although we
seldom admit this to ourselves, or only after a single colour has operated
on us for a long time, e.g., for prison inmates or lunatics). This is why
insects react differently to different colours: some they love, e.g., ants.

2[97]

Health and sickliness: be careful! The yardstick remains the body's ef-
florescence, the mind's elasticity, courage and cheerfulness – but also, of
course, *how much sickliness it can take upon itself* and *overcome* – can *make*
healthy. What would destroy more tender men is one of the stimulants of
great health.

2[103]

Distrust of self-observation. That a thought is the cause of a thought
cannot be established. On the table of our consciousness there appears a
succession of thoughts, as if one thought were the cause of the next. But
in fact we don't see the struggle going on under the table – –

2[104]

For Plato, as a man of overexcitable sensuality and enthusiasm, the magic
of the concept was so strong that he fell into revering and deifying the
concept as an ideal form. *Intoxication with dialectic* as the consciousness
of using it to exercise mastery over oneself – as a tool of the will to power.

2[105]

Pressing and pushing as something unutterably late, derived, unoriginal – for it presupposes something that *holds together* and *can* press and push! But why would it hold together?

2[106]

The significance of German philosophy (Hegel): to think up a *pantheism* in which evil, error and suffering are *not* felt to be arguments against divinity. *This grandiose project* has been misused by the existing powers (state, etc.), as if it sanctioned the reasonableness of the rulers at that particular time.

Schopenhauer, in contrast, appears as an obstinate man of morality who finally, so as to be right about his moral appraisal, becomes a *negator of the world*. Finally a 'mystic'.

I myself have attempted an aesthetic justification: how is the world's ugliness possible? – I took the will to beauty, to remaining fixed in *the same* forms, as being a temporary remedy and means of preservation: fundamentally, though, it seemed to me that the eternally-creating, as an *eternally-having-to-destroy*, is inseparable from pain. Ugliness is the way of regarding things that comes from the will to insert a meaning, a *new* meaning, into what has become meaningless: the accumulated force which compels the creating man to feel that what has gone before is untenable, awry, deserving of negation – is ugly? –

Apollo's deception: the *eternity* of the beautiful form; the aristocratic law that says *'Thus shall it be forever!'*
    Dionysos: sensuality and cruelty. Transience could be interpreted as enjoyment of the engendering and destroying force, as continual creation.

2[107]

NB. Religions perish through the belief in morality: the Christian-moral God is not tenable: hence 'atheism' – as if there could be no other kind of god.

Likewise, culture perishes through the belief in morality: once the necessary conditions are discovered from which alone morality grows, we no longer *want* it: Buddhism.

2[108]

That the *world's value* lies in our interpretation (– that somewhere else other interpretations than merely human ones may be possible –); that previous interpretations have been perspectival appraisals by means of which we preserve ourselves in life, that is, in the will to power and to the growth of power; that every *heightening of man* brings with it an overcoming of narrower interpretations; that every increase in strength and expansion of power opens up new perspectives and demands a belief in new horizons – this runs though my writings. The world *which matters to us* is false, i.e., is not a fact but a fictional elaboration and filling out of a meagre store of observations; it is 'in flux', as something becoming, as a constantly shifting falsity that never gets any nearer to truth, for – there is no 'truth'.

2[109]

The 'meaninglessness of what happens': belief in this results from an insight into the falseness of previous interpretations, a generalisation of weakness and despondency – it's not a *necessary* belief.

Man's lack of modesty – when he doesn't see meaning, he *denies* it exists!

2[110]

Regarding 'The Birth of Tragedy'

'Being' as a fabrication by the man suffering from becoming.

A book constructed entirely of experiences about states of aesthetic pleasure and unpleasure, with a metaphysics of the artiste in the background. At the same time the confession of a Romantic; finally, an early work full of youthful courage and melancholy. The most suffering man most deeply craves beauty – he *generates* it.

Fundamental psychological experiences: the name 'Apollonian' designates the enraptured lingering before a fabricated, dreamed-up world, before the world of *beautiful illusion* as a redemption from *becoming*.

Dionysos, on the other hand, stands namesake for a becoming which is actively grasped, subjectively experienced, as a raging voluptuousness of the creative man who also knows the wrath of the destroyer. Antagonism of these two experiences and the *desires* that underlie them: the first wants appearance *to be eternal*, and before it man becomes quiet, free of wishes, smooth as a still sea, healed, in agreement with himself and all existence; the second desire urges men towards becoming, towards the voluptuousness of making things become, i.e., of creating and annihilating. Becoming, felt and interpreted from within, would be continual creating by someone dissatisfied, over-wealthy, endlessly tense and endlessly under pressure, by a god whose only means of overcoming the torment of being is constant transformation and exchange – illusion as the temporary redemption achieved every moment; the world as the succession of divine visions and redemptions in illusion. – This metaphysics of the *artiste* stands counter to the one-sided view held by Schopenhauer, who cannot appreciate art from the standpoint of the artist but only from that of the recipient, because it bestows liberation and redemption in the enjoyment of the not-real, in contrast to reality (the experience of someone suffering and despairing at himself and his reality) – redemption through *form* and its eternity (as Plato may also have experienced it, except that for Plato the concept alone already meant the enjoyment of victory over his too excitable and suffering sensibility). Against this is set the second fact, art from the standpoint of the artist's experience, especially the musician's: the *torture* of having to create, as a *Dionysian drive*.

Tragic art, rich in both experiences, is described as a reconciliation of Apollo and Dionysos: appearance is given the most profound significance, through Dionysos; and yet this appearance is negated, and negated with *pleasure*. This opposes Schopenhauer's doctrine of *resignation* as a tragic view of the world.

Against Wagner's theory that music is the means and drama the end.

A craving for the tragic myth (for 'religion', namely pessimistic religion) (as a bell jar in which growing things flourish).

Distrust of science, although its momentarily soothing optimism is strongly felt. The bright mood of the theoretical man.

Deep distaste for Christianity: why? It is blamed for the degeneration of the German character.

Only aesthetically can the world be justified. Thorough suspicion of morality (it is part of the world of appearances).

Happiness with existence is only possible as happiness with *illusion*

Happiness with becoming is only possible in *annihilating* the reality of 'existence', of the beautiful semblance, in the pessimistic destruction of illusion.

Dionysian happiness reaches its peak in the annihilation of even the most beautiful illusion.

2[112]

A Romantic is an artist made creative by his great displeasure with himself – who looks away, looks back from himself and the rest of his world

2[114]

The work of art where it appears *without* an artist, e.g., as body, as organisation (Prussian officer corps, Jesuit order). How far the artist is only a preliminary stage. What does the 'subject' mean – ?

The world as a work of art giving birth to itself – –

Is art a consequence of *dissatisfaction with the real*? Or an expression of *gratitude for happiness enjoyed*? In the first case *Romanticism*, in the second glory and dithyrambs (in short, *art of apotheosis*): this includes Raphael too, except that he had that falsity of deifying the *appearance* of the Christian interpretation of the world. He was grateful for existence where it did *not* appear specifically Christian.

With the *moral* interpretation, the world is unbearable. Christianity was the attempt to overcome, i.e., to negate, the world with it. In practice, such an assassination attempt by insanity – an insane presumptuousness of man in the face of the world – amounted to clouding over, diminishing, impoverishing man: the most mediocre and harmless species, the herd-like species, was the only one to derive advantage from it, derive *encouragement*, if you will...

Homer as an artist of apotheosis; Rubens too. Music hasn't yet had one.

Idealisation of the *great transgressor* (the sense of his *greatness*) is Greek; disparagement, slander, contempt for the sinner is Judeo-Christian.

2[116]

That self-knowledge which is humility – for we are not our own work – but equally is gratitude – for we have 'turned out well' –

2[127]

Nihilism is standing at the gate: from where does this uncanniest of guests come to us? –

I. 1. Starting point: it is an *error* to point to 'social hardship' or 'physiological degeneration' or even corruption as the *cause* of nihilism. These can still be interpreted in very different ways. Instead, it's in a *very particular interpretation*, the Christian-moral one, that nihilism is found. This is the most decent, sympathetic age. Distress – psychological, bodily, intellectual distress – alone is by no means capable of bringing forth nihilism, i.e., the radical rejection of value, meaning, desirability.

2. The collapse of Christianity – brought about by its morality (indissoluble from it), which turns against the Christian God (the sense of truthfulness, highly developed by Christianity, is *disgusted* at the falseness and mendacity of the whole Christian interpretation of world and history. A backlash from 'God is truth' into the fanatical belief 'Everything is false'. Buddhism of the *deed*....

3. The decisive thing is scepticism towards morality. The collapse of the *moral* interpretation of the world, its *sanction* lost once it has tried to flee into a hereafter: ending up in nihilism, 'Everything is meaningless' (the impracticability of one interpretation of the world – one to which tremendous energies have been dedicated – arouses the suspicion that *all* interpretations of the world might be false). Buddhist trait, longing for nothingness. (Indian Buddhism does *not* have a fundamentally moral development behind it, which is why in its nihilism there is only morality which hasn't been overcome: existence as punishment and existence as error combined; thus, error as punishment – a moral valuation). The philosophical attempts to overcome the 'moral God' (Hegel, pantheism). Overcoming the popular ideals: the sage; the saint; the poet. Antagonism of 'true' and 'beautiful' and 'good' – –

4. Against 'meaninglessness' on the one hand and moral value judgements on the other: to what extent all science and philosophy up to now have stood under the aegis of moral judgements? And whether making an enemy of science isn't part of the bargain? Or antiscientism? Critique of Spinozism. Christian value judgements residually present everywhere in socialist and positivist systems. Lack of a *critique of Christian morality*.

5. The nihilist consequences of present-day natural science (as well as its attempts to slip away into the hereafter). Its practice finally *results in* its own disintegration, a turn against *itself*, an anti-scientism. – Since Copernicus, man has been rolling from the centre into the x

6. The nihilist consequences of the political and economic way of thinking where all 'principles' have virtually become affectations: the tinge of mediocrity, meanness, insincerity, etc. Nationalism, anarchism, etc. Punishment. Lack of a *redeeming* class and man, the justifiers –

7. The nihilist consequences of historiography and the '*practical* historians', i.e., the Romantics. The position of art: absolute *un*originality of its position in the modern world. Its new gloominess. Goethe's alleged Olympian status.

8. Art and the preparation of nihilism. Romanticism (the close of Wagner's Ring).

2[128]

I. Fundamental contradiction within civilisation and the heightening of man. It is the time of the *great midday, the most fruitful **breaking** of the clouds : my kind of pessimism* – the great starting point.

II. Moral valuations as a history of the lie and the art of slander in the service of a will to power (the *herd* will) which rebels against the stronger men.

III. The conditions of every heightening of culture (of making possible a *selection* at the expense of the crowd) are the conditions of all growth.

IV. The *ambiguity* of the world as a question of *force*, which looks at all things from the *perspective of its growth*.[79] *Moral-Christian* valuations as a slave revolt and slave deceitfulness (against the aristocratic values of the *classical* world).

How far does *art* reach down into the essence of *force*?

2[131]

Plan of the first book

The opposition is dawning between the world we revere and the world which we live, which we – are. It remains for us to abolish either our reverence or ourselves. The latter is nihilism.

[79] The German text would also allow the reading '*of their growth*'.

1. The emerging nihilism, theoretical and practical. Its faulty derivation. (Pessimism, its types: preludes to nihilism, although not necessary.) Ascendancy of the north over the south.
2. Christianity perishing by its morality. 'God is truth', 'God is love', 'the just God'. – The greatest event – 'God is dead' – felt obscurely. The German attempt to transform Christianity into a gnosis[80] has burgeoned into the profoundest suspicion, with 'untruthfulness' felt most strongly (– against Schelling, e.g.).
3. Morality, now without any sanction, is no longer able to preserve itself. The moral interpretation is finally let *go* – (though feeling continues everywhere to be full of the aftershocks of Christian value judgement –)
4. But it is on moral judgements that *value* has rested so far, especially the value of philosophy! ('of the will to truth' –)
   the popular ideals of 'the sage', 'the prophet', 'the saint' have fallen
5. *Nihilistic* trait in the natural sciences. ('Meaninglessness' –) Causalism, mechanicism. 'Conformity to laws' an intermezzo, a relic.
6. The same in politics: lack of a belief in one's *own* right, of innocence; lies, opportunism prevail
7. The same in political economy: the abolition of slavery: lack of a redeeming class, a *justifier* – Emergence of anarchism. 'Education?'
8. The same in history: fatalism, Darwinism, the last attempts to read reason and divinity into it have foundered. Sentimentality about the past; a biography could not be endured! – (phenomenalism here too: character as mask, there are no facts)
9. The same in art: Romanticism and its *reaction* (distaste for Romantic ideals and lies) – the pure artists, indifferent to content. This reaction, morally, as a sense of greater truthfulness, but pessimistic
   (Psychology of the father confessor and psychology of the Puritan, two forms of psychological Romanticism; but also the reaction to it, the attempt to take up a purely artistic position towards 'man' – there too the *reverse* valuation has not yet been *dared*!)
10. The whole European system of human endeavour *feels* in part meaningless, in part already 'immoral'. Likelihood of a new Buddhism. The greatest danger. 'How do truthfulness, love, justice relate to the *real* world?' Not at all! –

---

[80] A special knowledge of spiritual mysteries.

The signs.

European nihilism.

Its cause: the devaluation of values up to now.

The indistinct word 'pessimism': people who feel uneasy and people who feel too well – both have been pessimists.

Relationship of nihilism, Romanticism and positivism (the latter a re-action against Romanticism, the work of disappointed Romantics)

'Return to nature' 1. Its stages: its background Christian credulity (in some ways already Spinoza's 'deus sive natura'![81])

Rousseau, science after Romantic idealism

Spinozism extremely influential:

1. the attempt to acquiesce in the world *as it is*
2. happiness and knowledge naively posited in a relation of *dependence* (expresses a will *to* optimism which betrays the deeply suffering man –)
3. the attempt to *rid oneself* of the moral order of the world, *so as to have* 'God' remain, *a world that holds its ground in the face of reason* . . .

'When man no longer considers himself evil, he ceases to be so –' Good and evil are only interpretations, by no means facts or in-themselves. One can track down the origin of this kind of interpretation; one can try in this way to slowly liberate oneself from the deep-rooted compulsion to interpret morally.

Regarding the second book

Origin and *critique* of moral valuations. These two do *not* coincide, as is too easily believed (a belief which itself *results* from a moral appraisal: 'Something that originated thus and thus has little value, being of immoral origin').

Yardstick *with which* the value of moral valuations is to be measured: critique of the words 'improving, perfecting, heightening'.

The fundamental fact, which has been *overlooked*: contradiction be-tween 'becoming more moral' and the heightening and strengthening of the human type.

Homo natura.[82] The 'will to power'.

---

[81] See note to 36 [15].   [82] Man as nature.

Regarding the third book

The will to power.

How the men undertaking this revaluation of themselves would have to be constituted.

The order of rank as an order of power: war and danger required for a rank to maintain its conditions. The grandiose prototype: man in nature; the weakest, cleverest being making itself master, subjugating the more stupid forces

Regarding the fourth book

The *greatest* struggle: a new *weapon* is needed for it.

The hammer: conjure up a dreadful decision, face Europe with the *logical conclusion*: whether its will 'wills' ruin

Preventing mediocratisation. Ruin is preferable!

2[133]

Against the wish for reconciliation and the love of peace. This includes every attempt at monism.

2[135]

– Error veritate simplicior[83] –

2[139]

On 'causalism'

It's obvious that things-in-themselves cannot stand in a relation of cause and effect to one another, and *neither* can phenomena: from which it follows that within a philosophy which believes in things-in-themselves and in phenomena, the concept 'cause and effect' *cannot be applied*. Kant's mistakes – . . . In fact the concept 'cause and effect', considered psychologically, only arises from a way of thinking that believes will to be working upon will, always and everywhere – that believes only in what lives and at bottom only in 'souls' (and *not* in things). Within the mechanistic view of the world (which is logic and its application to space and time), that

---

[83] Error is simpler than truth. An attack on the motto 'simplex sigillum veri' (see note to 2 [77]).

concept reduces to the mathematical formula – using which, as must be emphasised again and again, nothing is ever understood, but is denoted, *distorted*.[84]

The unalterable sequence of certain phenomena does not prove a 'law' but a power relation between two or several forces. To say: 'But precisely this relation remains the same!' means nothing more than: 'One and the same force cannot be a different force as well'. – It's not a matter of *one after another* – but of *one in among another*, of a process in which the individual factors that succeed one another do *not* condition each other as causes and effects. . . .

The separation of 'doing' from the 'doer', of what happens from a something that *makes* it happen, of process from a something that is not process but is enduring, substance, thing, body, soul, etc. – the attempt to grasp what happens as a kind of displacement and repositioning of what 'is', of what persists: that ancient mythology set down the belief in 'cause and effect' once this belief had found a fixed form in the grammatical functions of language. –

2[140]

'Like can only be known by like' and 'Like can only be known by unlike': against both assertions, over which centuries of struggle were fought even in antiquity, the following objection can be made today, on the basis of a strict and cautious concept of knowledge: *nothing can be known at all* – and this for the very reason that neither can like know like, nor can like be known by unlike. –

2[141]

These divorces of doing and doer, of doing and being done to, of being and becoming, of cause and effect

   belief in change already presupposes the belief in *something which* 'changes'.

   reason is the philosophy of *what appears obvious*

---

[84] *bezeichnet, verzeichnet*: the prefix 'ver' adds a connotation of wrongness to the central element of 'denote'.

2[142]

The 'regularity' of a succession is only a figurative expression, *as if* here a rule were being obeyed: it is not a fact. Likewise 'conformity with a law'. We find a formula to express a kind of sequence that occurs again and again: doing this *doesn't* mean we have *discovered a 'law'*, and even less a force which is the cause of the recurrence of sequences. That something *always* happens thus and thus is here interpreted as if a being's always acting thus and thus resulted from obedience towards a law or a legislator, while without the 'law' it would be free to act otherwise. Yet precisely that thus-and-not-otherwise might originate in the being itself, which behaved thus and thus *not* on the prompting of some law but as constituted thus and thus. It only means: something cannot be something else as well; cannot do first this, then something different; is neither free nor unfree, but just thus and thus. *The mistake lies in a subject being invented in*

2[143]

Supposing the world had at its disposal a single quantum of force, then it seems obvious that every shift in power at any point would affect the whole system – thus, alongside causality, one *after* the other, there would be dependency, *one alongside and with the other*.

2[144]

Even if Christian belief could not be disproved, Pascal,[85] in view of a *dreadful* possibility that it might yet be true, considered it prudent in the highest sense to be a Christian. Today, indicating how much dreadfulness Christianity has lost, one finds this other attempt to justify it: that even if it were to be an error, still, great benefit and enjoyment could be had from that error one's whole life long. It seems, thus, that Christian belief is to be kept alive precisely for the sake of its soothing effects – not from dread of a menacing possibility but from dread of a life which misses out on a particular charm. This hedonistic turn, the proof based on *pleasure*, is a symptom of decline: it replaces the proof based on *force*, on that aspect of the Christian idea which shakes us, on *dread*. In fact, with this

---

[85] Nietzsche may be referring here to Pascal's wager, *Pensées*, ed. Lafuma, No. 418.

reinterpretation Christianity approaches exhaustion: one contents oneself with an *opiate* Christianity because one hasn't the strength either for searching, struggling, daring, wanting to stand alone – or for Pascalism, that brooding self-contempt, that belief in human unworthiness, that anxiety of the 'possibly condemned'.[86] But a Christianity which chiefly aims to soothe sick nerves has absolutely *no need* of that dreadful solution, a 'God on the cross': which is why quietly, everywhere in Europe, Buddhism is advancing.

2[148]

The will to power *interprets*: the development of an organ is an interpretation; the will to power sets limits, determines degrees and differences of power. Power differences alone wouldn't be able to feel themselves as such: there has to be a something that wants to grow, interpreting every other something that wants to grow in terms of its value. *In this* like – – In truth, *interpretation is itself a means of becoming master of something.* (*The organic process presupposes constant **interpreting**.*)

2[149]

A 'thing-in-itself' just as wrong-headed as a 'meaning-in-itself', a 'significance-in-itself'. There is no 'fact-in-itself'; *instead, for there to be a fact, a meaning must always first be projected in.*

The question 'What is that?' is the *positing of a meaning* from the viewpoint of something else. '*Essence*', '*essential being*', is something perspectival and presupposes multiplicity. At bottom there is always the question 'What is that for *me*?' (for us, for everything that lives, etc.).

A thing would be determined only when all beings had asked of it, and answered, their 'What is that?' If just one being, with its own relations to and perspectives on all things, were missing, then the thing wouldn't yet be 'defined'.

2[150]

In short, the essence of a thing, too, is only an *opinion* about the 'thing'. Or rather: '*This is considered to be*' is the real '*This is*', the sole 'This is'.

---

[86] Pascal, *Pensées*, ed. Lafuma No. 163.

2[151]

One mustn't ask: 'So *who* interprets?' – instead, the interpreting, as a form of the will to power, itself has existence (but not as a 'being'; rather as a *process*, as a *becoming*) as an affect.

2[152]

The genesis of 'things' is wholly the work of the imaginers, thinkers, willers, inventors – the very concept of 'thing' as well as all qualities. – Even 'the subject' is something created in this way, is a 'thing' like all the others: a simplification to designate as such the *force* which posits, invents, thinks, as distinct from all individual positing, inventing, thinking. Thus, the *capacity* is designated, as distinct from all individual cases: at bottom, it is action summarised with regard to all the action anticipated for the future (action and the likelihood of similar action).

2[153]

NB. The humanitarian God cannot be *demonstrated* from the world that is known to us: nowadays you can be forced and driven that far – but what's the conclusion you draw from it? This God cannot be demonstrated *by us*: epistemological scepticism. But you all *fear* the conclusion: 'From the world that is known to us a quite different God could be *demonstrated*, one who, at the very least, is *not* humanitarian' – – and so, in short, you hold fast to your God and invent for him a world *that is not known to us*.

2[155]

Deep disinclination to settle down comfortably once and for all in any single overall view of the world; charm of the opposite way of thinking; refusal to be robbed of the attraction of the enigmatic.

2[157]

Might not all *quantities* be signs of *qualities*? A greater degree of power corresponds to a different consciousness, feeling, desiring, a different perspectival view; growth itself is a craving *to be more*; the craving for an increase in quantity grows from a *quale*;[87] in a purely quantitative world all would be rigid, unmoving, dead. – Reducing all qualities to quantities is nonsense: what follows is that one thing and another stand side by side, an analogy –

2[158]

Psychological history of the concept of 'subject'. The body, the thing, the 'whole' constructed by the eye, awakens the distinction between a doing and a doer; the doer, the cause of the doing, was understood ever more subtly, finally leaving the 'subject' as residue.

2[159]

Has a force ever been ascertained? No, but effects have, translated into a completely foreign language. We are, though, so pampered by regularity in sequences that *its surprisingness doesn't surprise us*

2[165]

Regarding the *preface* to *'Daybreak'*

An attempt to think about morality without falling under its spell, mistrustful of the deception in its lovely gestures and glances.

A world we can revere, that accords with our drive to worship – that continually *proves* itself, by guiding the individual and the universal: this is the Christian view from which we are all descended.

A more and more precise, mistrustful, scientific attitude (and a more ambitious instinct for sincerity, thus again under Christian influence) has increasingly *disallowed* us *that* interpretation.

The subtlest way out: Kantian criticism. The intellect disputes its own right both to interpret in that spirit and to *reject* interpretations in that spirit. One is then content to fill up the gap with an *increase* in trust and belief, with a renunciation of all provability for one's belief, with an incomprehensible and superior 'ideal' (God).

The Hegelian way out, following Plato, is a piece of Romanticism and reaction, as well as a symptom of the historical sense, a new *force*: 'spirit' itself is the ideal, unveiling and realising itself: in 'process', in 'becoming',

[87] What something is like.

92

ever more of this ideal we believe in reveals itself – thus, the ideal realises itself, belief looks towards a *future* when it will be able to worship in accordance with its noble needs. In short,

1. God is unknowable and unprovable *to us* – deeper meaning of the epistemological movement
2. God is provable, but as something that becomes – and we are part of it, precisely with our urge towards the ideal – deeper meaning of the historicising movement

But the same historical sense, crossing over into nature, has – – –

As one can see: critique has *never* dared address the ideal itself, but only the problem of what gave rise to the objection against it, why it has not yet been achieved or why it is not provable in detail or in whole.

The ideal of the *sage* – to what extent has it been a fundamentally moral one till now? – – –

It makes the greatest difference whether out of passion, out of longing, one feels this crisis to be a crisis, or whether, by stretching to the very tip of thought and with a certain force of historical imagination, one just manages to reach it as a problem . . . .

Outside religion and philosophy we find the same phenomenon: utilitarianism (socialism, democratism) criticises the origins of moral valuations, *but it believes in them* just as the Christian does. (Naivety: as if morality remained when the sanctioning *God* is gone. The 'hereafter' is absolutely necessary if belief in morality is to be upheld.)

Fundamental problem: where does this unlimited power of *belief* come from? *Of belief in morality?*

(– which also betrays itself in the way even the fundamental conditions of life are misinterpreted in favour of morality, despite knowledge of the animal and plant worlds.)

'self-preservation': Darwinian perspective on the reconciliation of altruistic and egoistic principles.

(Critique of egoism, e.g., La Rochefoucauld)

My attempt to understand moral judgements as symptoms and sign languages in which appear processes of physiological thriving or failure as well as consciousness of the conditions of preservation and growth: as a way of interpreting that has the same value as astrology – prejudices prompted by the whispers of instincts (of races, communities, of different phases such as youth, withering, etc.)

Applied to the specific Christian-European morality: our moral judgements are signs of decay, of disbelief in *life*, a preparation for pessimism.

What does it mean that we have interpreted a *contradiction* into what exists? – Of decisive importance: behind all other valuations these moral valuations stand and command. Supposing they fall away, what yardsticks will we then measure by? And what value will knowledge, etc., etc., then have???

My main proposition: there are no moral phenomena, there is only a moral interpretation of those phenomena. This interpretation itself is of extra-moral origin.

2[171]

The *pang of conscience*, like all *ressentiments*,[88] absent where there is a great abundance of force (Mirabeau, B. Cellini, Cardanus[89]).

2[172]

'Being' – we have no other idea of this than '*living*'. How, then, can something dead 'be'?

2[174]

One finds nothing in things but what one has put into them oneself: this children's game is called science? But I don't want to denigrate it – on the contrary, let's proceed with both, both take courage: some are for finding, the others – *we* others – for putting in!

– In the end, man finds nothing in things but what he has put into them himself: the finding of them is called science, the putting in: art, religion, love, pride. In both, even if it were to be a children's game, – – –

2[175]

NB. *Against* the doctrine of the influence of milieu and external causes: the internal force is infinitely *superior*; much that looks like an influence

---

[88] Poisonous, jealous resentment, including an element of vengefulness.
[89] Honoré-Gabriel Riqueti, comte de Mirabeau (1749–1791): politician and orator in the early phase of the French Revolution; Benvenuto Cellini (1500–1571): Mannerist sculptor and goldsmith of the Italian Renaissance; Gerolamo Cardano (1501–1576): outstanding Italian mathematician and physician.

from outside is really only its adaptation from inside. One and the same milieu may be interpreted and made use of in opposite ways: there are no facts. – A genius is *not* explained by such conditions of his origin –

2[178]

It is good to take 'right', 'wrong', etc., in a certain narrow bourgeois sense, like 'Do right and fear nobody': i.e., fulfil one's obligations according to a particular crude schema within which a community exists.

2[182]

For something longer-lasting than an individual to endure, thus for a *work* to endure that was perhaps created by an individual: for this to happen, every possible kind of restriction, of one-sidedness, etc., must be imposed upon the individual. Using what means? Love, reverence, gratitude towards the person who created the work makes it easier; or that our forebears fought to gain it; or that my descendants will only be safeguarded if I safeguard this *work* (e.g., the πόλις[90]). *Morality* is essentially the means of making something endure beyond the individuals, or rather by *enslaving* the individuals. Obviously, the view upwards from below will produce quite other expressions than the view downwards from above.

A complex of power: how is it *preserved*? By many generations sacrificing themselves for it, i.e. – – –

2[189]

Questioning the origins of our valuations and tables of values is by no means the same thing as criticising them, as is so often believed – however much it's true that for our feelings, understanding some pudenda origo[91] reduces the value of the thing which originated that way, and prepares a critical mood and attitude towards it.

2[190]

what are our valuations and tables of moral values really worth? *What results from their rule?* For whom? With regard to what? – Answer: for life.

---

[90] 'polis'; see note to 34 [92].   [91] Shameful origin.

But *what is life*? Here a new, more definite version of the concept 'life' is needed. My formula for it is: life is will to power.

what does valuating mean itself? Does it refer back or down to a different, metaphysical world? As Kant (living before the great historical movement) still believed. In short, *where did it 'originate'*? Or did it not 'originate'? Answer: moral valuating is an *interpretation*, a way of interpreting. The interpretation itself is a *symptom* of particular physiological conditions, as well as of a particular intellectual level among the ruling judgements. *Who interprets*? – Our affects.

2[191]

My assertion: that one must subject moral valuations themselves to a critique. That one must curb the impulse of moral feeling with the question 'Why?' That this insistence on a 'Why?', on a critique of morality, is *itself our present form of morality*, as a sublime sense of honesty. That our honesty, our will not to deceive *ourselves*, must give an account of itself: 'Why *not*?' – before what forum? The will not to let ourselves be deceived has a different origin: caution against being overwhelmed and exploited, one of life's instincts for self-defence.

These are the demands I make of you – and you may not like the sound of them: that you subject the moral valuations themselves to a critique. That you curb the impulse of moral feeling, which here insists on submission and *not* criticism, with the question: 'Why submission?' That you view this insistence on a 'Why?', on a critique of morality, as being your *present* form of morality itself, as the most sublime kind of probity, which does honour to you and your age.

2[192]

the feeling: thou shalt!, the agitation when offending against it – question: 'Who is commanding here? Whose disfavour do we fear?'

2[193]

Our bad habit of considering a mnemonic token, an abbreviating formula, as an entity, and finally as a *cause*, e.g., saying of the lightning that 'it flashes'. Or, indeed, the little word 'I'. To make one perspective in seeing into *the cause of seeing as such*: that was the clever feat in the invention of the 'subject', of the 'I'!

2[196]

We without homeland – yes! But let's exploit the *advantages* of our situation and, far from being ruined by it, draw full benefit of the open air and the magnificent abundance of light.

2[197]

Unbelieving and godless, yes! – but without that bitterness and passion of the man torn loose, who out of disbelief makes himself a belief, a purpose, often a martyrdom: we've become hardened and cold-hearted from understanding that in the world things go on in anything but a godly way, in fact not even according to a reasonable, charitable, humane measure; we know that the world we live in is immoral, ungodly, inhumane – for far too long we have interpreted it in line with our veneration. The world is not worth what we believed: and we've broken off even the last gossamer thread of consolation that Schopenhauer spun when he said the meaning of the whole of history was its realising its own meaninglessness and becoming satiated with itself. This becoming tired of existence, this will to will no longer, the shattering of our own will, of our own utility, of the subject (as an expression of this reversed will) – this and nothing else is what Schopenhauer wanted to see honoured with the highest honour: he called it morality, decreeing that all selfless action – – – he thought he could secure even art's value by viewing the indifferent states it creates as a preparation for the complete detachment and satiety of nausea.

– but would the sight of an immoral world really make us *pessimists?* No, because we don't believe in morality – – we believe that charity, law, compassion, and obedience to the law are grossly *overvalued*, that their opposite has been slandered, and that both the exaggeration and the slander, the whole application of the *moral ideal* and measure, have involved a tremendous danger to man. Let's not, though, forget the profit they have yielded: finesse of *interpretation*, of moral vivisection, the pangs of conscience have raised man's *falsity* to the highest pitch and made him ingenious.

In itself, a religion has nothing to do with morality, but the two offspring of the Jewish religion are both *essentially* moral religions, ones that prescribe how we *ought* to live and gain a hearing for their demands with rewards and punishments.

2[200]

Likewise, we are no longer Christians: we've outgrown Christianity, not because we've lived too far from it but too near, and more than that because we've grown *out of* it – our stricter and more fastidious piety itself is what today *forbids* us to remain Christians –

2[201]

If I once wrote the word 'untimely' on my books, how much youth, inexperience, peculiarity that word expressed! Today I realise it was precisely this kind of complaint, enthusiasm and dissatisfaction that made me one of the most modern of the modern.

2[203]

And even today the philosophers, without knowing it, still provide the strongest proof of how far this authority of morality goes. With all their will to independence, all their habits or principles of doubt, even their vice of contradiction, of innovation at any price, of haughtiness before everything high – what becomes of them as soon as they start thinking about 'Thou shalt' and 'Thou shalt not'? All at once there's nothing humbler to be found on earth: morality, that Circe,[92] has breathed on them and caught them in her spell! Those proud men and lonely wanderers! – Now all at once they're lambs, now they want to be flocks. Initially they all want to share the same 'Thou shalt' and 'Thou shalt not' with everyone else – the first sign of having relinquished their independence. And what is the criterion they set for a moral prescription? Here they all agree: its general validity, its disregard for the individual. This I call the 'herd'. True, at that point they part ways, for each wants to serve morality with *his* best energies. Most of them hit upon 'justifying morality', as it's called, in other words reconciling and allying morality with reason, even to the point of unity; conversely, the subtler among them find in the very unjustifiability of morality the sign and privilege of its rank, its rank

---

[92] Circe was an enchantress who turned Odysseus' companions into swine.

superior to reason; others want to give it a historical derivation (for instance with the Darwinists, who've invented that handy household remedy for bad historians, 'First utility and constraint, then habit, finally instinct, even enjoyment'). Still others refute these derivations and deny in general that morality can be historically derived, this likewise to the honour of its rank, its higher type and destiny. But they all agree on the main thing: 'Morality exists, morality is given!' – they all believe, honestly, unconsciously and unabashed, in the value of what they call morality, that is: they are under its authority. Oh yes – the *value* of morality! Will anyone be allowed to take the floor who has doubts about just that value? Whose concern for morality's derivation, derivability, psychological possibility and impossibility is exclusively from this point of view?

2[205]

There is no egoism which stops at its own borders and doesn't encroach – consequently, the 'permitted', 'morally indifferent' egoism you speak of doesn't exist.

'One always furthers one's ego at the expense of others'; 'Life always lives at the expense of other life'. – Anyone who doesn't grasp that hasn't taken the first step in himself towards honesty.

2[206]

What a sensation of freedom it is to feel, as we freed spirits feel, that we are *not* harnessed up to a system of 'ends'! Likewise, that the concepts of 'reward' and 'punishment' do not have their seat in the nature of existence! Likewise, that the good or evil action is to be called good or evil not in itself but only from the perspective of what favours self-preservation among particular kinds of human community! Likewise, that our balance sheets of pleasure and pain have no cosmic significance, let alone a metaphysical significance! – The pessimism which undertakes to weigh up the pleasure and unpleasure of existence itself, with its arbitrary confinement to the pre-Copernican prison and horizon, would be something antiquated and regressive, if indeed it isn't just a bad joke made by a Berliner (Eduard von Hartmann's pessimism).[93]

93 Eduard von Hartmann (1842–1906), successful philosophical writer of the turn of the century whose pessimistic outlook follows Schopenhauer.

2[207]

Beginning

Conclusion

In what way this self-annihilation of morality is part of morality's own force. We Europeans have in our veins the blood of those who died for their beliefs; we have taken morality seriously and dreadfully, and there's nothing we haven't sacrificed for it in one way or another. On the other hand: our spiritual subtlety was achieved essentially through vivisection of the conscience. We don't yet know what 'Whither?' we'll be driven to, having torn ourselves from our old soil like this. But that soil itself has bred in us the force which now drives us far abroad, into adventure, which casts us out to the shoreless, the untried, the undiscovered – we have no choice but to conquer, now we no longer have a land where we're at home, where we would like to 'preserve'. No, you know better, my friends! The hidden Yes in you is stronger than all the Nos and Maybes with which you and your age are sickened and addicted; and if you have to go to sea, you emigrants, then what compels you is a *belief* . . .

Notebook 3, beginning of 1886 – spring 1886

3[13]

It is this loneliness which we *guard* when we speak up for the religious organisation of humanity – and perhaps nothing distinguishes us so unambiguously from the herd animals and apostles of equality wrongly called 'free spirits': not a single one of whom *would be able* to endure loneliness. Religion thought of as an extension and deepening of the basic political doctrine, which is always the doctrine of unequal rights and of the necessity of a social structure with high and low, with those who command and those who obey: religion means to us the doctrine of the difference in rank between souls, of the breeding and enabling of higher souls at the expense of the lower ones.

Notebook 4, beginning of 1886 – spring 1886

4[6]

Marriages in the *bourgeois* sense of the word, and I mean in the most respectable sense of the word 'marriage', haven't the least to do with love –
no kind of institution can be made from love – and just as little with money;
but rather with the social permission given to two people to satisfy their
sexual desires with each other, of course under certain conditions, but
such conditions as have the *interests of society* in view. It's clear that the
prerequisites for such a contract must include some degree of liking between the parties concerned and very much goodwill – the will to be
patient, conciliatory, to care for one another – but the word love should
not be misused to describe it! For two lovers in the whole and strong
sense of the word, sexual satisfaction is not the essential thing and really
just a symbol: for one party, as has been said, a symbol of unconditional
submission, for the other a symbol of assent to this, a sign of taking possession. – Marriage in the aristocratic sense, the old nobility's sense of the
word, is about *breeding* a race (is there still a nobility today? Quaeritur[94]),
in other words about maintaining a fixed, particular type of ruling men:
man and woman were sacrificed to this viewpoint. Obviously, the primary
requirement here was *not* love, on the contrary! – and not even that measure of mutual goodwill on which the good bourgeois marriage is based.
The decisive thing was first the interest of the dynasty, and above that
the class. Faced with the coldness, severity and calculating clarity of this

---

[94] One asks.

noble concept of marriage, which has ruled in every healthy aristocracy, in ancient Athens as in eighteenth-century Europe, we would shiver a little, we warm-blooded animals with our ticklish hearts, we 'moderns'! And this is precisely why love as passion, in the grand understanding of the word, was *invented* for the aristocratic world and within it – where coercion and privation were greatest . . .

4[7]

– 'Sickness improves a man': this famous assertion, heard throughout the centuries from the mouths of the wise as much as from the mouths, or the muzzles, of the populace, makes one think. And granting its validity one would like to ask: might there be a causal connection between morality and sickness in general? The 'improvement of man' seen as a whole, for example the European's undeniable softening, humanisation, charitablisation over the last thousand years – might this be the consequence of a long, strange and secret suffering and withering, being deprived, falling away? Has 'sickness' 'improved' the European? Or put another way: is our morality – our modern, tender-hearted morality in Europe, compare it with that of the Chinese – the expression of a physiological *decline*? . . . After all, as can hardly be denied, every point in history when the human type has shown itself in special magnificence and power at once took on an unexpected, dangerous, eruptive character where humaneness must fare ill; and perhaps in those cases which *seem to be different* there just wasn't enough courage or subtlety to drive psychology into the depths and even there dig out the general proposition: 'The healthier, the stronger, the richer, more fruitful, more enterprising a man feels, the "more immoral" he becomes'. An unpleasant thought! and certainly not one to be pondered on! But supposing we run with it for just a short moment, with what wonder we look into the future! What would then be more dearly paid for on earth than precisely the thing we demand with all our force – the humanisation, the 'improvement', the growing 'civilisation' of man? Nothing would be more expensive than virtue: for in the end it would give us the earth as an infirmary, and 'Everyone to be everyone else's nurse' would be the pinnacle of wisdom. True, that much-desired 'peace on earth' would have been achieved! But how little 'goodwill among men'! How little beauty, exuberance, daring, danger! How few 'works' for whose sake it would still be worth living on earth! And oh! absolutely no more 'deeds' whatsoever! All the *great* works and deeds which have remained standing and not been washed away by the waves of time – were they not all, in the deepest sense, great immoralities? . . .

4[8]

That a belief's strength alone guarantees nothing whatsoever about its truth, in fact is even capable of slowly, slowly distilling out of the most reasonable thing a concentrate of folly: this is our real European insight – in this, if in anything, we have become experienced, been made cautious, shrewd, *wise*, apparently through much injury . . . 'He that believeth shall be saved': fine! Now and again, at least! But he that believeth shall most certainly be made *stupid*, even in the rarer case that the belief is not *already* stupid, that it was an intelligent one in the first place. Every long-held belief finally *becomes* stupid, which means (to express it with the clarity of our modern psychologists) that its reasons sink 'into the unconscious', disappear there – from then on it no longer rests upon reasons but upon affects (that is, whenever it needs help it gets the affects, and *no longer* the reasons, to fight its cause). Supposing one could discover which was the most strongly believed, longest held, least disputed, most honest belief that exists among men: it would then be highly justified to conjecture that this belief could also be the most profound, most stupid, 'most unconscious', the most thoroughly defended against reasons, the longest abandoned by reasons. –

Agreed: but which is that belief? – Oh, you're curious! But since I've started setting you riddles, I'll be fair and come out quickly with the answer and solution – they won't be easily anticipated.

Man is above all a *judging* animal; but in judgement lies concealed our oldest and most constant belief. Every judgement rests on a holding-to-be-true and an asserting, on a certainty that something is thus and not otherwise, that in it man has really come to 'know': *what* is it that, in every judgement, is unconsciously believed to be true? – That we have a right to *distinguish* between subject and predicate, between cause and effect – that is our strongest belief; in fact, at bottom even the belief in cause and

104

effect itself, in conditio and conditionatum,[95] is merely an individual case of the first and general belief, our primeval belief in subject and predicate (as the assertion that every effect is a doing and that every conditioned presupposes something that conditions, every doing a doer, in short a subject). Might not this belief in the concept of subject and predicate be a great stupidity?

[95] Condition and conditioned.

Notebook 5, summer 1886 – autumn 1887

5[3]

We place a word at the point where our ignorance begins – where we can't see any further, e.g., the word 'I', the words 'do' and 'done to': these may be the horizons of our knowledge, but they are not 'truths'.

5[7]

The happiness whose proper name on earth the modest believe is: 'Well, not bad.'

5[9]

Exoteric – esoteric
1. Everything is will against will
2. There is no will at all
1. Causalism
2. There is no such thing as cause and effect.
1.

All causality goes back psychologically to the belief in *intentions*:
Precisely the effect of an intention is *un*provable.

(Causa efficiens is tautological with causa finalis[96]) looked at psychologically –

---

[96] See note to 34 [53].

5[10]

What is 'knowing'? Tracing something alien back to something one is acquainted[97] and familiar with. First principle: what we have *got used to* we no longer consider a riddle, a problem. The feeling of the new, of the discomfiting, is dulled: everything that happens *regularly* no longer seems questionable to us. This is why the knower's first instinct is to *look for the rule* – whereas, of course, finding the rule doesn't yet mean anything at all is 'known'! – Hence the superstition of the physicists: where they can stand still, i.e., where the regularity of phenomena allows them to apply abbreviating formulas, they think *knowing* has taken place. They have a feeling of 'security', but behind this intellectual security is the soothing of their fearfulness: *they want the rule* because it strips the world of dreadfulness. *Fear of the unpredictable* as the *hidden instinct* of science.

Regularity lulls to sleep the questioning (i.e., fearing) instinct: to 'explain' is to show a rule in what happens. Belief in the 'law' is belief in the dangerousness of the arbitrary. The good *will* to believe in laws has helped science to victory (particularly in democratic eras).

5[12]

Fundamental question: whether the *perspectival* is part of the *essence*, and not just a form of regarding, a relation between various beings? Do the various forces stand in relation to one another, in such a way that this relation is tied to the viewpoint of perception? This would be possible *if everything that is were **essentially** something that perceives.*

5[13]

That similarity of form indicates kinship, indicates origin in a shared form – that similarity in the sound of words indicates kinship between the words – this is a way of inferring prompted by sluggishness: as if it were *more probable* for a form to have originated just once rather than several times...

The succession of phenomena, however precisely described, cannot render the *essence* of a process – but at least the *constancy* of the falsifying medium (our 'I') is there. It's as if rhymes from one language were lost

---

[97] *bekannt*: known or familiar (cf. *erkennen*, to know, cognise, in the opening sentence).

in translation into another, while the *belief* was evoked *that* the poem did rhyme in the original language. Thus sequence, succession, arouses the belief in a kind of 'coherence' *beyond* the fluctuation we see.

5[14]

The development of science increasingly dissolves the 'known' into an unknown: yet it *wants* exactly the *opposite*, and starts from the instinct to trace the unknown back to the known.

In short, science prepares the way for a *sovereign ignorance*,[98] a feeling that there is no 'knowing', that it was a kind of arrogance to dream of it; still more: that we don't have left the least concept that would let us even consider 'knowing' to be a *possibility* – that 'knowing' is itself a contradictory idea. We *translate* an ancient mythology and vanity of man into the hard fact that not only thing-in-itself but also 'knowledge-in-itself' has ceased to be *permissible* as a concept. Seduction by 'number and logic'

– – by 'laws'

'Wisdom' as an attempt to get *beyond* perspectival appraisals (i.e., beyond the 'wills to power'), a principle that is disintegratory and hostile to life, a symptom as in India,[99] etc. A *weakening* of the appropriating force.

5[15]

Just as in our senses the attempt is made to translate everything into the dead, the lifeless (thus, e.g., to break it down into movements, etc.), it is equally permissible to break down everything seen, heard, everything our senses offer us, into our *vital* functions, thus as desiring, perceiving, feeling, etc.

5[16]

Scientific precision is achievable first in the case of the *most superficial* phenomena, in other words where things can be counted, calculated, touched, seen, where quantities can be *ascertained*. Thus, the most impoverished

---

[98] *Wissenschaft* (science), *Unwissenheit* (ignorance).
[99] Nietzsche appears to be thinking of Buddhism here.

fields of existence were the first to be fruitfully cultivated. The demand that everything must be explained in mechanistic terms is the instinctive idea that it's precisely there that the most valuable and fundamental insights are *first* reached: which is a piece of naivety. In fact, nothing that can be counted and grasped is worth much to us: what we can*not* reach with our 'grasp' is what we consider 'higher'. Logic and mechanics can only be applied to what is *most superficial*, and are really only an art of schematising and abbreviating, a coping with multiplicity through an art of expression – not an 'understanding', but a designating in order to *make oneself understood*. Thinking the world as reduced to its surface means above all making it 'graspable'.

Logic and mechanics *never* touch on causality – –

5[19]

The world which matters to us is only illusory, is unreal. – But the concept 'really, truly there' is one we drew out of the 'mattering-to-us': the more our interests are touched on, the more we believe in the 'reality' of a thing or being. 'It exists' means: I feel existent through contact with it. – Antinomy.

To the same degree that this feeling produces life, we posit *meaning* in what we believe is the cause of the stimulation. Thus, we construe 'what is' as what exerts an effect on *us*, what *proves itself by exerting its effect*. – 'Unreal', 'illusory', would be that which is incapable of producing effects, yet appears to produce them. –

Supposing, though, we put certain values into things, then these values have effects *back* on us after we've forgotten we were the ones who put them in.

Supposing I think someone is my father, then much follows from that concerning everything he says to me: it's *interpreted* differently. – Thus, given the way we comprehend and construe things, the way we interpret them, it follows that all the 'real' actions of these things upon us then appear different, newly interpreted – in short, that they *exert different effects on us*.

But if all construals of things have been false, it follows that all the actions of those things upon us are felt and interpreted in terms of *a false causality*: in short, that we measure value and disvalue, benefit and harm, in terms of errors, that the world *which matters to us* is false.

5[22]

Fundamental solution:

we believe in reason, but this is the philosophy of grey *concepts*; language is built in terms of the most naive prejudices

now we read disharmonies and problems into things because we *think only* in the form of language – thus believing in the 'eternal truth' of 'reason' (e.g., subject, predicate, etc.)

we cease thinking when we no longer want to think within the constraints of language, we just manage to reach the suspicion that there might be a boundary here.

Thinking rationally is interpreting according to a scheme we cannot cast away.

5[24]

People in whose body there's a constant grunting and uproar from the inner brute

5[34]

The most intellectual men feel the stimulus and spell of sensual things in a way that other men, those with 'hearts of flesh', can't even imagine – and had better not imagine. They are sensualists in the best of faith, because they accord a more fundamental value to the senses than to that fine filter, the apparatus of dilution and miniaturisation, or however one should describe what the common people's language calls 'mind'. The force and power of the senses – this is the most essential thing in a well-constituted and complete man: there has to be a magnificent 'animal' first – what else would be the point of all 'humanisation'!

5[36]

Our 'knowing' restricts itself to ascertaining quantities, i.e.

but we can't stop ourselves experiencing these quantitative distinctions as qualities. *Quality* is a *perspectival* truth for *us*; not an 'in-itself'.

Our senses have a particular quantum as a medium span within which they function, i.e., we experience large and small in relation to the conditions of our existence. If we sharpened or blunted our senses tenfold, we would perish. That is, we experience even *relations of magnitude* as *qualities* with regard to the necessary conditions of our existence.

5[38]

The antinomy of my existence lies in the fact that everything I, as a radical philosopher, have radical *need* of – freedom from profession, wife, child, friends, society, fatherland, home country, faith; freedom almost from love and hate – I equally feel to be privations, inasmuch as I am, fortunately, a living creature and not a mere apparatus of abstraction. I must add that, in any case, I lack *robust health* – and only in moments of health do these privations weigh on me *less heavily*. Also, I still don't know how to gather together the five conditions on which a bearable medium state of my shaky health could be based. Even so it would be a disastrous mistake if in order to provide myself with the five conditions, I robbed myself of those eight freedoms: that is an *objective* view of my situation. –

The matter is complicated by my being a poet as well, with, as is just, the needs of all poets, which include sympathy, excellent housekeeping, fame and so on (in respect to which needs I can only describe my life as a dog-kennel existence). The matter is complicated further by my being a musician as well: so that actually nothing in life – – –

5[39]

– that I speak the language of the popular moralists and 'holy men' and speak it with insouciant originality, with enthusiasm and merriness, but also with an artiste's pleasure in it which isn't too far from irony – irony about the fact that the modern thought in its most sophisticated form is continually translated back into the language of naivety – thus with a secret feeling of triumph about the defeated difficulties and apparent impossibility of such an undertaking

5[41]

Overture to Parsifal, greatest gift I've been granted for a long time. The power and severity of feeling, indescribable, I know nothing else that grasps Christianity so deeply and presents it so distinctly for our sympathy. Entirely exalted and moved – no painter has painted such an indescribably melancholy and tender *gaze* as Wagner

the greatness in capturing a terrifying certainty out of which something like compassion wells up:

the greatest masterpiece of the sublime I know, the power and severity in capturing a terrifying certainty, an indescribable expression of greatness *in* the very compassion for it; no painter has painted such a dark, melancholy gaze as Wagner does in the last part of the overture. Nor has Dante, nor has Leonardo.

It's as if for the first time in many years someone were speaking to me about the problems that trouble me; not, of course, with the answers I hold ready but with Christian answers – which ultimately have been the answers of stronger souls than those brought forth by our past two centuries. Admittedly, when listening to this music one sets one's Protestantism aside like a misunderstanding: just as, I won't deny, Wagner's music in Monte Carlo made me set aside even the *very good* other music (Haydn, Berlioz, Brahms, Reyer's Sigurd overture) that could be heard there like a misunderstanding of music. Strange! As a lad I intended for myself the mission of bringing the Eucharist to the stage; – – –

5[54]

The principle of the conservation of energy demands *eternal recurrence*.

5[55]

The psychologists' chief error: they take the indistinct idea to be a lower *species* of idea than the luminous one: but what moves away from our consciousness and thus *becomes obscure may* yet be perfectly clear in itself. *Becoming obscure is a matter of the perspective of consciousness.*

'Obscurity' is something produced by the apparatus of consciousness, not *necessarily* something inherent to 'what is obscure'.

5[56]

Everything which enters consciousness as 'unity' is already tremendously complicated: we only ever have a *semblance of unity*.

The phenomenon of the *body* is the richer, more distinct, more comprehensible phenomenon: to be given methodological priority, without determining anything about its ultimate significance.

NB. Even if the *centre of 'consciousness'* doesn't coincide with the physiological centre, it would still be possible that the *physiological* centre is also the *psychic* centre.

The *intellectuality of feeling* (pleasure and pain), i.e., it is *ruled* from that centre.

5[58]

Morality as *an illusion of the species*, to incite the individual to sacrifice himself to the future: seeming to accord him an infinite value so that, armed with this *self-confidence*, he tyrannises and suppresses other sides of his nature and finds it hard to be contented with himself.

Deepest gratitude for what morality has achieved so far: but *now* it's *only a pressure* that would prove disastrous! *Morality itself*, as honesty, *compels* us to negate morality.

5[59]

Precondition for *scientific*[100] *work*: a belief in the shared and lasting character of scientific work, so that the individual can work away on even the smallest point, confident of *not working in vain*. This – – –

There is one *great paralysis*: *working in vain*, struggling *in vain*. – –

The ages of *accumulation*, where force and means of power are found which will one day be used by the future. *Science as an intermediate stage* which gives the intermediate, more multifarious, more complicated beings their most natural discharge and satisfaction: *all those for whom the deed is inadvisable*.

---

[100] *wissenschaftlich*: in the wide meaning, covering humanities and social sciences as well as natural sciences.

5[61]

A point in time when man has a superabundance of *force* at his disposal: the aim of science is to bring about this *slavery of nature*.

Then man acquires *leisure*: to *educate* himself for something new, higher. *New aristocracy*

Then many *virtues* which were formerly *conditions of existence* will have become *obsolete*.

No longer needing qualities, and *consequently* losing them.

*We no longer **need** virtues: consequently* we lose them – whether the morality of 'One thing is needful', of the soul's salvation, or of immortality: means of *making possible* for man a tremendous *self-conquering* (through the affect of a tremendous *dread*: : :

the various kinds of *hardship* through whose discipline man is shaped: hardship teaches us to work, to think, to restrain ourselves

Physiological purifying and strengthening

the *new aristocracy* needs an opposite against which it struggles: it must have a dreadful pressure to preserve itself.

the two futures for humanity:

1. the consequence of mediocratisation
2. conscious distinction, self-shaping

a doctrine that creates a *chasm*: it preserves the *uppermost and* the *lowest* species (and destroys the middle one)

the aristocracies up to now, spiritual and secular, *in no way* disprove the necessity of a new aristocracy.

Not *sociology* but theory of *structures of domination*

5[63]

Let there be no inventing of false persons, e.g., no saying: 'Nature is cruel'. Precisely the realisation *that there is no* such *central organ of responsibility is a relief!*

Development of mankind

A. To gain power over nature and *to that end* a certain power over oneself. Morality was necessary *in order* for man to prevail in the struggle with nature and the 'wild animal'.

B. Once power over nature *has been* gained, one can use this power to continue freely shaping *oneself*: will to power as self-heightening and strengthening.

5[64]

What is 'passive'? resisting and reacting. Being *hindered* in one's forward-reaching movement: thus, an act of resistance and reaction

What is 'active'? reaching out for power

'Nourishment' is only a derivation; the original phenomenon is wanting to enclose everything in oneself

'Procreation' only a derivation; originally: where one will is not enough to organise everything that's been appropriated, a *counter-will* comes into force which does the releasing, a new organisational centre, after a struggle with the original will

Pleasure as a feeling of power (presupposing unpleasure)

5[65]

All thinking, judging, perceiving as *likening* presupposes a '*positing as alike*', earlier still a '*making alike*'.[101] This making alike is the same thing as the amoeba's incorporation of appropriated material.

Memory a late phenomenon, inasmuch as here the drive to make alike already appears in a *tamed* form: difference is preserved. Remembering as categorising, packing into boxes, active – who?

5[67]

What is needed is not a 'moral education' of the human race, but the harsh school of errors, because 'truth' disgusts and makes life wearisome, assuming man has not already started irrevocably on his *course* and accepts his honest *insight* with tragic pride.

5[68]

Both physiologists and philosophers believe that *consciousness* grows in *value* in the same measure as it *increases* in lucidity: the most lucid consciousness, the coldest and most logical thinking, they say, is of the *first*

---

[101] *vergleichen* (compare, liken), *gleichsetzen* (equate, posit as alike), *gleichmachen* (level, equalise, make alike).

rank. Yet – on what basis is this value determined? The most superficial, most *simplified* thinking is the most useful as regards *triggering the will* (because it leaves so few other motives over) – it might therefore, etc. NB.

the *precision of action* stands in antagonism to *circumspection*, which is *far-sighted* and often uncertain in its judgements: circumspection guided by the *deeper* instinct.

NB. *Value to be measured* according to the *reach* of its usefulness.

5[71]

European Nihilism

Lenzer Heide, 10th June 1887

1

What *advantages* did the Christian moral hypothesis offer?

1. It endowed man with an absolute *value*, in contrast to his smallness and contingency in the flux of becoming and passing away.
2. It served the advocates of God by conceding to the world, despite suffering and evil, the character of *perfection*, including that 'freedom' – evil seemed full of *meaning*.
3. It posited that man *knows* about absolute values, thus giving him *adequate knowledge* precisely of what is most important.

It shielded man from despising himself as man, from taking sides against life, from despairing of knowledge: it was a *means of preservation* – in sum, morality was the great *antidote* to practical and theoretical *nihilism*.

2

But among the forces that morality cultivated was *truthfulness: this*, in the end, turns against morality, discovers its *teleology*, the *partiality* of its viewpoint – and now the *insight* into this long-ingrained mendacity, which one despairs of ever shedding from oneself, is what acts as a stimulus: a stimulus to nihilism. We notice needs in ourselves, planted there by the long-held moral interpretation, which now appear to us as needs for the untrue; on the other hand, it is these needs on which depends the value for whose sake we endure living. This antagonism – *not* esteeming what we know and no longer being *permitted to* esteem what we would like to pretend to ourselves – results in a process of dissolution.

3

In fact we no longer have so much need of an antidote to the *first* nihilism: in our Europe, life is no longer quite so uncertain, contingent, nonsensical. Such a tremendous *potentiation* of the *value* of man, the value of evil, etc., is now less necessary: we can endure a considerable *moderation* of that value, we can concede much nonsense and contingency. The *power* man has achieved now allows a *reduction* of those means of discipline of which the moral interpretation was the strongest. 'God' is far too extreme a hypothesis.

4

However, an extreme position is replaced not by a moderated one but by a new extreme one, its *converse*. Thus belief in the absolute immorality of nature, in the absence of purpose and meaning, becomes the psychologically necessary *affect* once belief in God and an essentially moral order can no longer be sustained. Nihilism appears now *not* because unpleasure in existence is greater than it used to be, but because we have become more generally mistrustful of a 'meaning' in evil, indeed in existence itself. *One* interpretation has perished; but because it was regarded as *the* interpretation, there now seems to be no meaning at all in existence, everything seems to be *in vain*.

5

It remains to be shown that this 'In vain!' constitutes the character of our present nihilism. Mistrust of our previous valuations intensifies until it arrives at the question: 'Are not all "values" just decoys that prolong the comedy without ever getting closer to a denouement?' *Continuing* with an 'In vain', without aim and purpose, is the *most paralysing* thought, especially when one realises one's being fooled and yet has no power to prevent oneself being fooled.

6

Let us think this thought in its most terrible form: existence as it is, without meaning or goal, but inevitably recurring, without any finale into nothingness: 'eternal recurrence'.

That is the most extreme form of nihilism: nothingness ('meaningless-ness') eternally!

European form of Buddhism: the energy of knowledge and of strength *compels* such a belief. It is the *most scientific* of all possible hypotheses. We deny final goals: if existence had one, it could not fail to have been reached.

7

It now becomes clear that here an opposite to pantheism is being sought: because 'Everything perfect, divine, eternal' *likewise* compels *a belief in 'eternal recurrence'.* Question: once morality becomes impossible, does the pantheistic affirmative stance towards all things become impossible as well? After all, fundamentally it's only the moral God that has been overcome. Does it make sense to conceive of a God 'beyond good and evil'? Would a pantheism in *this* sense be possible? If we remove the idea of purpose from the process do we *nevertheless* affirm the process? – This would be the case if something within that process were *achieved* at every moment of it – and always the same thing.

Spinoza attained an affirmative stance like this insofar as every moment has a *logical* necessity: and with his fundamental instinct for logic he felt a sense of triumph about the world's being constituted *thus*.

8

But his is only a single case. *Every fundamental trait* which underlies *everything* that happens, which expresses itself in everything that hap-pens, ought to lead an individual who felt it as *his* fundamental trait to welcome triumphantly every moment of general existence. The point would be precisely to experience this fundamental trait in oneself as good, as valuable, with pleasure.

9

Now, *morality* protected life from despair and from the plunge into nothingness for those men and classes who were violated and oppressed by *men*: for powerlessness against men, *not* powerlessness against nature, is what engenders the most desperate bitterness against existence. Morality treated the despots, the men of violence, the 'masters' in general, as the enemies against whom the common man must be protected, i.e., *first of all encouraged, strengthened*. Consequently, morality taught the deepest *hatred* and *contempt* for what is the rulers' fundamental trait: *their will to power*. To abolish this morality, to deny it, corrode it: that would be to imbue the most hated drive with an *opposite* feeling and evaluation. If the suffering, oppressed man *lost his belief* in being *entitled* to despise the will to power, he would enter the phase of hopeless desperation. This would be the case if the masters' trait were essential to life, if it turned out that even the 'will to morality' only disguised the 'will to power', that even this hating and despising is a power-will. The man oppressed would realise that he stands *on the same ground* as the oppressors and that he has no *privilege*, no *higher rank* than them.

10

Rather *the reverse!* There is nothing to life that has value except the degree of power – assuming, precisely, that life itself is the will to power. For *those who have come off badly*, morality provided protection from nihilism by conferring on *each* an infinite value, a metaphysical value, and positioning him within an order that does not coincide with the worldly order of rank and power: it taught submission, meekness, etc. *If belief in this morality fell into ruin*, those who come off badly would lose their consolation – and *would be ruined too*.

11

This *ruin* takes the form of – *ruining oneself*, as an instinctive selection of what *must destroy*. *Symptoms* of this self-destruction of those who have come off badly: self-vivisection, poisoning, intoxication, Romanticism, above all the instinctive compulsion to act in ways that make *mortal enemies* of the powerful (– breeding one's own executioners, so to speak); the *will to destruction* as the will of a still deeper instinct, the instinct for self-destruction, the *will into nothingness*.

12

Nihilism as a symptom of the badly off having lost all consolation: that they destroy in order to be destroyed, that once separated from morality they no longer have any reason to 'submit' – that they settle on the ground of the opposite principle and themselves *want* to have *power* by *forcing* the powerful to become their executioners. This is the European form of Buddhism, *doing No* after all existence has lost its 'meaning'.

13

It is not that 'hardship' has become greater: on the contrary! 'God, morality, submission' were remedies applied at terrible, profound levels of misery: *active nihilism* appears under conditions much more favourable compared with these. Indeed, the fact that morality is felt to be overcome presupposes quite some degree of intellectual culture, and this, in turn, relative prosperity. Likewise, a certain intellectual fatigue, brought by the long struggle of philosophical opinions to the point of hopeless scepticism *towards* all philosophy, characterises the position, by no means *lowly*, of these nihilists. Consider the situation in which the Buddha appeared. The doctrine of eternal recurrence would have *scholarly* presuppositions (as did the Buddha's doctrines, e.g., the concept of causality, etc.).

14

Now, what does 'come off badly' mean? Above all *physiologically* – no longer politically. The *most unhealthy* kind of man in Europe (in all classes) is fertile ground for this nihilism: they will feel belief in eternal recurrence to be a *curse*, struck by which one no longer shrinks from any action: not passively dying down, but *extinguishing* everything which lacks aim and meaning in this degree: although it's only a convulsion, a blind rage at the insight that everything has existed for eternities – including this moment of nihilism and lust for destruction. – The *value of such a crisis* is that it *cleanses*, that it crowds related elements together and has them bring about each other's destruction, that it assigns common tasks to men with opposite ways of thinking – bringing to light the weaker, more uncertain of them as well and thus initiating *an order of rank among forces*, from the point of view of health: recognising those who command as commanders, those who obey as obeyers. Of course, outside all existing social orders.

15

In this process, who will prove to be the *strongest?* The most moderate, those who have no *need* of extreme articles of faith, who not only concede but even love a good deal of contingency and nonsense, who can think of man with a considerable moderation of his value and not therefore become small and weak: the richest in health, who are equal to the most misfortunes and therefore less afraid of misfortunes – men who *are sure of their power* and who represent with conscious pride the strength man has achieved.

16

What would such a man think of eternal recurrence? –

5[82]

Right originates only where there are contracts; but for there to be contracts, a certain *balance of power* must exist. If there is no such balance, if two quantities of power that are too different collide, then the stronger encroaches on the weaker and weakens it further, until in the end it submits, adapts, conforms, is incorporated: with the end result, thus, that two have become one. For two to remain two, as has been said, a balance of power is necessary: and therefore all right goes back to a preceding process of *weighing*. Thus the representation of Justice with a pair of scales in her hand cannot be accepted, for it's misleading: the correct allegory would be to make Justice stand at the centre of a pair of scales in such a way that she *kept* the two pans *balanced*. But Justice is wrongly represented – and the wrong words are put into her mouth as well. Justice doesn't say: 'Give everyone his due', but always only: 'Tit for tat'. That two powers in a relation to each other rein in the reckless will to power, and not only leave each other be as *equal* but even *want* each other to be equal, is the beginning of all 'good will' upon earth. For a contract contains not just a mere affirmation with respect to an *existing* quantum of power, but also the will to affirm this quantum on both sides as something *lasting* and thus, to a certain extent, themselves to maintain it. In this, as I say, is to be found a *germ* of all 'good will'.

5[87]

Pour qu'un homme soit au-dessus de l'humanité, il en coûte trop cher à tous les autres.

Montesquieu.[102]

5[89]

Against the *great error* of thinking that our era (Europe) represents the *highest human type*. Instead: the men of the Renaissance were higher, as were the Greeks; in fact, perhaps we are at a *rather low* level: 'understanding' is not a sign of highest force but of *thorough fatigue*; *moralisation* itself is a *'décadence'*.

5[98]

1.

Anyone considering how the human type can be raised to its greatest magnificence and power will understand first of all that man must place himself outside morality: for morality has essentially directed itself towards the opposite goal – to hamper or destroy that magnificent development wherever it was in progress. For indeed, a development of this kind consumes such a tremendous quantity of men in its service that a *reverse* movement is only too natural: the weaker, more tender, middling existences find it necessary to band together *against* that glory of life and force, and to do that they must acquire a new appreciation of themselves which enables them to condemn, and possibly destroy, life in this highest plenitude. A hostility to life is thus characteristic of morality inasmuch as it wants to overpower the strongest types of life.

---

[102] Montesquieu, *Dialogue de Sylla et d'Eucrate* (1722): 'One man's being raised above humanity costs all the rest too dear.'

5[100]

On the *critique of ideals*: begin this in such a way that the word '*ideal*' is abolished: critique of *desirabilities*.

5[105]

An action *good* if the conscience has said Yes to it! – as if a work were beautiful simply because the artist was thoroughly pleased with it! '*Value*' dependent on the doer's accompanying *feelings of pleasure*! (– and who will disentangle comfort in the traditional, vanity, etc., from the calculation!)

On the other hand, all *crucial* and valuable actions have been done *without* that security . . .

One must try to judge according to *objective* values. Is the community's 'benefit' one of these? Yes, only it's usually *confused* with the community's 'pleasurable feelings'. A 'wicked action' which provided a stimulus to the community and initially aroused very disagreeable feelings would, in this respect, be a *valuable* action.

5[107]

Critique of 'justice' and 'equality before the law': what are these really supposed to *eliminate*? Tension, enmity, hatred – but it's an error to think that '*happiness*' is *increased* that way: the Corsicans enjoy more happiness than their continental neighbours[103]

---

[103] A reference to the Corsicans' supposed lawlessness and tendency to blood feuds.

Notebook 6, summer 1886 – spring 1887

6[9]

If there is no goal in the whole history of man's lot, then we must put one in: assuming, on the one hand, that we have *need* of a goal, and on the other that we've come to see through the illusion of an immanent goal and purpose. And the reason we have need of goals is that we have need of a will – which is the spine of us. 'Will' as the compensation for lost 'belief', i.e., for the idea that there is a *divine* will, one which has plans for us . . .

6[11]

The inventive force that thought up categories was working in the service of needs – of security, of quick comprehensibility using signs and sounds, of means of abbreviation – 'substance', 'subject', 'object', 'being', 'becoming' are not metaphysical truths. – It is the powerful who made the names of things law; and among the powerful it is the greatest artists of abstraction who created the categories.

6[13]

The last thing in metaphysics we'll rid ourselves of is the oldest stock, assuming we *can* rid ourselves of it – that stock which has embodied itself in language and the grammatical categories and made itself so indispensable that it almost seems we would cease being able to think if we relinquished it. Philosophers, in particular, have the greatest difficulty in freeing themselves from the belief that the basic concepts and categories of reason belong without further ado to the realm of metaphysical certainties: from ancient times they have believed in reason as a piece of the metaphysical world itself – this oldest belief breaks out in them again and again like an overpowering recoil.

6[14]

Qualities are our insurmountable barriers; we have no way to stop ourselves feeling mere quantitative distinctions to be something fundamentally different from quantity, namely to be qualities, no longer reducible to one another. But everything for which the word 'knowledge' makes any sense refers to the realm where there can be counting, weighing, measuring, refers to quantity – while conversely all our feelings of value (i.e., all our feelings) adhere to qualities, that is, to the perspectival 'truths' that are ours and nothing more than ours, that simply cannot be 'known'. It is obvious that every being different from us feels different qualities and consequently lives in another world from the one we live in. Qualities are our real human idiosyncrasy: wanting our human interpretations and values to be universal and perhaps constitutive values is one of the hereditary insanities of human pride, which still has its safest seat in religion. Need I add, conversely, that quantities 'in themselves' do not occur in experience, that our world of experience is only a qualitative world, that consequently logic and applied logic (such as mathematics) are among the artifices of the ordering, overwhelming, simplifying, abbreviating power called life, and are thus something practical and useful, because life-preserving, but for that very reason not in the least something 'true'?

6[18]

We no longer eat a particular dish for moral reasons; one day we will no longer 'do good' for moral reasons either.

6[23]

It matters little to me whether someone says today with the modesty of philosophical scepticism or with religious submission: 'The essence of things is unknown to me,' or whether another, bolder man, who has not yet learned enough of criticism and mistrust, says: 'The essence of things is to a large extent unknown to me.' I maintain towards both of them that they certainly still pretend to know, or imagine they know, far too much, as if the distinction they both assume were justified: the distinction between an 'essence of things' and a world of appearances. To make such a distinction, one would have to conceive of our intellect as afflicted with a contradictory character: on the one hand adapted to a perspectival way of seeing, as precisely creatures of our species must be to preserve their existence; on the other, capable of grasping this perspectival seeing as perspectival, the appearance as appearance. In other words, equipped with a belief in 'reality' as if it were the only one, and yet also with knowledge about this belief, the knowledge that it's only a perspectival restriction with respect to a true reality. Yet a belief looked at with this knowledge ceases to be belief, is dissolved as belief. In short, we must not conceive of our intellect as being so contradictory that it is simultaneously both a belief and a knowledge of that belief as belief. Let's abolish the 'thing-in-itself' and with it one of the least clear concepts, that of 'appearance'! This whole antithesis, like the older one of 'matter and spirit', has been proven unusable

Notebook 7, end of 1886 – spring 1887

7[1]

Psychology of error

From times of old we have placed the value of an action, of a character, of an existence in the intention, the purpose for the sake of which there was doing, acting, living. This ancient idiosyncrasy of taste finally takes a dangerous turn – assuming, that is, we become ever more conscious of the lack of intention and purpose in what happens. With that process a general devaluation seems to be preparing itself. 'Everything is without meaning' – a melancholy statement which signifies: 'All meaning lies in the intention, and if there is no intention at all, then there is no meaning at all either'. This appraisal had made it necessary to displace the value of life into a 'life after death'; or into the progressive development of ideas or of mankind or of the people or beyond man; but this meant entering a progressus in infinitum[104] of purposes, and it finally became necessary to find oneself a place in the 'world process' (perhaps with the dysdaemonistic[105] perspective that it was the process into nothingness).

However, 'purpose' requires a more severe critique: one must realise that an action *is never caused by a purpose*; that ends and means are interpretations, with certain elements of what happens being underscored and selected at the expense of others, in fact of most; that every time something

---

[104] Infinite series.
[105] Nietzsche has adapted the word 'eudaemonistic' (a system of ethics guided by the question of how to become happy) by replacing the prefix 'eu' (well) with 'dys' (ill).

is done with a view to a purpose, something other and fundamentally different occurs; that the case of every purposive action is like the supposed purposiveness of the sun's heat – the huge mass of it is wasted, and a part barely worth considering has 'purpose', has 'meaning'; that an 'end' with its 'means' is an inexpressibly indeterminate outline which, although it can command as precept, as '*will*', presupposes a system of obedient and trained tools that replace the indeterminate with fixed quantities. That is, we imagine a system of *shrewder* but more restricted intellects that posit ends and means, so as to be able to attribute to the 'purpose', the only thing we know, the role of the 'cause of an action': to which we really have no right (it would mean trying to solve a problem by putting the solution in a world inaccessible to our observation –). Lastly: why could 'a purpose' not be an *attendant phenomenon* in the series of changes of the effecting forces that bring about the purposive action – a pale sign-image anticipated in consciousness, which gives us orientation about what happens, itself a symptom of what happens and *not* its cause? – But with this, we have subjected the *will itself* to critique: is it not an illusion to take as a cause what appears in consciousness as an act of will? Are all the phenomena of consciousness not merely final phenomena, last links in a chain which, however, give the appearance of conditioning each other in their succession on a single plane of consciousness? That could be an illusion. –

Opposition to the alleged 'facts of consciousness'. Observation is a thousand times more difficult, error perhaps a condition of observation in general.

I have the intention of stretching out my arm; supposing I know as little about the physiology of the human body and the mechanical laws of its motion as a common man does, is there really anything vaguer, fainter, more uncertain than this intention compared to what follows upon it? And if I had the most acute mind for mechanics and special instruction in the relevant formulae, I wouldn't stretch out my arm a jot better or worse. In this case our 'knowing' and our 'doing' lie coldly apart, as if in two different realms. – On the other hand: Napoleon carries out his plan of campaign – what does that mean? Here everything is *known* that pertains to the plan's execution, because everything has to be commanded; yet this too presupposes subordinates who interpret the general plan and adapt it to immediate necessities, the measure of force, etc.

It is *not* the case that the world is thus and thus, and living beings see it as it appears to them. Instead: the world consists of such living beings, and for each of them there is a particular little angle from which it measures, notices, sees and does not see. There *is no* 'essence': what 'becomes', the 'phenomenal', is the only king of being. |?

'It changes', no change without a reason – this always presupposes a something that stands, and remains, behind the change.

'Cause' and 'effect': calculated psychologically, this is the belief which expresses itself in the *verb*, in active and passive, doing and being done to. In other words: it is preceded by the separation of what happens into a doing and a being done to, by the supposition of something that does. Belief in the *doer* is behind it: *as if once all doing were subtracted from the 'doer', the doer itself would remain over.* Here we are always prompted by the 'notion of I': all that happens has been interpreted as *doing*: with the mythology that a being corresponding to the 'I' – – –

7[2]

Value of *truth* and *error*

The origin of our valuations: out of our needs

Whether the origin of our apparent 'knowledge', too, oughtn't to be sought solely in *older valuations*, ones so firmly incorporated in us that they're part of our basic substance? So that it's really just a grappling of *more recent* needs with the *results of the oldest needs*?

The world seen, felt, interpreted in such a way that organic life preserves itself with this perspective of interpretation. Man is *not* just an individual but what lives on, all that is organic in one particular line. That *he* exists proves that one species of interpretation (albeit one always under further construction) has also kept existing, that the system of interpretation has not switched. 'Adaptation'

Our 'discontent', our 'ideal', etc., is perhaps the *consequence* of this incorporated piece of interpretation, of our perspectival viewpoint; perhaps in the end organic life will perish through it – just as the division of labour within organisms brings with it a withering and weakening of the parts, finally the death of the whole. There must be a potential for the *ruin* of organic life in its highest form just as for the ruin of the individual.

7[3]

Interpretation

How far interpretations of the world are symptoms of a ruling drive

Contemplating the world *artistically*: to sit down in front of life. But here the analysis of the aesthetic gaze is missing, its reduction to cruelty, its feeling of security, of sitting in judgement and being outside, etc. One must take the artist himself, and his psychology (critique of the drive to play as a release of force, pleasure in change and in stamping one's own soul on something else, the absolute egoism of the artist, etc.). What drives does he sublimate?

Contemplating the world *scientifically*: critique of the psychological need *for* science. The wish to make comprehensible; the wish to make practical, useful, exploitable: to what extent anti-aesthetic. Value only in what can be counted and calculated. Extent to which an average kind of man tries to gain ascendancy this way. Dreadful when even *history* is appropriated like this – the realm of the superior, of the one who sits in judgement. What drives he sublimates!

Contemplating the world religiously: critique of the religious man. He is *not* necessarily the moral man but the man of high peaks and deep depressions, who interprets the former with gratitude or suspicion and does not consider them to have issued from *himself* (– the same for the latter –). Essentially the man who feels 'unfree', who sublimates his states, his instincts of subjection.

Contemplating the world *morally*. The social feelings of the order of rank are displaced into the universe: immovability, law, fitting in and equating are, because they are most highly valued, also *sought* in the highest places, above the universe, or behind the universe, likewise – – –

What they have *in common* is: the ruling drives want *to be viewed* as *the highest pronouncers of value in general* – yes, as *creative* and *governing powers*. It goes without saying that these drives either attack or submit to each other (synthetically, probably bind each other together as well) or alternate in rule. However, their profound antagonism is so great that where they all try to be satisfied, a man of profound *mediocrity* can be assumed.

7[4]

What is the *criterion* of moral action? (1) its selflessness (2) its universal validity, etc. But that's armchair moralising. One must study the peoples of the world, and see what the criterion is in each case and what is expressed in it. A belief that 'to behave like this is among the first conditions of our existence'. Immoral means 'bringing ruin'. Now, all the communities in which these propositions were found have perished; certain of the propositions have been insisted on again and again, because each newly forming community had need of them afresh, e.g., 'Thou shalt not steal'. In periods when no collective feeling for society could be demanded (e.g., the Roman Empire), the drive threw itself into the 'soul's salvation', to put it in religious terms; or 'the greatest happiness' to put it philosophically. For even the Greek moral philosophers were no longer attuned to their πόλις.[106]

7[5]

The priest, for periods of time, himself the god, at least its deputy

In themselves, ascetic habits and exercises are still far from indicating an anti-natural attitude, a hostility to existence, or degeneration and sickness

self-overcoming, with harsh and dreadful inventions: a means of having and demanding respect for oneself: ascesis as a means of *power*

7[6]

The good men

Danger in modesty. – To adapt too early to a milieu, to tasks, societies, orders of work and everyday life where chance has put us, at a time when neither our force nor our goal has entered our consciousness as legislator; the security of conscience, the refreshing, sociable life thus all too early gained, this premature, modest making-do that wheedles its way into our feelings as an escape from inner and outer unrest, spoils us and keeps us

---

[106] 'polis'. See note to 34[92].

down in the most dangerous way; learning to feel respect after the manner of 'one's peers', as if we had no measure and right within ourselves to posit values, the endeavour to esteem like the others, *against* the inner voice of taste, which is also a conscience – these become dreadful, subtle fetters. If there is not finally an explosion, where all the bonds of love and morality are blown apart at once, then a spirit like this withers and becomes petty, becomes effeminate and prosaic. – The opposite is quite bad enough, but at least better than that: suffering from one's environment, its praise as well as its disparagement, wounded by it and beginning to fester without letting on; defending oneself against its love with involuntary suspicion; learning silence, perhaps veiling it with speech; creating nooks and unguessable solitudes for the moments of relief, of tears, of sublime consolation – until at last one is strong enough to say: 'What have I to do with *you?*' and goes *one's own* way.

The virtues are as dangerous as the vices, to the extent that one allows them to rule as authority and law from outside instead of generating them from within oneself, as would be right: as the most personal self-defence and necessity, as a condition of precisely *our* existence and benefit to others, which we know and acknowledge regardless of whether others grow with us under the same or different conditions. This law of the dangerousness of a virtue understood as impersonal and *objective* applies to modesty as well: many exquisite spirits perish through such modesty.

The morality of modesty is the worst softening in those souls for whom it only makes sense to quickly become *hard*.

7[7]

Physiology of *art*

The sense of and pleasure in nuance (which is real *modernity*), in what is *not* general, runs counter to the drive that takes its pleasure and force in grasping the *typical*: like the Greek taste of the best period. There is in it an overwhelming of the abundance of what lives; moderation comes to rule; at its base is that *calm* of the strong soul which moves slowly and has an aversion to what's too lively. The general case, the law is *honoured* and *high*lighted; the exception, conversely, is set aside, the nuance wiped away. What's firm, powerful, solid, life that rests broad and massive and encloses its force – that '*is pleasing*': i.e., that corresponds to how one sees oneself.

7[9]

Principle of life

Consciousness, beginning quite externally, as a coordination and becoming conscious of 'impressions' – initially furthest away from the biological centre of the individual; but a process that becomes deeper, more inward, moves constantly closer to that centre.

7[15]

Ethics or 'philosophy of desirability': 'It *ought* to be different', it *shall* become different; dissatisfaction would thus be the germ of ethics.

One could save oneself firstly by choosing what does *not* arouse that feeling, secondly by understanding its presumption and silliness: for to demand that *something* be different from what it is means demanding that *everything* be different – it includes a damning criticism of the whole – and to this extent . . . *Yet life itself is such a demand!*

To determine *what* is, what it's *like*, appears unutterably higher and more serious than any 'It ought to be so': because the latter, as human criticism and presumption, seems condemned from the start to be ridiculous. It expresses a need which demands that the disposition of the world should accord with our human well-being, and the will to do as much as possible towards this task. On the other hand, it was only this demand 'It ought to be so' which called forth that other demand, the demand for what *is*. Our knowledge of what is, was only the outcome of our asking: 'How? Is it possible? Why precisely like that?' Our wonder at the discrepancy between our wishes and the course of the world has led to our becoming acquainted with the course of the world. Perhaps it's different again: perhaps that 'It ought to be so', our wish to overwhelm the world, is – – –

7[18]

'*Every activity* as such gives pleasure' – say the physiologists. In what way? Because dammed-up force brought with it a kind of *stress* and *pressure*, a state compared with which action is experienced as a *liberation*? *Or* in that every activity is an *overcoming* of difficulties and resistances? And many small resistances, overcome repeatedly, easily, as in a rhythmic dance, bring with them a kind of *stimulation of the feeling of power*?

Pleasure as a *stimulation* of the *feeling of power*: always presupposing something that resists and is overcome.

All pleasurable and unpleasurable phenomena are intellectual, are overall assessments of some inhibitive phenomenon, interpretations of it

7[23]

NB. In a psychological respect I have *two senses*:

first: *the sense of the **naked***
then: *the **will** to the **grand** style* (few main propositions, these in the strictest relationship to one another; no esprit, no rhetoric).

7[24]

For me, all the drives and powers that morality *praises* turn out to be essentially *the same* as the ones it slanders and rejects, e.g., justice as will to power, will to truth as a means used by the will to power

7[25]

Against Darwinism

– the utility of an organ does *not* explain its origin, on the contrary!
– for the longest time while a quality is developing, it does not preserve or prove useful to the individual, least of all in the struggle with external circumstances and enemies
– what, after all, is 'useful'? One must ask, 'Useful in regard *to what*?' E.g., something useful for maintaining the individual *over time* might be unfavourable to its strength and magnificence; what preserves the individual might simultaneously hold it fast and bring its evolution to a standstill. On the other hand a *deficiency*, a *degeneration* may be of the highest use, inasmuch as it has a stimulatory effect on other organs. Likewise, a *state of distress* may be a condition of existence, in that it makes the individual smaller to the point where it *coheres* and doesn't squander itself.

– The individual itself as a struggle between its parts (for food, space, etc.): its evolution dependent on some parts *conquering, prevailing*, and the others *withering*, 'becoming organs'.

– Darwin absurdly *overestimates* the influence of 'external circumstances'; the essential thing about the life process is precisely the tremendous force which shapes, creates form from within, which *utilises* and *exploits* 'external circumstances'...

– that the *new* forms created from within are *not* shaped with a purpose in view, but that in the struggle of the parts, it won't be long before a new form begins to relate to a partial usefulness, and then develops more and more completely according to how it is *used*

– if only what proved *lastingly* useful has been preserved, then primarily the damaging, destroying, dissolving capacities, the meaningless, the accidental, – – –

7[28]

The strong human being, powerful in the instincts of strong health, digests his deeds exactly as he digests his meals; he can manage heavy fare himself: chiefly, though, he is guided by a strict, undamaged instinct not to do anything repugnant to him, just as he doesn't eat anything he doesn't like.

7[36]

Supposing our usual conception of the world were a *misunderstanding*: could a *perfection* be imagined within which even such *misunderstandings* were *sanctioned*?

The idea of a new perfection: what does *not* accord with our logic, our 'beautiful', our 'good', our 'true' could be perfect in a higher sense than our ideal itself is.

7[38]

The first question is by no means whether we are satisfied with ourselves, but whether we are satisfied with anything at all. If we say Yes to a single moment, this means we have said Yes not only to ourselves, but to all existence. For nothing stands alone, either in us ourselves or in things:

and if just once our soul has quivered and resounded with happiness like a harpstring, then all eternity was needed to condition that one event – and in that one moment of our saying Yes, all eternity was welcomed, redeemed, justified and affirmed.

7[39]

A full and powerful soul can not only cope with painful, even terrible losses, privations, dispossessions and disdain: from such hells it emerges fuller and more powerful and – the crucial thing – with a new growth in the blissfulness of love. I believe that the man who has sensed something of the deepest conditions of every growth in love will understand Dante when he wrote over the gate to his Inferno: 'I too was created by eternal love'.

7[41]

The soil of desires from which grew *logic*: herd instinct in the background, the assumption of like cases presupposes the 'like soul'. *For the purpose of communication and mastery.*

7[42]

The antagonism between the 'true world', as pessimism reveals it, and a world capable of being lived in: one must test the claims of *truth*, the meaning of all these 'ideal drives' must be measured against *life* if we are to understand what that antagonism really is: the struggle of the sickly, despairing *life* which clings to the beyond, with the life which is healthier, more stupid, more mendacious, richer, more intact. Not, then, 'truth' struggling with life, but one type of life struggling with another. – But it wants to be the *higher* type! – Here one must begin with the proof that an order of rank is needed – that the primary problem is *the order of rank among the types of life.*

7[44]

'Useful' in the sense of Darwinist biology, i.e., proving advantageous in the struggle with others. But it seems to me that the *feeling of increase,* the feeling of *becoming stronger* is, quite irrespective of its usefulness in the struggle, itself the real *progress*: it is from this feeling that the will to struggle springs, –

7[46]

The kind of man whose mouthpiece I am:

suffering not from unfulfilled ideals but from fulfilled ones! – namely, from the fact that the ideal *which we represent*, and about which such a fuss is made, we ourselves treat with slight disdain –

dangerously homesick for the old 'wilderness' of the soul, for the conditions of greatness as well as devilry –

we enjoy our wilder, crazier, more disorderly moments; we would be capable of committing a crime just to see what this talk of the pangs of conscience is about –

we are inured to the everyday charms of the 'good man', of good social order, of well-behaved erudition –

we don't suffer because of 'corruption', we are very different from Rousseau and have no longing for the 'good natural man' –

we are *tired of the good, not* of suffering: we *no longer* take sickness, misfortune, old age, death seriously enough, and certainly not with the seriousness of the Buddhists, as if the objections to life were given.

7[48]

Intellectuality of *pain*: pain does not indicate what is momentarily damaged but what *value* the damage has with regard to the individual as a whole.

whether there are kinds of pain in which 'the species' and *not* the individual suffers –

What do *active* and *passive* mean? Is it not becoming *master* and being *defeated*?

and subject and object?

7[53]

The struggle fought among ideas and perceptions is not for existence but for mastery: the idea that's overcome is *not annihilated* but only *driven back* or *subordinated. In matters of the mind there is no annihilation* . . .

7[54]

To *imprint* upon becoming the character of being – that is the highest *will to power*.

A *dual falsification*, by the senses and by the mind, to obtain a world of things that are, that remain, that have equal value, etc.

That *everything recurs* is the most extreme *approximation of a world of becoming to one of being: pinnacle of contemplation*.

From the values attributed to what is derives the condemnation and dissatisfaction with what becomes: such a world of being having been invented in the first place.

The metamorphoses of what is (body, God, forms, laws of nature, formulae, etc.)

'What is' as illusion; reversal of values: the illusion was *what conferred value* –

Knowledge as such impossible within becoming; so how is knowledge possible? As error about itself, as will to power, as will to deception.

Becoming as inventing, willing, self-negating, self-overcoming: no subject, but a doing, positing, creative, no 'causes and effects'.

Art as a will to overcome becoming, as 'eternalisation', but short-sighted depending on perspective: reiterating in the detail, as it were, the tendency of the whole

To regard what *all life* shows as a repetition in miniature of the total tendency: hence a new definition of the concept 'life', as will to power

Instead of 'cause and effect', the struggle between elements that are becoming, which often includes swallowing up the opponent; the number of those becoming is not constant.

The old ideals no use for interpreting the whole of what happens, now that their animal origins and utility have been understood; all, moreover, contradict life.

Mechanistic theory no use – creates the impression of *meaninglessness*.

The whole *idealism* of humanity until now is on the point of tipping over into *nihilism* – into the belief in absolute *value*lessness, that is, *mean-ing*lessness . . .

The annihilation of ideals, the new wasteland, the new arts of enduring it, we *amphibians*.

Prerequisite: bravery, patience, no 'going back', no ardent rush forwards
NB. Zarathustra, constantly in a parodic relation to all previous values,
out of plenitude.

7[60]

Against the positivism which halts at phenomena – 'There are only
facts' – I would say: no, facts are just what there aren't, there are only
interpretations. We cannot determine any fact 'in itself': perhaps it's nonsensical to want to do such a thing. 'Everything is subjective,' you say:
but that itself is an *interpretation*, for the 'subject' is not something given
but a fiction added on, tucked behind. – Is it even necessary to posit the
interpreter behind the interpretation? Even that is fiction, hypothesis.

Inasmuch as the word 'knowledge' has any meaning at all, the world
is knowable: but it is variously *interpretable*; it has no meaning behind it,
but countless meanings. 'Perspectivism'.

It is our needs *which interpret the world*: our drives and their for and
against. Every drive is a kind of lust for domination, each has its perspective, which it would like to impose as a norm on all the other drives.

7[62]

Very few people make it clear to themselves what is implied by the standpoint of *desirability*, by every 'It ought to be so, but it is not' or even 'It
ought to have been so': a condemnation of the entire course of things. For
in that course nothing is isolated, the smallest element carries the whole,
upon your little injustice stands the whole edifice of the future, every
criticism of the smallest part condemns the whole as well. Assuming even
that the moral norm, as Kant himself supposed, has never been perfectly
fulfilled and remains like a kind of beyond, hanging over reality without
ever falling into it: then morality would imply a judgement of the whole,
which would, however, permit the question: *where does it get its right to
this?* How does the part come to sit in judgement on the whole? – And
if this moral judging and discontent with the real were indeed, as has
been claimed, an ineradicable instinct, might that instinct not then be one
of the ineradicable stupidities or indeed presumptions of our species? –
But by saying this we're doing exactly what we rebuke: the standpoint of
desirability, of unwarrantedly playing the judge, is part of the character

of the course of things, as is every injustice and imperfection – it's only our concept of 'perfection' which loses out. Every drive that wants to be satisfied expresses its dissatisfaction with the present state of things – what? Might the whole be composed entirely of dissatisfied parts, all of which have their heads full of what's desirable? Might the 'course of things' be precisely the 'Away from here! Away from reality!', be eternal discontent itself? Might desirability itself be the driving force? Might it be – deus?[107]

It seems to me important to get rid of *the* universe, unity, any force, anything unconditional; one could not avoid taking it as the highest agency and naming it God. The universe must be splintered apart; respect for the universe unlearned; what we have given the unknown and the whole must be taken back and given to the closest, what's ours. Kant, e.g., said: 'Two things remain forever worthy of admiration and awe'[108] – today we would rather say: 'Digestion is more venerable.' The universe would always bring with it the old problems, 'How is evil possible?', etc. Thus: *there is no universe, there is no* great sensorium,[109] or inventory, or storehouse of forces: *in that* [+ + +]

7[63]

Must not all philosophy finally bring to light the assumptions on which the movement of *reason* depends? Our *belief in the I* as substance, as the only reality on the basis of which we attribute reality to things in general? At last the oldest 'realism' comes to light: at the moment when the whole religious history of humanity recognises itself as the history of the soul-superstition. *Here there is a barrier*: our thinking itself involves that belief (with its distinction between substance and accident, doing, doer, etc.), abandoning it means no longer being allowed to think.

But that a belief, however necessary it is in order to preserve a being, has nothing to do with the truth can be seen even from the fact, e.g., that we *have to* believe in space, time and motion, without feeling compelled here to absolute [+ + +]

---

[107] God.
[108] Paraphrase of a sentence in the Conclusion of Immanuel Kant's *Critique of Practical Reason* (1788): 'Two things fill the mind with ever new and increasing admiration and awe, the oftener and more steadily they are reflected on: the starry heavens above me and the moral law within me'.
[109] The sensory faculties considered as a whole.

Notebook 8, summer 1887

8[2]

On the psychology of metaphysics

This world is illusory – *consequently* there is a true world.

This world is conditioned – *consequently* there is an unconditioned world.

This world is contradictory – *consequently* there is a world free of contradiction.

This world is a world that becomes – *consequently* there is a world that is.

All false conclusions (blind trust in reason: if A *is*, then its opposite concept B must *be* as well)

These conclusions are *inspired by suffering*: at bottom they are *wishes* that there might be such a world; in the same way, hatred of a world that makes us suffer expresses itself in the imagining of a different world, a *valuable* one: here, the metaphysicians' *ressentiment*[110] towards the real is creative.

Second series of questions: *what* is suffering *for*? . . . and here a conclusion is reached about the relationship of the true world *to* our illusory, changeable, suffering and contradictory world.

1. suffering as a consequence of error: how is error possible?

2. suffering as a consequence of guilt: how is guilt possible?

(– all experiences from the natural sphere or society, universalised and projected into the 'in-itself')

---

[110] See note to 2[171].

However, if the conditioned world is causally conditioned by the un-conditioned one, then the *freedom to err* and *to be guilty* must be conditioned by it as well: and again one asks *What for?* ... The world of illusion, of becoming, of contradiction, of suffering is thus *willed: what for?*

The mistake in these inferences: two antithetical concepts are formed – and *because* a reality corresponds to one of them, a reality 'must' also correspond to the other. *'Where* else could its counterpart have come from?' – *Reason* thus as a source of revelation about what is-in-itself.

But the *origin* of these oppositions *need not necessarily* go back to a supernatural source of reason: it's enough to set up against it the *true genesis of these concepts* – this comes from the practical sphere, from the sphere of usefulness, which is precisely where it gets the *strong belief* in them (one *perishes* if one does not conclude in line with this kind of reason: but that doesn't 'prove' what it asserts).

The metaphysicians' *preoccupation with suffering*: very naive. 'Eternal bliss': psychological nonsense. Brave and creative men *never* see pleasure and suffering as ultimate questions of value – they are accompanying states, one must *want* both if one wants to *achieve* anything. – Something weary and sick in the metaphysicians and religious men is expressed in their foregrounding problems of pleasure and suffering. *Morality*, too, *only* has such *importance* for them because it's considered an essential condition for the abolition of suffering.

Likewise the preoccupation with illusion and error: cause of suffering, superstition that happiness is connected with truth (confusion: happiness in 'certainty', in 'belief').

8[3]

on 'homines religiosi'[III]

What do ascetic ideals mean?

Preliminary form of the still new *contemplative* way of life; extreme, in order to find respect and *get* respect *for oneself* (*against* the 'bad conscience' of inactivity); its conditions are sought

---

[III] Religious men.

A sense of the *cleanliness* of the soul, to put it rather floridly

A *convict-like state* (planning all sorts of delicacies for oneself), as a remedy for an over-wild sensual appetite (which takes pains to avoid 'seductions') – expressing itself as *hatred* against the senses, against life.

An *impoverishment of life*, a need for indolence, peace and quiet. The fakir's trick. 'Old age'

A *pathological thin-skinnedness*, sensibility, something old-maidish that takes pains to avoid life: occasionally a mischannelled eroticism and hysteria of 'love'

Critique of *meekness* ('absolute obedience'), occasionally the instinct of power to look for absolute 'tools' or to achieve most as a tool. The prudence in that, the laziness (just as in poverty and chastity)

Critique of *poverty* (illusory renunciation and competition, as a prudent means on the path to mastery.

Critique of *chastity. Usefulness*: it provides time, independence – intellectually pampered state which can't stand being among the womenfolk – families are great nests of chatter. It conserves force, wards off various illnesses. Freedom from wife and child wards off many temptations (luxury, servility towards power, conformity.

A man in whom the mysterious multiplicity and plenitude of nature exerts its effect, a synthesis of the terrible and the delightful, something promising, something knowing more, something capable of more. The ascetic ideal always expresses something going awry, a deprivation, a physiological contradiction. It's thought-provoking that really only this one ascetic species, the priest, is still known to contemporary men: it's an expression of man in general having degenerated and turned out badly. – And just as we speak of Romantic artists, one could say that we really only know the *Romantic priest* – that, as such, the *classical* priest is perfectly possible, and has probably existed, as well. With this possibility of the classical priest in mind, look at Plato in the Museo Borbonico in Naples: the archaeologists are unsure whether he isn't a bearded Dionysos. That need not concern us: what's certain is that here a priestly type – *not* an ascetic type – is presupposed...

The priest of Christianity represents anti-nature, the power of wisdom and goodness, but anti-natural power and anti-natural wisdom, anti-natural goodness: animosity to power, knowledge and – – –

power as miracle-power
wisdom as anti-reason
love as anti-sexuality

hatred of the powerful of the earth and a hidden, fundamental contest and competition – the soul is what's wanted, the body they're allowed to keep –
hatred of the mind, of pride, of courage, of the freedom, exuberance of the mind
hatred of the senses, of the joys of the senses, of joy in general, and mortal enmity towards sensuality and sexuality

it's on the conscience of the Christian priesthood – the slanderous and despicable will to misunderstanding with which, in cults and mysteries, sexuality has always...

the Christian priest has been the mortal enemy of sensuality from the very beginning: one can't imagine a greater contrast than the solemn attitude of innocent foreboding which, e.g., in the most venerable female cults of Athens accompanied the presence of sexual symbols. The act of procreation is the mystery itself in all non-ascetic religions: a kind of symbol of perfection and of mysterious intention, of the future (rebirth, immortality)

8[7]

Pleasure in lying as the mother of art, fear and sensuality as the mother of religion, nitimur in vetitum[112] and curiosity as the mother of science, cruelty as the mother of unegoistic morality, remorse as the origin of the movement for social equality, the will to power as the origin of justice, war as the father of honesty (of good conscience and cheerfulness), the master of the house as the origin of the family; mistrust as the root of justice and contemplation

---

[112] We strive for what is forbidden (Ovid, *Amores*, III, 4, 17).

Notebook 9, autumn 1887

9[22]

The great *lies* in history:

as if it was the *corruption* of paganism that paved the way for Christianity! Instead, it was the weakening and *moralisation* of the man of antiquity! The reinterpretation of natural drives as *vices* had already gone before!

– as if the *corruption of the Church* was the *cause* of the Reformation; it was only the pretext, the lies its agitators told themselves – there were strong needs, whose brutality very much required a cloak of spirituality.

9[23]

the mendacious interpretation of the words, gestures and states of *the dying*: e.g., the customary confusion of fear of death with fear of the 'after death' . . .

9[26]

against the *value* of what remains eternally the same (see the naivety of *Spinoza*, also of *Descartes*), the value of the shortest and most fleeting, the seductive flash of gold on the belly of the snake vita[113] –

---

[113] Life.

9[27]

Replacement of morality by the *will* to our goal, and *consequently* to the *means* of gaining it.

Replacement of the categorical imperative by the *natural imperative*

Not to want *praise*: one does what profits one, what one enjoys, or what one *has to* do.

9[34]

Workers should learn to feel in the same way as *soldiers*. A honorarium, an income, but no being paid! No relation between what one is paid and what one *achieves*! Instead, placing the individual *each according to his kind* in such a way that he can *achieve the highest* which lies in his sphere.

9[35]

1. *Nihilism as a **normal** condition.*
   Nihilism: the goal is lacking; an answer to the 'Why?' is lacking. What does nihilism mean? – *That the highest values are devaluated*.
   It is **ambiguous**:

(A) Nihilism as a sign of the *increased power of the spirit*: as **active nihilism**.
   It may be a sign of *strength*: the force of the spirit may have grown so much that the goals it has had *so far* ('convictions', articles of faith) are no longer appropriate
   – for a belief generally expresses the constraints of *conditions of existence*, submission to the authority of the circumstances under which a being *prospers, grows, gains in power* ...
   On the other hand a sign that one's strength is *insufficient* to productively *posit* for oneself a new goal, a 'Why?', a belief.
   It achieves its **maximum** of relative force as a violent force of **destruction**: as *active nihilism*. The opposite would be the weary nihilism that no longer *attacks*: its most celebrated form Buddhism: as *passivist* nihilism
   Nihilism represents a pathological *intermediate state* (what is pathological is the tremendous generalisation, the inference *that there is no*

meaning at all): whether because the productive forces are not yet strong enough or because décadence is still hesitating and has not yet invented the resources it needs.

(B) Nihilism as a *decline and retreat of the spirit's power: passive nihilism*:

as a sign of weakness: the force of the spirit may be wearied, *exhausted*, so that the goals and values that have prevailed *so far* are no longer appropriate and are no longer believed –

that the synthesis of values and goals (on which every strong culture rests) dissolves, so that the individual values wage war on each other: disintegration

that everything which revives, heals, soothes, benumbs comes to the fore in a variety of *disguises*: religious, or moral or political or aesthetic, etc.

2. *Presupposition of this hypothesis*

That there is no truth; that there is no absolute nature of things, no 'thing-in-itself'

– *this is itself a nihilism*, and indeed *the most extreme one*. It places the *value* of things precisely in the fact that *no* reality corresponds and has corresponded to that value, which is instead only a symptom of force on the part of the *value-positers*, a simplification for *the purposes* of *life*

9[38]

the *valuation* 'I believe that such and such is the case' as the *essence* of '*truth*'

in *valuations, conditions of preservation* and *growth* express themselves

all our *organs and senses of knowledge* are developed only with a view to conditions of preservation and growth

trust in reason and its categories, in dialectics, thus the *valuing* of logic, only proves logic's *usefulness* for life, proved by experience – and *not* its 'truth'.

That there must be a large measure of *belief*, that *judging* must be allowed, that doubt regarding all essential values *is absent*: –

these are the preconditions for everything that lives and for its life. In other words, what's necessary is that something *must* be held to be true; *not* that something *is true*.

'the *true* and the *illusory* world' – I trace this antithesis back to *relations of value*

we have projected the conditions of *our* preservation as *predicates of being* in general

we have taken the fact that in order to prosper we have to be stable in our belief, and made of it that the 'true' world is not one which changes and becomes, but one which *is*.

9[39]

values and their changes stand in relation to the *growth in power of the value-positer*

the measure of *unbelief*, of 'freedom of the mind' that is admitted, as an *expression of the growth in power*

'nihilism' as the ideal of the *highest powerfulness* of spirit, of the greatest over-abundance of life: part destructive, part ironic

9[40]

That things have *qualities in themselves*, irrespective of interpretation and subjectivity, is *a perfectly idle hypothesis*: it would presuppose that *interpreting and being subjective* are *not* essential, that a thing once released from all relations is still a thing. Conversely, the apparently *objective* character of things: might this not amount merely to a *difference of degree* within the subjective? – that, for example, what slowly changes might become for us something 'objectively' lasting, being, an 'in-itself'

– that the objective would be only a false category and opposition *within* the subjective?

9[41]

What is a *belief*? How does it originate? Every belief is a *holding-to-be-true*.

The most extreme form of nihilism would be that *every* belief, every holding-to-be-true, is necessarily false: *because there simply is no true world*. Thus: a *perspectival illusion* whose origins lie within us (inasmuch as we have constant *need* of a narrower, abridged and simplified world)

– that the *measure of force* is how far we can admit to ourselves *illusoriness*, the necessity of lies, without perishing.

*To this extent nihilism, as the **denial** of a true world, of a being, might be a divine way of thinking:* – – –

9[42]

Around 1876 I had the terrible experience of seeing *compromised* everything I had previously willed, when I realised which way Wagner was going: and I was very closely bound to him by all the bonds of a profound unity of needs, by gratitude, by the irreplaceability and absolute privation I saw ahead of me.

Around the same time I seemed to myself almost irretrievably *incarcerated* in my philology and teaching – in something accidental and makeshift in my life: I no longer knew how to escape and was tired, worn out, used up.

Around the same time I realised that my instinct was after the opposite of Schopenhauer's: it aspired to a justification of life, even in its most dreadful, ambiguous and mendacious forms – for this I had ready the formula 'Dionysian'.

(– against the view that an 'in-themselves of things' must necessarily be good, blissful, true, one, Schopenhauer's interpretation of the in-itself as will was an essential step: but he didn't know how to *deify* this will, and remained caught in the moral, Christian ideal

Schopenhauer was still so much dominated by Christian values that once the thing-in-itself had ceased to be 'God' to him, it must now be bad, stupid, absolutely reprehensible. He didn't understand there are endless ways that one can be different, ways even that one can be God.

The curse of that narrow-minded duality: good and evil.

9[44]

(Regarding the *third* treatise)

Main consideration: that one does not see the *task* of the higher species as being to *guide* the lower one (as, e.g., Comte[114] does) but the lower one as a *base* upon which a higher species devotes itself to its *own* task – upon which it *can stand*.

---

[114] Auguste Comte (1798–1857), French founder of positivism.

The conditions under which the *strong* and *noble* species preserves itself (in regard to intellectual discipline), are the reverse of those of the 'industrial masses' of little shopkeepers à la Spencer.[115]

What is open only to the *strongest* and *most fruitful* natures, to make possible *their* existence – leisure, adventure, unbelief, even dissipation – would, if open to middling natures, necessarily destroy them, indeed does destroy them. Here industriousness, rules, moderation, firm 'conviction' are appropriate – in short, the herd virtues: under them this middling kind of man becomes perfect.

Causes of **nihilism**:

1. *lack of the higher species*, i.e., the one whose inexhaustible fruitfulness and power sustains belief in humanity. (Think what is owed to Napoleon: almost all the higher hopes of this century)

2. *the lower species*, 'herd', 'mass', 'society', forgets how to be modest, and puffs up its needs into *cosmic* and *metaphysical* values. Through this the whole of existence is *vulgarised*: for to the degree that the *mass* rules, it tyrannises the *exceptions*, who thus lose their belief in themselves and become *nihilists*

All attempts to *imagine higher types having failed* ('Romanticism', the artist, the philosopher, against Carlyle's attempt to ascribe the highest moral values to them).

Resistance to the higher type as a result.

Decline and *insecurity of all higher types*; the struggle against the genius ('folk poetry', etc.). Compassion with the lower and the suffering as a *measure* of the *height of the soul*

What we lack is the philosopher, one who interprets the deed and does *not* merely rewrite it in a different form

9[48]

The *ascertaining of 'true'* versus *'untrue'*, in general the *ascertaining* of facts, differs fundamentally from creative *positing*, from the forming, shaping, overwhelming, *willing* which is of the essence of *philosophy*. **Putting in a meaning** – this task still remains *to be done* whatever happens, assuming there *isn't a meaning* already *there*. Thus it is with sounds, as well as with

---

[115] Herbert Spencer (1820–1903), English evolutionist, social reformer and positivist.

the destinies of peoples: they are *capable* of very different interpretations and of being directed towards *different goals*. The still higher stage is to *posit goals* and mould reality accordingly; thus, the *interpretation of the deed* and not merely its conceptual *rewriting*

9[52]

The most courageous among us does not have courage enough for what he really *knows*... The point where a man comes to a halt or does not *yet* do so, where he judges 'Here is the truth', is decided by the degree and strength of his valour; more, at least, than by any keenness or dullness of eye and mind.

9[64]

the *salesman philosophers* who build a philosophy not out of their lives but out of collections of bits of evidence for particular hypotheses

Never want to see *for the sake of* seeing! As a psychologist one must live and wait – until the *sifted* result of many experiences has come to its conclusion by itself. One must never know *how* one came to know something

Otherwise there is a distorted view and artificiality.

– *Forgetting* the individual case involuntarily is philosophical – but *wanting* to forget it, deliberate abstraction is *not*: rather, the latter characterises the *non*-philosophical nature.

9[66]

Revaluating values – what would that be? All the *spontaneous* movements must be there, the new, stronger ones of the future: only they still bear false names and estimations and have not yet *become conscious* of themselves

courageously becoming conscious and *saying Yes* to what has been *achieved*

extricating ourselves from the lazy routine of old valuations which degrade us in the best and strongest things we have achieved.

9[75]

A period where the old masquerade and moral finery of the affects arouses repugnance: *nature stripped bare*, where the *quantities of power* are simply accepted as *decisive* (as *determining rank*), where the *grand style* makes a new appearance, as a consequence of *grand passion*.

9[77]

Every doctrine is superfluous unless everything lies ready for it, all the accumulated forces, the dynamite. A revaluation of values is achieved only when there is a tension of new needs, of new needers who suffer under the old valuation without becoming aware – – –

9[79]

What is praising? –

Praise and *gratitude* on the occasions of harvest, good weather, victory, weddings, peace – all these festivals require a *subject* towards which the feeling is discharged. One wants everything good that happens to one to have been *done to* one, one wants the doer. The same contemplating a work of art: the piece itself is not enough, its maker is praised. – What, then, is *praising*? A kind of *settling up* in respect of benefits received, a *giving in return*, a demonstration of *our* power – for the praiser affirms, judges, estimates, *passes sentence*: he grants himself the right to *be able to* affirm, to *be able to* mete out honour . . . The heightened feeling of happiness and life is also a heightened *feeling of power*: it is out of this that man *praises* (– out of this he invents and seeks a *doer*, a '*subject*' –)

    Gratitude as the *good revenge*, most strictly required and practised where equality and pride must both be maintained, where revenge is practised best.

9[84]

The great nihilist counterfeiting, with shrewd misuse of moral values
a. Love as depersonalisation; likewise compassion.
b. Only the *depersonalised intellect* ('the philosopher') knows the *truth*, 'the true being and essence of things'

c. the genius, the *great men* are *great* because they do not seek themselves and their own concerns: the *value* of man *grows* in proportion to his self-denial. Schopenhauer II 440 ff.[116]

d. art as the work of the *'pure will-free subject'*, misunderstanding of 'objectivity'.

e. *happiness* as life's objective; *virtue* as a means to this end

the pessimistic condemnation of life in Schopenhauer's work is a *moral* transfer of the herd's yardsticks to the realm of metaphysics.

The 'individual' meaningless; consequently giving him an origin in the 'in-itself' (and a significance of his existence as an aberration); parents only as 'accidental cause'.

Science's failure to comprehend the individual is now taking its toll: the individual is *the whole of life up to now in a single line*, and *not* its *result*.

9[86]

moralistic naturalism: tracing the apparently emancipated, supranatural moral value back to its 'nature', that is, to *natural immorality*, natural 'usefulness', etc.

I may call the tendency of these observations *moralistic naturalism*: my task is to translate moral values which merely appear to have become emancipated and *without nature* back into their nature – that is, into their natural 'immorality'

NB. Comparison with Jewish *'holiness'* and its basis in nature: the same applies to *moral law made sovereign*, detached from its *nature* (– to the point of becoming the *antithesis* of nature –)

Steps in the 'denaturalisation of morality' (known as *'idealisation'*)

as path to individual happiness

as consequence of knowledge

as categorical imperative, detached from – – –

as path to sanctification

as negation of the will to life

morality's step-by-step *hostility to life*.

---

[116] The reference is to the *Parerga* in the 1862 Frauenstädt edition.

9[91]

On combating determinism

From the fact that something happens regularly and predictably, it does not follow that it happens *necessarily*. That in every determinate case a quantum of force behaves and determines itself in a single way does not make it an 'unfree will'. 'Mechanical necessity' is not a fact: it is *we* who have interpreted it into what happens. We have interpreted the fact that what happens *can be expressed in formulae* as resulting from a necessity that governs what happens. But from the fact that I do a particular thing, it by no means follows that I do it under compulsion. *Compulsion* in things cannot be demonstrated at all: regularity proves only that one and the same happening is not another happening as well. Only our having interpreted subjects, '*doers*', into things makes it appear that everything which happens is the consequence of a *compulsion* exerted on subjects – exerted by whom? Again, by a 'doer'. Cause and effect – a dangerous concept if one conceives of a *something* that *causes* and a something upon which there *is* an *effect*.

(A) Necessity is not a fact but an interpretation.

(B) Once one has understood that the 'subject' is not something that *effects* but merely a fiction, many things follow.

It is only after the model of the subject that we invented *thingness* and interpreted it into the hubbub of sensations. If we cease to believe in the *effecting* subject, then the belief in things *that exert effect*, in reciprocal effect, cause and effect between those phenomena we call 'things', falls as well.

This, of course, also means the fall of the world of **atoms that exert effect**, the assumption of which always presupposes that one needs subjects.

Finally, the '*thing-in-itself*' also falls, because at bottom this is the concept of a 'subject-in-itself', yet we have understood that the subject is fictitious. The antithesis of 'thing-in-itself' and 'appearance' is untenable; with this, however, the concept '*appearance*' collapses too.

(C) If we give up the effecting *subject*, then also the *object* on which effects are exerted. Duration, conformity with itself, being, inhere neither in what is called subject nor in what is called object. They are complexes of what happens which appear to have duration in relation to other complexes – for example due to a difference in tempo (rest-motion, fixed-slack: all these are oppositions which don't exist in themselves and in fact only express *differences of degree* that look like oppositions when viewed through a particular prism.)

There are no oppositions: we have only acquired the concept of oppositions from those of logic, and from there wrongly transferred it to things.

(D) If we give up the concept 'subject' and 'object', then also the concept '*substance*' – and consequently its various modifications, e.g., 'material', 'spirit' and other hypothetical entities, 'the eternity and immutability of matter', etc. We have then rid ourselves of *materiality*.

Put in moral terms: *the world is false* – but inasmuch as morality itself is a piece of this world, morality is false

The will to truth is a *making* fixed, a *making* true and lasting, a removing from sight of that *false* character, its reinterpretation into something that *is*.

Truth is thus not something that's there and must be found out, discovered, but something *that must be made* and that provides the name for a *process* – or rather for a will to overcome, a will that left to itself has no end: inserting truth as a processus in infinitum,[117] an *active determining, not* a becoming conscious of something that is 'in itself' fixed and determinate. It is a word for the 'will to power'

Life is founded on the presupposition of a belief in things lasting and regularly recurring; the more powerful the life, the wider must be the divinable world – the world, so to speak, that is *made* to *be*. Logicising, rationalising, systematising as life's resources.

In a certain sense man projects his drive to truth, his 'goal', outside himself as a world that *is*, as a metaphysical world, as a 'thing-in-itself', as an already existing world.

His needs as a maker already invent the world he's working on, anticipate it: this anticipation ('this belief' in truth) is his mainstay.

All that happens, all movement, all becoming as a determining of relations of degree and force, as a *struggle* . . .

The 'well-being of the individual' is just as imaginary as the 'well-being of the species': the former is *not* sacrificed to the latter; regarded from a distance, the species is something quite as fluid as the individual.

---

[117] Process to infinity.

The '*preservation* of the species' is only a consequence of the *growth* of the species, i.e., of *overcoming the species* on the path to a stronger type

As soon as we *imagine* someone who is responsible for us being thus and thus, etc. (God, nature), attributing our existence, our happiness and misery to it as its *intention*, we corrupt for ourselves the *innocence of becoming*. We then have someone who wants to achieve something through us and with us.

That what appears to be '*purposiveness*' ('*the purposiveness infinitely superior to all human art*') is merely the consequence of the *will to power* played out in everything that happens

that *becoming stronger* brings with it orderings which resemble outlines of purposiveness

that what appear to be *purposes* are not intended; instead, as soon as a slighter power has been overwhelmed and made to work as a function of the greater one, there is an order of *rank*, of organisation, which is bound to produce the appearance of an order of means and ends.

Against what appears to be '*necessity*'

– this only an *expression* of the fact that a force is not also something else.

Against what appears to be '*purposiveness*'

– this only an *expression* of an ordering of spheres of power and their interplay.

Logical determinacy, transparency, as criterion of truth ('omne illud verum est, *quod clare et distincte percipitur*',[118] Descartes): this makes the mechanicist hypothesis of the world desirable and credible.

But that is a crude confusion, like simplex sigillum veri.[119] How does one know that the true nature of things stands in *this* relation to our intellect? – Could it not be different? That the hypothesis which most gives the intellect the feeling of power and security is the one it most *favours, values, and consequently* calls **true**? – The intellect posits its freest and *strongest capacity and skill* as the criterion of what is most valuable, consequently *true* . . .

'true':

---

[118] All that is true which is perceived clearly and distinctly.   [119] See note to 2[77].

from the perspective of feeling: what most strongly stimulates feeling ('I')

from the perspective of thinking: what gives thinking the greatest feeling of force

from the perspective of touching, seeing, hearing: what calls forth the strongest resistance

Thus the *highest degrees of effort* arouse for the *object* the belief in its own 'truth', i.e., *reality*. The feeling of force, of struggle, of resistance, prompts the conviction that *there is* something which is being resisted.

9[94]

To greatness belongs dreadfulness: let no one be deceived about that.

9[97]

We do not succeed in both affirming and negating one and the same thing: that is a subjective empirical proposition which expresses not a 'necessity' *but only a non-ability*.

If, according to Aristotle, the *principle of non-contradiction* is the most certain of all principles, if it is the final and most fundamental one upon which all proofs are based, if the principle of all other axioms lies within it: then one ought to examine all the more carefully what it actually *presupposes* in the way of theses. Either, as if it already knew the real from somewhere else, it asserts something with respect to the real, to what is: namely, that opposite predicates *can*not be ascribed to the real. Or does the principle mean that opposite predicates *shall* not be ascribed to it? Then logic would be an imperative, *not* to know the true, but to posit and arrange a world *that shall be called true by us*.

In short, the question remains open: are the axioms of logic adequate to the real, or are they measures and means to *create* for us the real, the concept 'reality'? ... But to be able to affirm the former one would, as I have said, already need to be acquainted with what is; and that's simply not the case. The principle thus contains not a *criterion of truth*, but rather an *imperative* about *what shall count as true*.

Supposing there were no A identical with itself, such as that presupposed by every logical (including mathematical) principle, supposing A were already an *illusion*, then logic would have as its presupposition a merely *illusory* world. And indeed we believe in that principle under the impression of endless experience which seems continually to *confirm* it. The 'thing' – that is the real substratum of A: *our belief in things* is the precondition for our belief in logic. The A of logic is, like the atom, a re-construction of the 'thing'...By not grasping that, and by making of logic a criterion of *true being*, we are well on the way to positing all those hypostases – substance, predicate, object, subject, action, etc. – as realities: i.e., to conceiving a metaphysical world, i.e., a 'true world' (– *but this is the illusory world once again...*).

The most basic acts of thought – affirming and negating, holding-to-be-true and holding-to-be-not-true – are, inasmuch as they presuppose not only a habit but a *right* to hold-to-be-true or hold-to-be-not-true in general, themselves ruled by a belief *that there is knowledge for us*, that *judging really can reach the truth*. In short, logic does not doubt its ability to state something about the true-in-itself (namely, that this *can*not have opposite predicates).

Here the crude, sensualist prejudice *reigns* that sensations teach us *truths* about things – that I cannot say at the same time of one and the same thing that it is *hard* and it is *soft* (the instinctive proof 'I cannot have two opposite sensations at the same time' – *quite crude and false*). The conceptual ban on contradiction proceeds from the belief that we *are able* to form concepts, that a concept doesn't merely name what is true in a thing but *encompasses* it...In fact *logic* (like geometry and arithmetic) only applies to *fictitious truths* **that we have created**. Logic is the attempt *to understand the real world according to a scheme of being that we have posited, or, more correctly, the attempt to make it formulatable, calculable for us...*

9[98]

Psychological derivation of our belief in reason

The concept of 'reality', of 'being', is drawn from our feeling of '*subject*'.

'Subject': interpreted from the standpoint of ourselves, so that the I is considered subject, cause of all doing, *doer*.

The logical-metaphysical postulates, belief in substance, accident, attribute, etc., draw their persuasive power from the habit of regarding all our doing as a consequence of our will – so that the I, as substance, is not absorbed into the multiplicity of change. – *But there is no will.* –

We don't have the categories to allow us to separate a 'world-in-itself' from a world as appearance. All our *categories of reason* have sensual origins: read off from the empirical world. 'The soul', 'the I' – the history of this concept shows that here too the oldest separation ('breath', 'life') – – –

If there is nothing material, then neither is there anything immaterial. The concept no longer *contains* anything...

No subject-'atoms'. The sphere of a subject constantly becoming *larger* or *smaller* – the centre of the system constantly *shifting* – if it cannot organise the mass it has appropriated, it divides into two. On the other hand, it can transform a weaker subject into a functionary without destroying it, and to a certain degree form a new unit together with it. No 'substance', but rather something that as such strives for more strength, and only indirectly wants to 'preserve' itself (it wants to *surpass* itself...)

9[99]

NB. Not to want to be shrewd, as psychologists; indeed we *mustn't* be shrewd... Anyone who wants to snatch little advantages from his knowledge, from his experience of men (– or large advantages, like the politician –) moves back from the general to the most particular case; but this kind of viewpoint is contrary to that other one, the only one we can make use of: we look *outwards* from the most particular –

9[102]

Aesthetica

The states in which we put a *transfiguration and plenitude* into things and work at shaping them until they reflect back to us our own plenitude and lust for life:

the sexual drive
intoxication
meals
springtime

victory over the enemy, derision

the daring feat; cruelty; the ecstasy of religious feeling.

Three elements most of all:

the sexual drive, intoxication, cruelty: all part of man's oldest *joy* in *festival*: likewise all predominating in the original 'artist'

Conversely: when we encounter things that show this transfiguration and plenitude, our animal existence responds with an *arousal of the spheres* where all those states of pleasure have their seat – and the mixture of these very delicate nuances of animal well-being and desires is the *aesthetic state*. This state occurs only in natures capable of that generous and overflowing plenitude of bodily vigour; it's there the primum mobile[120] is always to be found. The sober man, the weary man, the exhausted, the desiccated one (e.g., a scholar) can receive absolutely nothing of art, because he doesn't have the primordial artistic force, the pressure of wealth: a man who can't give won't receive anything either.

'*Perfection*': in those states (especially in sexual love, etc.) there is naively revealed what the deepest instinct acknowledges to be the higher, more desirable, more valuable in general, the upward movement of its type; likewise, *which* status it's really *striving for*. Perfection: that is the extraordinary expansion of its feeling of power; it is wealth; it is the necessary bubbling and brimming over all limits...

Art reminds us of states of animal vigour; it's on the one hand a surplus and overflow of flourishing corporeality into the world of images and wishes; on the other a rousing of the animal function through images and wishes of intensified life – a heightening of the feeling of life, a stimulus for it.

In what way can the ugly, too, possess this power? In that it still communicates something of the victorious energy of the artist who has become master of the ugly and dreadful; or in that it quietly rouses our pleasure in cruelty (sometimes even our pleasure in causing *ourselves* pain, self-violation: and thus the feeling of power over ourselves.)

9[103]

NB. When one is sick, one should creep away and hide in some 'cave': that is what's reasonable, that is the only animal way.

---

[120] Prime source of motion.

9[106]

Our psychological perspective is determined by

1. *communication* being necessary, and that for communication something has to be fixed, simplified, specifiable (especially in *identical cases*...). However, for it to be communicable, it must be experienced in a *trimmed* form, as '*recognisable*'. The material of the senses trimmed by the intellect, reduced to the broadest strokes, made similar, subsumed under related headings. Thus: the indistinctness and chaos of the sensory impression is, so to speak, *logicised*.
2. the world of 'phenomena' is the trimmed world which we *experience as real*. This 'reality' lies in the constant recurrence of the same, familiar, related things, in their *logicised character*, in the belief that here we can calculate, ascertain by calculation.
3. the opposite of this phenomenal world is *not* 'the true world' but the formless, unformulatable world of the chaos of sensations – thus, *a different kind* of phenomenal world, one not 'knowable' by us.
4. questions about what 'things-in-themselves' may be like, aside from our sensory receptivity and the activity of our intellect, must be parried by the question: how could we know *that things exist*? It was we who created 'thingness' in the first place. The question is whether there might not be many other ways of creating such an *illusory* world – and whether this creating, logicising, trimming, falsifying is not itself the best-guaranteed *reality*: in short, whether that which 'posits things' is not the sole reality; and whether the 'effect of the external world upon us' is not also just a consequence of such subjects that will...

'Cause and effect': false interpretation of a *war* and of a relative *victory*
Other 'beings' act upon us; our *trimmed* illusory world is a trimming and *overpowering* of their actions; a kind of *defensive* measure.
   The *subject alone is demonstrable: **hypothesis** that there are only subjects –* that 'object' is only a kind of effect of subject upon subject... *a mode of the subject*

9[121]

That one gives men back the *courage* for their natural drives

That one curbs their *underestimation of themselves* (*not* of man as an individual but of man as *nature*...)

That one takes the *oppositions* out of things, having understood that we put them there.

That one takes the *idiosyncrasies of society* out of existence in general (guilt, punishment, justice, honesty, freedom, love, etc.)

To raise the problem of *civilisation*.

Progress towards '*naturalness*': in all political questions, including the relationships between parties, even between the parties of the merchants or the workers or the entrepreneurs, questions of *power* are at stake – 'What *can* one do?' and only then 'What *ought* one to do?'

The fact that here, in the midst of the machinery of grand politics, the Christian fanfare is still sounded (e.g., in victory bulletins or the Kaiser's addresses to the people) increasingly belongs to what's becoming impossible: because it offends good taste. 'The Crown Prince's larynx'[121] is no business of God's.

Progress of the nineteenth century against the eighteenth.

*– basically we **good Europeans** are waging a war against the eighteenth century. –*

1. 'return to nature' understood more and more decidedly in the reverse sense of Rousseau's. *Away from idyll and opera!*

2. more and more decidedly anti-idealist, more concrete, fearless, industrious, moderate, suspicious of sudden changes, *anti-revolutionary*

3. more and more decidedly prioritising the question of *bodily health* over the health of 'the soul': understanding the latter as a state that results from the former, the former at the very least the precondition – – –

9[137]

The struggle against *great* men: justified on economic grounds. They are dangerous, accidents, exceptions, storms, strong enough to cast doubt on things that have been built and established slowly. Not only to discharge the explosive harmlessly, but if possible even to *prevent* it from forming... fundamental instinct of civilised society.

---

[121] The Prince, later to become Frederick III, had recently fallen ill with throat cancer.

9[138]

NB. To take everything terrible *into service*, part by part, step by step, experimentally: that's how culture sees its task; but until it is *strong enough* for this it will have to combat the terrible, moderate it, mystify it, even curse it...

– wherever a culture *posits evil*, it is giving expression to a relation of *fear*, thus to a *weakness*...

Thesis: everything good is a past evil now made serviceable.

Measure: the more terrible and the greater are the passions which an age, a people, which an individual can permit himself because he is capable of using them *as means, the higher is the level of his culture*. (– the realm of evil becomes ever *smaller*...)

– the more mediocre, weaker, more servile and cowardly a man is, the more he will posit as *evil*: for him the realm of evil is broadest. The lowest man will see the realm of evil (i.e., of what is forbidden and hostile to him) everywhere.

9[139]

Summa: to master the passions, *not* to weaken or exterminate them! the greater the mastering force of the will, the more freedom may be given to the passions.

the 'great man' is great through the free play he gives his desires and the even greater power that is capable of taking these magnificent monsters into its service.

– the 'good man' is, at every stage of civilisation, *at once the harmless and the useful one*: a kind of *mean*; the expression in the common consciousness of *who it is one need not fear and yet must not despise*...

Upbringing: essentially the means of *ruining* the exception – a distraction, seduction, enfeeblement – in favour of the rule.

This is harsh, but from an economic point of view perfectly reasonable. At least for that long period – – –

Education: essentially the means of directing taste against the exceptional in favour of the average.

A culture of the exception, of experiment, danger, nuance, as a consequence of a great *wealth of forces: every* aristocratic culture tends towards *this*.

Not until a culture has a surplus of forces at its command can, on its ground, a hothouse of luxury culture – – –

9[140]

Attempt on my part to understand the *absolute reasonableness* of social judging and valuating: of course, without wanting to calculate moral conclusions out of this.

: the degree of *psychological falseness* and opacity needed to *sanctify* the affects essential for preservation and the enhancement of power (to build oneself a *good conscience* regarding them)

: the degree of *stupidity* needed for common regulating and valuing to remain possible (to this effect: upbringing, supervision of the elements of education, drilling)

: the degree of *inquisition, mistrust and intolerance* needed to treat the exceptions as criminals and oppress them – to imbue them with bad conscience so that inwardly they fall sick with their own exceptionality.

Morality essential as a *shield*, a means of defence: to this extent a sign that a man is not yet fully grown p. 123[122]

(armour-clad; stoical;

a man fully grown has, above all, *weapons*, he is *on the attack*

the tools of war transformed into the tools of peace (scales and plates become feathers and hair)

In sum: morality is precisely as 'immoral' as every other thing on earth; morality itself is a form of immorality.

The great *liberation* this insight brings, the opposition is removed from things, the homogeneity of all that happens is *rescued* – –

9[141]

Overwork, inquisitiveness and compassion – our *modern vices*

---

[122] It is unclear what text Nietzsche is referring to here.

9[147]

What are the means by which a virtue comes to power?

By exactly the same means as a political party: slander, insinuations, undermining the opposing virtues that are already in power, changing their name, systematically persecuting and deriding them: in other words, *by means of nothing but 'immoralities'.*

What does a *desire* do to itself to become a *virtue?* It changes its name; denies its intentions as a matter of principle; practises misunderstanding itself; allies itself with existing and established virtues; advertises its enmity towards their opponents. If possible buying the protection of sanctifying powers; intoxicating, inspiring, the hypocrisy of idealism; gaining a party that *either* rises to the top with it *or* perishes . . . , becoming *unconscious, naïve.*

9[151]

The will to power can only express itself against *resistances*; it seeks what will resist it – this is the original tendency of protoplasm in sending out pseudopodia and feeling its way. Assimilation and incorporation is, above all, a willing to overwhelm, a training, shaping and reshaping, until at last the overwhelmed has passed entirely into the power of the attacker and augmented it. – If this incorporation fails, the formation will probably fall apart; and *duality* appears as a result of the will to power: to avoid letting go of what it has captured, the will to power divides into two wills (in some circumstances not entirely giving up the connection between them)

'Hunger' is only a closer adaptation, once the fundamental drive for power has gained a more intellectual form.

9[152]

The *preoccupation with morality* locates a man low in the order of rank: with it, he lacks the instinct for special privilege, for standing apart, the feeling of freedom known to creative natures, to the 'children of God' (or of the devil –). And regardless of whether he preaches the ruling morality or applies his ideal to *criticise* the ruling morality: it makes him part of the herd – even if as their most pressing need, as 'shepherd' . . .

9[153]

The strong of the future

What has been achieved here and there partly by hardship, partly by chance, the conditions for a *stronger species* to emerge, we can now understand and deliberately *will*: we can create the conditions under which such a heightening is possible.

Up till now 'education' had society's benefit in view: *not* the greatest possible benefit for the future but the benefit of the society existing at that moment. What was wanted were 'tools' for its use. Supposing the *wealth of force were greater*, then one could imagine some *forces being drawn off*, for the sake *not* of benefiting the present society but of a future benefit –

Such a task would be set more urgently the more it was understood how far the present form of society is in the throes of a deep transformation, and will some day *no longer be able to exist for its own sake*, but only as a *tool* in the hands of a stronger race.

The progressive diminishment of man is what drives one to think about the breeding of a *stronger race*, a race whose surplus would lie precisely in those areas where the diminished species was becoming weak and weaker (will, responsibility, self-assurance, the capacity to set itself goals).

The *means* would be those taught by history: *isolation* through interests of preservation that are the opposite of the average ones today; learning opposite valuations by practice; distance as pathos;[123] a free conscience regarding what is most undervalued and forbidden today.

The *levelling out* of European man is the great process which cannot be impeded: it should be speeded up even further.

The necessity of *a chasm opening*, of *distance*, of an *order of rank* is thus given: *not* the necessity of slowing down the process.

As soon as it is achieved, this *levelled* species requires *justification*: that justification is the service of a higher, sovereign type which stands upon it and can only rise to its own task from that position.

Not merely a master race, whose task would be limited to governing; but a race with *its own sphere of life*, with a surplus of force for beauty, valour, culture, manners, right up to the highest intellectual realm; an *affirming* race which can grant itself every great luxury . . . strong enough

---

[123] See note to 35[24].

not to need the tyranny of the virtue-imperative, rich enough not to need thrift and pedantry, beyond good and evil; a hothouse for strange and exquisite plants.

9[155]

Virtue no longer meets with any belief, its attraction has disappeared; someone would have to think of a way to market it afresh, perhaps as an unusual form of adventure and excess. Virtue requires of its believers so much eccentricity and blinkered stupidity that the conscience is bound to object to it today. Of course, for those without conscience and free of all scruples, this is precisely what may become its new magic – it's now what it has never been before, a *vice*.

9[156]

Forgery in psychology

The great *crimes* in *psychology*:

1 that all *unpleasure, all unhappiness*, has been adulterated with wrong and guilt – (pain has been robbed of its innocence).

2 that all *strong feelings of pleasure* (exuberance, voluptuousness, triumph, pride, audacity, knowledge, self-assurance and happiness in oneself) have been branded as sinful, as seduction, as suspect.

3 that *feelings of weakness*, the most inward cowardices, the lack of courage towards oneself have been provided with sanctifying names and taught as desirable in the highest sense.

4 that everything *great* in man has been reinterpreted as a renunciation of self, as self-sacrifice for something else, for someone else; that even in the case of the knower, even that of the artist, *depersonalisation* has been falsely held out as the cause of his highest knowledge and ability.

5 that *love* has been falsified as a giving of oneself (and as altruism), whereas it is a taking in addition, or a giving away that follows from an over-abundance of personality. Only the *most whole* person can love; the depersonalised, the 'objective' ones are the worst lovers (– ask the ladies!). The same applies to love of God, or of the 'fatherland': one must be firm and steady on one's feet,

Egoism as *I*-ification, altruism as *other*-ification[124]

6 life as punishment, happiness as temptation; the passions as devilish, confidence in oneself as godless

NB. *This whole psychology is a psychology* of **obstruction**, a kind of *immurement* out of fear; on the one hand the crowd (those who've come off badly and the mediocre) want to use it to defend themselves from the stronger (– and to *destroy* them in their development...), on the other they want to sanctify all the drives with which they themselves best prosper, and to ensure that these alone are honoured. Cf. the Jewish priests.

9[162]

Causes of the *rise of pessimism*

1. that up to now the most powerful and promising drives of life have been *slandered*, so that life has a curse upon it
2. that man's growing bravery and honesty and his bolder mistrust realises these instincts are *inseparable* from life, and turns against life
3. that only *the most mediocre* prosper, those who do not even *feel* that conflict, while the higher species goes awry and makes itself unappealing as a product of degeneration – that on the other hand what's mediocre, naming itself as goal and meaning, arouses *indignation* (– that no one can answer a *What for?* any more –)
4. that diminution, painfulness, restlessness, bustle, haste become constantly greater – that it becomes ever easier to *have in view* this whole commotion and so-called 'civilisation', that in the face of this tremendous machinery the individual *desponds* and *submits*.

9[165]

The *modern spirit's lack of discipline*, underneath all sorts of moral finery:
Those decorative words are:

---

[124] *Ver- Ichlichung* and *Ver- Änderung* – the first of these is a neologism based on the second, which is a typographically highlighted version of the common German word *Veränderung*: alteration, making other.

tolerance (for 'incapacity to say Yes and No')

la largeur de sympathie[125] = one third indifference, one third curiosity, one third pathological excitability

objectivity = lack of personality, lack of will, incapacity to love

'freedom' versus rules (Romanticism)

'truth' versus falsification and lies (naturalisme[126])

'scientific attitude' (the 'document humain'[127]), in plain words the cheap serial and addition instead of composition

'passion' for disorder and immoderation

'profundity' for confusion, the chaotic welter of symbols

On 'modernity'

a. the ill-discipline of the spirit
b. histrionics
c. pathological irritability (milieu as 'fatum'[128])
d. colourful jumble
e. overwork

The *most promising curbs* and *remedies* for *'modernity'*

1. universal *military service*, with real wars and no more joking
2. *national* bigotry (simplifying, focusing; admittedly sometimes also squeezing dry and exhausting with overwork)
3. improved *nutrition* (meat)
4. increasingly *clean* and healthy dwellings
5. domination of *physiology* over theology, moralism, economics and politics
6. military severity in demanding and dealing with 'what one is expected to do' (no more *praising...*)

9[170]

Aesthetica

the modern *counterfeiting* in the arts: understood as **necessary**, namely as appropriate to the *most genuine need* of the *modern soul*

---

125 The breadth of sympathy.
126 Nietzsche uses the French word to connect his point to the naturalist movement in French literature.
127 The human document, a term used by the French naturalists.   128 Destiny.

one stops the gaps in *talent*, even more so the gaps in *education*, tradition, *training*

firstly: one finds oneself a *less artistic* audience, one that's unconditional in its love (– and which at once kneels down before the *person*...). This is aided by the superstition of our century, the superstitious belief in the *genius*...

secondly: one harangues the dark instincts of those men of a democratic era who are dissatisfied, ambitious, disguised from themselves: importance of the *pose*

thirdly: one transfers the methods of one art into another, mixes the intentions of art with those of knowledge or of the church or of the racial interest (nationalism) or of philosophy – one strikes every bell at once and arouses the obscure suspicion that one could be a 'God'

fourthly: one flatters women, the suffering, the outraged; one helps narcotics and opiates to prevail in art as well. One tickles the 'educated', the readers of poets and ancient stories

9 [173]

Morality in the valuation of races and classes

Bearing in mind that the *affects* and *fundamental drives* of every race and every class express something of their conditions of existence (– or at least of the conditions under which they have asserted themselves for the longest time)

: demanding they be 'virtuous' means: that they switch their character, change their spots and erase their past

: means they are to cease differing from one another

: means they are to become similar to one another in needs and demands – more clearly: *that they are to perish*...

The will to *one* morality thus proves to be the *tyranny* of the type to which this one morality is tailored, over the other types: it is annihilation or standardisation in favour of the prevailing type (whether with the aim of ceasing to be dreadful to it, or of being exploited by it).

'Abolition of slavery' – allegedly a tribute to 'human dignity', in fact the *annihilation* of a fundamentally different species (– the undermining of its values and its happiness –)

The element where an *antagonistic* race or an antagonistic class is most strong is interpreted as being what's *most evil*, most wicked about it: for this is what it harms us with (– its 'virtues' are slandered and renamed).

It is considered an *objection* against a man and a people if they *harm us*: but from their point of view *we* are desirable, because we are such as they can make use of.

The call for 'humanisation' (which very naively believes itself in possession of the formula 'What is human?') is a piece of hypocrisy, under cover of which a very particular kind of man tries to gain mastery – more precisely, a very particular instinct, the *herd instinct*.

'Equality of men': what *is hidden* behind the tendency more and more to posit men *as equal* simply because they are men.

'*Interestedness' in respect to common morality* (the *trick*: making the great desires avarice and lust for power into patrons of virtue).

How far all kinds of *businessmen* and the avaricious, all those who have to grant and request credit, *need* to insist on sameness of character and sameness of value concepts: *world trade* and *exchange* of all kinds enforces and, as it were, *buys* itself virtue.

Likewise the *state* and every kind of lust for power in respect to civil servants and soldiers; likewise science, to work with confidence and economy of forces

Likewise the *priests*.

– Here, then, common morality is enforced because it procures a benefit; and war and violence are waged against immorality to bring it to victory – by what 'right'? By no right at all, but in accordance with the instinct of self-preservation. The same classes make use of *immorality* whenever that serves their purpose.

9[177]

To circumnavigate the whole of the modern soul, to have sat in every one of its corners – my ambition, my torment and my happiness

Really to *overcome* pessimism – the result being a gaze like Goethe's, full of love and good will.

NB. My work shall include a *total over*view over our century, over the whole of modernity, over the 'civilisation' *attained*

Notebook 10, autumn 1887

10[2]

My five 'Nos'

1 My struggle against *guilt* and against mixing the concept of *punishment* into the physical and metaphysical world, likewise into psychology and the interpretation of history. Insight into the *moralisation* of all previous philosophy and valuation.

2 My recognition and extraction of the ideal that has been *handed down* to us, the Christian ideal, even where the dogmatic form of Christianity has been run down completely. The *danger posed by the Christian ideal* lies in its feelings of value, in what can do without conceptual expression: my struggle against *latent Christianity* (e.g., in music, in socialism).

3 My struggle against *Rousseau's* eighteenth century, against its 'nature', its 'good man', its belief in the rule of feelings – against the softening, weakening, moralisation of man: an ideal that was born of *hatred of aristocratic culture* and is in practice the rule of unbridled feelings of ressentiment,[129] invented as a banner for the struggle.
– the Christian's morality of guilt
the morality of ressentiment (a pose of the mob)

4 My struggle against *Romanticism*, which combines Christian ideals and the ideals of Rousseau, but also with a longing for the *old days* of priestly-aristocratic culture, for virtù,[130] for the 'strong

---

[129] See note to 2[171].   [130] See 10[45] for Nietzsche's own definition of this term.

man' – something extremely hybrid; a false and imitated kind of *stronger* humanity, which values extreme states as such, seeing in them the symptom of strength ('cult of passion').

– the desire for stronger men, for extreme states

an imitation of the most expressive forms, *furore espressivo*[131] *not* out of plenitude but out of *lack*

(among writers, Stifter and Keller,[132] for example, show signs of more strength, inner well-being, than – – –)

5 My struggle against the *dominance of the herd instincts*, now that science is joining forces with them; against the inner hatred with which all kinds of order of rank and distance are treated.

– what was born of a relative plenitude in the nineteenth century, with *relish* . . .

technology, cheerful music, etc.,	products of the relative
great technology and inventiveness	strength, self-confidence
the natural sciences	of the nineteenth century.
history (?)	

10[3]

My new path to 'Yes'

My new version of *pessimism*: willingly to seek out the dreadful and questionable sides of existence: which made clear to me related phenomena of the past. 'How much "truth" can a spirit endure and dare?' – a question of its strength. The *outcome* of a pessimism like this *could be* that form of a Dionysian *saying Yes* to the world as it is, to the point of wishing for its absolute recurrence and eternity: which would mean a new ideal of philosophy and sensibility.

Understanding that those aspects of existence previously *negated* are not only necessary, but also desirable; and desirable not merely with respect to the aspects which have previously been affirmed (perhaps as their complement and precondition) but for their own sake, as the more powerful, more fruitful, truer aspects of existence, in which the will of existence expresses itself more clearly.

---

[131] Expressive frenzy.
[132] Adalbert Stifter (1805–1868), Austrian narrative writer; Gottfried Keller (1819–1890), German-Swiss realist writer of novels and stories.

To devalue those aspects of existence that have previously been the only ones *affirmed*; to draw out what it is that actually says Yes here (first the instinct of those who suffer, second the instinct of the herd, and that third instinct, the instinct of the majority against the exception).

Conception of a *higher* kind of being as 'immoral' according to existing ideas: the beginnings of this in history (the pagan gods, the ideals of the Renaissance)

10[6]

NB. A man is not one of us until he's ashamed of catching himself with some residual Christianity of feeling: *for us, conscience is against the old ideal...*

10[7]

To think about: how far the disastrous belief in *divine Providence* still continues to exist – that *most paralysing* belief for hand and mind there's ever been; how far what's behind the formulas 'nature', 'progress', 'perfecting', 'Darwinism', behind the superstition that happiness is somehow associated with virtue, unhappiness with guilt, is still the Christian presupposition and interpretation, living out its afterlife. That absurd *trust* in the course of things, in 'life', in the 'life instinct', that stolid *resignation* which believes every man has only to do his duty for *everything* to turn out well – this kind of thing only makes sense if we suppose that things are guided sub specie boni.[133] Even *fatalism*, our present-day form of philosophical sensibility, is a consequence of that *longest-held* belief in divine dispensation, an unconscious consequence: as if it were not precisely up to *us* how everything turned out (– as if we *could* let things run as they run: each *individual* himself merely a mode of absolute reality –)

What we owe to Christianity:
the mixing of the concept of guilt and punishment into all concepts
cowardice in the face of morality
the *stupid* trust in the course of things (for the 'better')
psychological falsity towards oneself.

[133] With a view to the good.

10[8]

A *division of labour* of the *affects* within society, so that individuals and classes breed *incomplete*, but for that very reason *more useful*, kinds of soul. How far in each type within society some affects have become almost rudimentary (towards the more vigorous development of another affect).

On justifications of morality:

economic (the intention to exploit individual force as fully as possible, against the wastage caused by everything exceptional)

aesthetic (the formation of fixed types together with the pleasure in one's own type)

political (as the art of tolerating the severe tensions between different degrees of power –

physiological (as an imaginary predominance of esteem in favour of those who've come off badly or indifferently – to preserve the weak

10[9]

Every ideal presupposes *love* and *hatred, veneration* and *contempt.* Either the positive feeling is the primum mobile[134] or the negative feeling is. *Hatred* and *contempt* are, e.g., the primum mobile in all the ideals of ressentiment.[135]

10[10]

The *economic* evaluation of the existing ideals

The legislator (or the instinct of society) selects a number of states and affects whose action guarantees regulated performance (a machinism, as a consequence of the regular needs of those affects and states).

Supposing these states and affects begin to touch painful chords, then a means must be found to overcome this painful element through a notion of value, to make unpleasure experienced as valuable, and thus as pleasurable in a higher sense. In formulaic terms: '*How does something disagreeable become agreeable?*' For example, when it can serve as a proof of strength,

---

[134] See note to 9[102].   [135] See note to 2[171].

power, self-overcoming. Or when in it our obedience, our submission to the law, come to be honoured. Likewise as a proof of public spirit, neighbourly spirit, patriotic spirit, of our 'humanisation', 'altruism', 'heroism'.

That one enjoy doing disagreeable things – the *intention of ideals.*

10[11]

I attempt an economic justification of virtue. – The task is to make man as useful as possible, and to have him approximate as far as possible the infallible machine: to this end he must be equipped with *machine virtues* (– he must learn to experience as most valuable those states in which he works in a mechanically useful way: for this to happen, the *other* states have to be made as repellent, as dangerous and disreputable as possible to him...)

The first stumbling block here is the *boredom*, the *monotony*, which all mechanical activity involves. Learning to tolerate *this*, and not just to tolerate it, but learning to see boredom lit up by a higher charm: so far, this has been the task of all higher schooling. Learning something which doesn't concern us; and feeling that our 'duty' lies precisely there, in that 'objective' activity; learning to assess pleasure and duty separately – that is the invaluable task and achievement of the higher school system. This is why up till now the philologist has been the educator *per se*: because his activity itself provides the pattern of an activity that is monotonous, sometimes on a grand scale. Under his banner, a young man learns to 'swot': the first condition for later efficiency in the machine-like fulfilment of duty (as state functionary, spouse, office hack, newspaper reader and soldier). This kind of existence perhaps requires philosophical justification and transfiguration even more than any other: the *agreeable* feelings must, by some infallible authority, be devalued as of lower rank; 'duty in itself', perhaps even the pathos[136] of reverence for everything disagreeable – and this demand speaking as if it were beyond all profitability, amusement, expediency – in the imperative form... The mechanical form of existence as the highest, most venerable form of existence, worshipping itself. (– Type: Kant as a fanatic of the formal concept 'Thou shalt'.)

[136] See note to 35[24].

10[17]

To show that an ever more economical use of men and mankind, a 'machinery' of interests and actions ever more firmly intertwined, *necessarily implies a counter-movement*. I call this the *secretion of a luxurious surplus from mankind*, which is to bring to light a *stronger* species, a higher type, the conditions of whose genesis and survival are different from those of the average man. As is well known, my concept, my *metaphor* for this type is the word 'superman'.

That first path, which can now be perfectly surveyed, gives rise to adaptation, flattening-out, higher Chinesehood,[137] modesty in instincts, contentment with the miniaturisation of man – a kind of *standstill* in *man's level*. Once we have that imminent, inevitable total economic administration of the earth, mankind will *be able* to find its best meaning as a piece of machinery in the administration's service: as a tremendous clockwork of ever smaller, ever more finely 'adapted' cogs; as an ever-increasing superfluity of all the dominating and commanding elements; as a whole of tremendous force, whose individual factors represent *minimal forces, minimal values*. Against this miniaturisation and adaptation of men to more specialised usefulness, a reverse movement is required – the generation of the *synthesising*, the *summating*, the *justifying* man whose existence depends on that mechanisation of mankind, as a substructure upon which he can invent for himself *his higher way of being* . . .

Just as much, he needs the *antagonism* of the masses, of the 'levelled-out', the feeling of distance in relation to them; he stands upon them, lives off them. This higher form of *aristocratism* is that of the future. – In moral terms, this total machinery, the solidarity of all the cogs, represents a maximum point in the *exploitation of man*: but it presupposes a kind of men for whose sake the exploitation has *meaning*. Otherwise, indeed, it would be just the overall reduction, *value* reduction of the human *type* – a *phenomenon of retrogression* in the grandest style.

– It can be seen that what I'm fighting is *economic* optimism: the idea that everyone's profit necessarily increases with the growing costs *to everyone*. It seems to me that the reverse is the case: *the costs to everyone add up to an overall loss*: man becomes *less* – so that one no longer knows what this

---

[137] Here, Nietzsche seems to mean an obedient and uniform existence as a cog in an administrative machine.

tremendous process was actually *for*. A 'What for?', a *new* 'What for?' – that is what mankind needs...

10[18]

'*Modernity*', using the metaphor of feeding and digestion.

Sensibility unutterably more excitable (– the increase in excitability dressed in moralistic finery as the increase of *compassion* –), the abundance of disparate impressions greater than ever before – the *cosmopolitanism* of dishes, of literatures, newspapers, forms, tastes, even landscapes, etc.

the *tempo* of this influx is *prestissimo*;[138] the impressions efface each other; one instinctively resists taking something in, taking something *deeply*, 'digesting' something

– this results in a *weakening* of the digestive power. A kind of *adaptation* to this overload of impressions occurs: man forgets how to *act* and **now only re-acts** to stimuli from outside. *He spends his force* partly in *appropriation*, partly in *defence*, partly in *responding*.

Profound weakening of spontaneity: the historian, critic, analyst, the interpreter, the observer, the collector, the reader – all *reactive* talents: *all* science!

Artificial *adjustment* of one's nature into a 'mirror'; interested, but only, as it were, epidermally interested; a fundamental coolness, an equilibrium, a *lower* temperature kept steady just below the thin surface on which there's warmth, motion, 'storm', the play of the waves

Contrast between *outward* mobility and a certain *deep weariness and heaviness*.

10[19]

The concept of *substance* a consequence of the concept of *subject, not* the other way around! If we give up the soul, 'the subject', there's no basis for any 'substance'. One gets *degrees of being*, one loses *being* as such.

Critique of '*reality*': where does it lead, this '*more or less of reality*', the gradation of being, that we believe in?

The degree of our *feeling* of *life* and *power* (logic and coherence of what we have experienced) gives us our measure of 'being', 'reality', non-illusion.

---

[138] Extremely fast.

Subject: that is the terminology of our belief in a *unity* among all the diverse elements of the highest feeling of reality: we regard this belief as the *effect* of one cause – we believe in our belief to such an extent that for its sake we imagine 'truth', 'reality', 'substantiality' in general.

'Subject' is the fiction that many *like* states in us are the effects of one substratum: yet it was *we* who created the 'likeness' of these conditions in the first place; the *fact* is our *likening* these and *making* them fit, *not* the likeness itself (– which, rather, must be *denied* –)

10[21]

Religion

In the inner psychological economy of *primitive* man, what predominates is the *fear* of *evil*. What is *evil*? Three things: chance, the uncertain, the sudden. How does primitive man combat evil? – He conceives of it as reason, as power, even as person. He thus obtains the possibility of entering a kind of contract with these, and in general of influencing them in advance – of acting preventively.

– Another course is to assert that its evilness and harmfulness is merely illusion: one interprets the consequences of the chance, the uncertain, the sudden as being *well-meant*, as meaningful...

– one interprets especially what's bad as 'deserved': one justifies evil as a punishment...

– In sum: *one subjugates oneself to it*: the whole moral-religious interpretation is merely a form of subjugation to evil.

– the belief that there is a good meaning in evil implies a renunciation of the struggle against it.

Now the whole history of culture represents a waning of that *fear of chance*, of the uncertain, of the sudden. Culture precisely means learning to *calculate*, learning to think causally, learning to act preventively, learning to believe in necessity. As culture grows, man becomes able to dispense with that *primitive* form of subjugation to evil (known as religion or morality), that 'justification of evil'. Now he wages war on 'evil' – he abolishes it. Indeed, there may be a state of feeling secure, of believing in law and calculability, which enters consciousness as *ennui* – where *pleasure in chance, in the uncertain* and *in the sudden* becomes a stimulant...

Let's stay a moment with this symptom of *highest* culture – I call it the *pessimism of strength*.

Man now *no longer* needs a 'justification of evil'; 'justifying' is exactly what he abhors: he enjoys evil raw, undiluted, he finds *meaningless evil* the most interesting form. If he used to need a God, now he's delighted by a world disorder without God, a world of chance in which the dreadful, the ambiguous, the seductive is of the essence...

In a state like this, it's precisely *good* that needs a 'justification', i.e., it must be rooted in evil and danger or else imply a great stupidity: *then it can still be pleasing.*

Animality now no longer arouses horror; in times like these, a brilliant and happy exuberance in favour of the animal in man is the most triumphant form of intellectuality.

Man is now strong enough to be ashamed of *believing in God* – he may once again play the devil's advocate.

If in practice he recommends the upholding of virtue, he does so for the reasons that reveal in virtue a subtlety, cunning, a form of covetousness and of lust for power.

This *pessimism of strength* also culminates in a *theodicy*,[139] i.e., in an absolute saying Yes to the world, but for the very reasons that used to prompt one's No to it: and thus a Yes to the conception of this world as the actually *attained, highest possible ideal*...

10[22]

Global insight

Every great growth indeed brings with it a tremendous *crumbling* and *falling into ruin*:

suffering, the symptoms of decline, *belong* to the periods of great advances.

every fruitful and powerful movement of mankind has also *produced alongside it* a nihilistic movement.

it would perhaps be the sign of a decisive and most essential growth, of the transition into new conditions of existence, that the *most extreme* form of pessimism, real *nihilism*, would be born.

This I have understood.

[139] A vindication of God in view of the existence of evil.

10[23]

Global insight: the *ambiguous* character of our *modern world* – the very same symptoms might indicate either *decline* or *strength*. And the emblems of strength, of hard-won adulthood, might, due to a handed-down (*residual*) devaluation of feeling, be **misunderstood** as *weakness*. In short, *feeling* as *value-feeling is not quite abreast of the times.*

Generalised: the *feeling of value is always* **antiquated**, it expresses a much earlier era's conditions of survival and growth: it battles against new conditions of existence, ones it hasn't grown from and which it necessarily misunderstands and teaches to view mistrustfully, etc. It hampers, it arouses suspicion against the new ...

Examples: – – –

10[31]

The Revolution made Napoleon possible: that is its justification. For a similar prize one would have to wish for the anarchic collapse of our whole civilisation. Napoleon made nationalism possible: that is his limitation.

Setting aside morality and immorality, as is fair – for these concepts don't even begin to touch the *value* of a man.

One begins – – –

The value of a man does not lie in his being useful, for it would continue to exist even if there were no one he could be useful to. And why couldn't precisely the man who gave rise to the most pernicious effects be the pinnacle of the whole human species: so high, so superior, that everything would perish from envy of him

10[33]

– Artists are *not* the men of *great* passion, whatever they try to tell us and themselves. And that's for two reasons: they lack shame towards themselves (they watch themselves *living*; they spy on themselves, they are too curious...) and they also lack shame towards great passion (they exploit it as artistes, the avarice of their talent...)

But secondly: (1) their vampire, their talent, usually begrudges them that squandering of force which is passion (2) their artists' *miserliness* shelters them from passion.

Having a talent, one is also the victim of a talent: one lives under the vampirism of one's talent, one lives – – –

One doesn't get over one's passions by representing them: instead, one has got over them *when* one represents them. (Goethe teaches something different: he *wanted* to misunderstand himself here: a man like Goethe felt the lack of delicacy

10[43]

The *perfect nihilist* – the eye of the nihilist *that idealises in the direction of ugliness*, that is faithless to its memories (– it lets them fall, shed their leaves; it doesn't protect them from the corpse-like pallor with which weakness bleaches what's remote and past); and what he doesn't practise towards himself, he doesn't practise towards mankind's whole past either – he lets it fall

10[45]

The realm of morality should be reduced and restricted, step by step; one should bring to light and honour the names of the instincts really at work in it, instincts concealed for the longest time under hypocritical names of virtue; the ever more commanding voice of one's 'honesty' should shame one into unlearning that shame which would like to deny and lie away the natural instincts. It is a measure of strength how far one can rid oneself of virtue; and heights could be imagined where the concept of 'virtue' would have been rethought so that it sounded like virtù, the virtue of the Renaissance, virtue free of moralin.[140] For the present, though – how far we still are from this ideal!

The diminishment of morality's domain: a sign of its progress. Wherever people were not yet capable of thinking *causally*, they thought *morally*.

10[47]

Restoration of 'nature': in itself an action is perfectly empty of value; everything depends on who does it. One and the same 'crime' can in one case be the highest privilege, in another the mark of shame. Indeed, it's the egotism of those who judge which interprets an action *or* its doer

---

[140] *moralinfrei*: Nietzsche's coinage *Moralin* – self-righteous, priggish morality – is analogous to word forms like *Anilin*, a poisonous chemical.

in relation to their own profit or disadvantage (– or in relation to the similarity or lack of kinship with themselves).

10[50]

Crime belongs under the heading: 'Rebellion against the social order'. A rebel is not 'punished': he is *suppressed*. A rebel may be a wretched and contemptible man, but in itself there is nothing to despise about a rebellion – and to be rebellious with regard to our kind of society does not, in itself, lower a man's value. There are cases where one would even have to honour such a rebel, because he senses something about our society against which war is needed: cases where he rouses us from our slumber.

That the criminal does an individual thing to an individual man does not contradict his whole instinct being at war with the whole order: the deed as merely a symptom

The concept of punishment should be reduced to the concept of putting down a rebellion, security measures against the one put down (total or partial imprisonment). But the punishment should not express *contempt*: at any rate a criminal is a man who risks his life, his honour, his freedom – a man of courage. Likewise, punishment should not be taken as penance; or as clearing a debt, as if there were a relation of barter between guilt and punishment – punishment does not purify, *for* crime does not pollute.

The criminal should not be refused the possibility of making his peace with society: assuming he doesn't belong to the *criminal race*. In that case war should be declared upon him even before he's done anything hostile (first step once one has him in one's power: castrate him).

The criminal's bad manners or the low level of his intelligence should not be held against him. Nothing is more common than for him to misunderstand himself: in particular, his outraged instinct, the rancune des déclassés,[141] has often not reached his consciousness, faute de lecture;[142] that under the impression of fear and failure he slanders and dishonours his deed – quite apart from those cases where, calculated psychologically, the criminal gives way to an uncomprehended drive and foists a false motive on his deed through some subsidiary act (for instance a robbery, when his real concern was the blood...).

---

[141] The rancour of people who have lost social status.   [142] For lack of reading.

One should take care not to treat a man's value according to a single deed. Napoleon warned against this. In particular, the high-profile deeds are especially insignificant. If someone like us has no crime, e.g., no murder, on his conscience – why is that? Because we lacked one or two circumstances that would have favoured it. And if we did do it, what would that say about our value? Would our value be lessened if we committed a few crimes? On the contrary: not everyone is capable of committing a few crimes. Actually we would be despised if we weren't credited with the force to kill a man in certain circumstances. Almost all crimes involve the expression of qualities that a man should not lack. Not unjustly, Dostoevsky said of the inmates of the Siberian prisons that they made up the strongest and most valuable component of the Russian people. If in our case the criminal is an ill-nourished and stunted plant, this reflects discredit on our social relations; in Renaissance times the criminal flourished and acquired for himself his own kind of virtue – virtue in the Renaissance style, to be sure: virtù, moralin-free[143] virtue.

One can only elevate those men one does not treat with contempt; moral contempt is a greater degradation and damage than any crime.

10[52]

The *nihilism* of *artistes*

Nature cruel in its serenity; cynical with its sunrises
    we are hostile to *feeling touched*
    we seek refuge where nature moves our senses and our imagination; where we have nothing to love, where nothing reminds us of the moral illusions and niceties of this northern nature – and it's the same in the arts. We prefer what no longer reminds us of 'good and evil'. Our moralist thin-skinnedness and capacity for pain seem redeemed in a dreadful and happy nature, in the fatalism of the senses and forces. Life without goodness
    the comfort consists in the sight of nature's magnificent *indifference* to good and evil
    No justice in history, no goodness in nature: that's why the pessimist, if he is an artiste, goes to that point in historicis[144] where the absence of justice still displays itself with magnificent naivety, where it is precisely *perfection* that finds expression . . .

---

143 See note to 10[45].   144 In historical matters.

and in the same way, in *nature* he goes to where its evil and indifferent character makes no secret of itself, where it represents the character of *perfection* ...

The nihilistic artist is revealed by his will and preference for cynical history, cynical nature.

10[53]

How man has become more natural in the nineteenth century

(the eighteenth century is the century of elegance, refinement and généreux sentiments[145])

Not 'back to nature': for there has never been a natural mankind. The scholasticism of unnatural and *anti*-natural values is the rule, is the beginning; man arrives at nature after a long struggle – he never comes 'back' ... Nature: i.e., daring to be immoral as nature is.

We are cruder, more direct, full of irony towards generous feelings, even when we succumb to them.

More natural is our first *society*, that of the rich, the idle: they hunt one another, sexual love is a kind of sport where marriage provides a hurdle and enticement; they entertain themselves and live for the sake of amusement; they esteem physical advantages first of all, they are curious and audacious

More natural is our attitude to *knowing*: we possess the libertinage of the mind in all innocence, we hate sentimental and hieratic manners, we delight in what's most forbidden, we would soon lose our interest in knowledge if we had to be bored on the way to gaining it.

More natural is our attitude to *morality*. Principles have become ridiculous; no one any longer permits himself to speak without irony of his 'duty'. But a helpful, benevolent disposition is esteemed (– one sees morality in *instinct* and disdains the rest –). And a few notions of points of honour.

More natural is our attitude in *politicis*:[146] we see problems of power, of one quantum of power against another. We do not believe in any right that doesn't rest on the power to enforce itself: we feel all rights to be conquests.

---

145 Generous feelings.   146 In political matters.

More natural is our esteem for *great men and things*: we count passion as a prerogative, we find nothing great that doesn't include a great crime; we conceive of all greatness as a placing oneself outside morality.

More natural is our attitude to *nature*: we no longer love it for the sake of its 'innocence', 'reason', 'beauty' but have nicely turned it 'devilish' and 'stupid'. But instead of making us despise nature, this has made us feel more kindred, more at home in it. Nature does *not* aspire to virtue, and we respect it for that.

More natural is our attitude to *art*: we don't demand of it the lovely lies of illusion, etc.; that brutal positivism reigns which observes without becoming agitated.

In sum: there are signs that the European of the nineteenth century is less ashamed of his instincts; he has taken a substantial step towards admitting to himself his unconditional naturalness, i.e., his immorality, *without becoming embittered*: on the contrary, strong enough to endure this sight alone.

To certain ears this sounds as if *corruption* had advanced: and what's certain is that man has not moved closer to the '*nature*' Rousseau spoke of but has taken a further step in the civilisation he *abhorred*. We have become *stronger*: we have come closer to the seventeenth century again, particularly to the taste of its close (Dancourt, Le Sage, Regnard[147]).

10[63]

Chief viewpoint: to open up *distances*, but *not to create oppositions*.

to dismantle the *intermediate forms* and reduce their influence: the chief means of preserving distances.

10[68]

Not to make men 'better', *not* to talk some kind of morality to them as if 'morality in itself', or an ideal kind of man, even existed: instead, to *create the conditions* under which *stronger men are necessary*, who in turn will need, and consequently *have*, a *morality* (put more clearly: a *discipline of body and mind*) *that makes them strong!*

---

[147] Florent Carton Dancourt (1661–1725), pioneer of the French comedy of manners; Alain-René Lesage (1668–1747), French satirist; Jean-François Regnard (1655–1709), French comic dramatist.

Not to be seduced by blue eyes or a swelling bosom: *the greatness of the soul has nothing romantic* about it. And, unfortunately, *nothing amiable whatsoever*!

10[83]

Above all, my dear virtuous sirs, you are not superior to us: let us nicely help you learn some *modesty*: it's miserable self-interest and prudence that recommends your virtue to you. And if you had more strength and courage in your bodies, you wouldn't reduce yourselves to virtuous nullity like this. You make of yourselves what you can: partly what you must – what your circumstances force upon you – partly what gives you pleasure, partly what seems useful to you. But if you do merely what suits your inclinations or what your necessity demands of you, or what benefits you, then you must *neither be allowed to praise yourselves for it nor have yourselves praised!* ... It's a *thoroughly small* type of person who is *only* virtuous: nothing must disguise that fact! Men in any way notable have never been such donkeys of virtue: it did not satisfy their innermost instinct, that of their quantum of power, while your own tiny portion makes nothing seem wiser to you than virtue. But you have *numbers* on your side: and as long as you *tyrannise* us we will wage war on *you* ...

10[84]

The hypocritical gloss with which all *civil institutions* are covered as if they were *outgrowths of morality* ... e.g., marriage, work, profession, fatherland, family, order, law. But as they are all designed for the *most mediocre* type of man, to guard against exceptions and exceptional needs, it is only fitting that here many lies are told.

10[85]

A *virtuous man* is a *lower* species if only because he is not a 'person' but acquires his value from conforming to a schema of man that has been fixed once and for all. He does not possess his value apart: he can be compared, he has peers, he is not *supposed* to be singular ...

Count the qualities of the *good* man – why are they so agreeable to us? Because we have no need to battle, because the good man imposes upon us no mistrust, no caution, collectedness or severity: our laziness, good nature, irresponsibility can *have a good time*. This *sense of well-being* of ours is what *we project out of ourselves* and attribute to the good man as a *quality*, as a *value*.

10[86]

What I'm not at all fond of in that Jesus of Nazareth or his apostle Paul is that they *put so much into the heads of little people*, as if there were anything of interest in their modest virtues. This has been paid for too dearly, for they have brought into discredit the more valuable qualities of virtue and of man; they have pitted bad conscience against the noble soul's sense of itself, they have led the *brave, generous, audacious, excessive* inclinations of the strong soul astray to the point of self-destruction...

touching, childlike, devoted, with feminine infatuation and shyness; the charm of virginal, ardent pre-sensuality – for chastity is only a form of sensuality (– the form of its pre-existence)

10[87]

All questions of *strength*: how far to assert oneself against the conditions for the preservation of *society* and its prejudices? – how far to let loose *one's terrible qualities*, which cause the downfall of most? – how far to approach *truth* and contemplate its most dubious aspects? – how far to go forward to meet *suffering*, self-contempt, pity, sickness, vice, with the question mark over whether one will master them?... (what does not kill us makes us *stronger*...) – finally: how far to make concessions in one's own mind to the ordinary, the mean, the petty, good, decent, the average nature, without being vulgarised by them?... The hardest test of character: not to let oneself be ruined through seduction by the good. The *good* as luxury, over-refinement, as *vice*...

10[89]

Moral values have hitherto been the highest values: can anyone doubt that?... If we remove moral values from that position then we change all values: it overturns the principle of the existing *order of rank*...

10[90]

Let us remove the highest goodness from the concept of God: it is unworthy of a god. And let us likewise remove the highest wisdom – the vanity of the philosophers is to blame for this folly of God as a monster of wisdom: they want him to look as much as possible like themselves. No! God *the highest power* – that is enough! From it everything follows, from it follows – 'the world'! Symbolice,[148] to have a mark of recognition D.O.[149]   omnipotens

10[91]

Christianity as *emancipated Judaism* (just as a locally and racially conditioned nobility in the end emancipates itself from those conditions and *goes in search* of related elements...)

1. as church (religious community) within the state, as an apolitical structure;
2. as life, discipline, practice, an art of living;
3. as *religion of sin* (of transgression *against God* as *the only* kind of transgression, the one and only cause of all suffering), along with a cure-all for it. There can only be sin against God; as for transgressions against men, man shall not pass judgement on or demand account of them, except in the name of God. The same for all commandments (love): everything is tied to God and done to men for God's sake. There is a high form of prudence in this (– living in very cramped surroundings, like the Eskimos, is only bearable with the most peaceable and forbearing disposition: Judeo–Christian dogma turned against sin in favour of the 'sinner' –).

10[94]

the European princes should really ask themselves whether they can do without our support. We immoralists – today we are the only power which

---

[148] Symbolically. The phrase that follows is an allusion to the earliest meaning of the Greek word 'symbolon': two segments of an earthenware token that served as a mark of identification between two parties.

[149] Deus omnipotens, i.e., God almighty.

needs no allies to reach victory: that makes us by far the strongest among the strong. We do not even need lies: what other power could dispense with them? A strong seduction fights for us, perhaps the strongest there is: the seduction of truth . . . of 'truth'? Who put that word into my mouth? But I take it out again – I spurn the proud word: no, we don't need even that, we would gain power and victory even without truth. The magic that fights for us, the eye of Venus that ensnares and blinds even our opponents, is the *magic of the extreme*, the seduction that every extreme exercises: we immoralists, we are *extreme* . . .

10[96]

Christian-Jewish life: here ressentiment[150] did *not* predominate. It may have been only the great persecutions that forced forth passion like this – both the *fire* of *love* and that of *hatred*.

Seeing one's dearest sacrificed for one's faith makes one *aggressive*; Christianity's victory is owed to its persecutors.

NB. *Asceticism* in Christianity is not specific – Schopenhauer misunderstood this: asceticism merely permeates Christianity wherever it already existed even without Christianity.

NB. Likewise, *hypochondriac* Christianity, the vivisection and tormenting of the conscience, merely inheres in a particular soil where Christian values have taken root: it is not Christianity itself. Christianity has absorbed all sorts of diseases from corrupt soils: the only possible reproach would be that it didn't manage to resist a single infection. Yet precisely *that* is its essence: Christianity is a type of décadence.

The *deep contempt* with which the still noble world of antiquity treated the Christian belongs just where the instinctual repugnance for the Jews belongs today: it is the hatred of the free and self-confident classes for those *who make their way forward unobtrusively* and combine shy, awkward gestures with an absurd sense of self-worth.

The New Testament is the gospel of a wholly *ignoble* kind of man; their claim to have more value, indeed to have all value, is actually rather outrageous – even today.

---

[150] See note to 2[171].

10[103]

On the kind of men *who matter to me* I wish suffering, isolation, sickness, ill-treatment, degradation – I wish they may become acquainted with deep self-contempt, the torment of self-mistrust, the misery of the overcome: I have no compassion for them, because I wish them the only thing that today can prove whether a man has any *value* or not – *his ability to stand his ground* . . .

I've never yet met an idealist, but plenty of liars – –

10[105]

On the nineteenth century's strength

We are *more medieval* than the eighteenth century; not merely more curious or more easily stimulated by the strange and rare. We have revolted against the *revolution* . . .

We have emancipated ourselves from the *fear of 'raison'*,[151] the spectre of the eighteenth century: we dare to be lyrical, absurd and childish again . . . in a word: 'We are musicians'

– we *fear* the *ridiculous* as little as the *absurd*

– the *devil* finds God's tolerance to his advantage: more than that, he has an interest in it, having been misunderstood, slandered for many an age – we are the champions of the devil's honour

– we no longer separate what's great from what's terrible

– we count up the *good* things in their complexity together with the *worst*: we have *overcome* the absurd 'desirability' of the past (which wanted the growth of good without the growth of evil –)

– *cowardice* before the ideal of the Renaissance has diminished – we dare to aspire even *to its mores* –

– *intolerance* towards the priests and the Church has reached its end at the same time: 'It is immoral to believe in God', but precisely that seems to us the best way of justifying this belief.

We have admitted the *right* of all these things in us. We do not fear the *reverse side* of 'good things' (– we seek it . . . we are brave and curious enough to do so), e.g., of Greek culture, of morality, reason, of good taste (– we calculate the losses incurred for all those precious things: such

[151] Reason.

preciousness *almost reduces one to poverty* –). Just as little do we conceal from ourselves the reverse side of *bad* things...

10[108]

Against *remorse*. I don't like this kind of cowardice towards one's own deed; one should not desert oneself when attacked by unexpected disgrace and distress. Extreme pride is more fitting here. In the end, what good is it! Remorse can't undo any deed; neither can 'forgiveness' or 'atonement'. One would have to be a theologian to believe in a power that cancels guilt; we immoralists prefer not to believe in 'guilt'. We hold that every kind of action is at root identical in value – likewise that actions directed *against* us may yet, considered economically, be useful and *generally desirable* actions. – In individual cases we'll admit that we could easily have *been spared* a particular deed – only circumstances favoured our committing it. – Which of us, *favoured* by circumstances, wouldn't already have run the entire gamut of crimes?... One should therefore never say: 'You shouldn't have done this or that,' but only ever: 'How strange that I haven't done that a hundred times.' – In the end very few actions are *typical* actions and really abbreviations for a personality; and considering how little personality most people have, a man is rarely *characterised* by a single deed. A deed of circumstance, merely epidermal, merely a reflex triggered by a stimulus: before the depths of our being have been touched by it, consulted on it. A rage, a grasp, a knife-thrust: what is there of personality in that! – The deed often brings with it a kind of fixed stare and unfreedom: so that the doer seems transfixed by the memory of it and sees himself as no longer anything more than an *appendage* of it. This disturbance of the mind, a form of hypnosis, is what one must combat most of all: after all, a single deed, whatever it may be, is *zero* compared to the entirety of what one has done, and may be counted out without falsifying the calculation. The fair interest which society may have in calculating our whole existence in just one direction, as if its whole aim had been to produce one single deed, should not infect the doer himself: unfortunately this happens almost constantly. That is because every deed with unusual consequences is followed by a disturbance of the mind: regardless even of whether those consequences are good or bad. Look at a man in love who's gained a promise; a writer applauded by the whole house: as far as their intellectual torpor is concerned, they differ not at all from the anarchist surprised by a raid. – There are actions that are *unworthy* of us: actions that, if we took them as typical, would push us down into a lower species. Here the one mistake to be avoided is *taking* them to be typical. There is the converse kind of action, of which *we* are unworthy: exceptions born of a special plenitude of happiness and health, our highest tidal waves, driven that high by a storm, a chance: such actions and 'works' (–) are not typical. One should never measure an artist by the yardstick of his works.

10[109]

One should defend virtue against the preachers of virtue: they are its worst enemies. For they teach virtue as an ideal *for everyone*; they take from virtue the charm of the rare, the inimitable, the exceptional and unaverage – its *aristocratic magic*. Likewise, one should take a stand against the unregenerate idealists who eagerly tap on every pot they find and are gratified when the sound it makes is hollow: what naivety, to *demand* greatness and rarity and ascertain its absence with wrath and contempt for mankind! – It's obvious, for example, that a *marriage* is worth as much as those who enter it, i.e., that on the whole it will be something wretched and improper: no pastor, no mayor can make anything different of it.

All the instincts of the average human being are ranged against *virtue*: it's disadvantageous, imprudent, it isolates, it's kin to passion and not easily accessible to reason; it corrupts character, brain, sense – always according to the standards of the mediocre part of mankind; it incites to enmity against order, against the *lies* hidden in every order, institution, reality – it is the *worst vice*, assuming we judge it by the harmfulness of its effect on *others*.

– I recognise virtue by (1) its not demanding to be recognised, (2) its not everywhere assuming virtue, but precisely something else, (3) its *not suffering* from the absence of virtue but on the contrary, regarding that absence as the relation of distance on the basis of which something about virtue can be honoured: it does not communicate itself, (4) its not using propaganda...(5) its allowing no one to sit in judgement on it, because it is always a virtue *for itself*, (6) its doing precisely everything that's otherwise *forbidden*: virtue as I understand it is the real vetitum[152]

---

[152] What is forbidden.

in every herd legislation, (7) in short, its being virtue in the Renaissance style, virtù, moralin-free[153] virtue...

10[112]

Every society has the tendency to drag its opponents down to the level of *caricature* and, as it were, to starve them – at least in its *imagination*. Our '*criminal*' is one such a caricature. Within the Roman aristocratic order of values, the *Jew* was reduced to a caricature. Among artists the 'bourgeois philistine' becomes a caricature; among the pious it is the godless man; among aristocrats the man of the people. Among immoralists it is the moralist: in my case Plato, for example, becomes a caricature.

10[119]

We who are 'objective' –

What opens the gates to the furthest-flung and most alien kinds of being and culture *for us* is not 'compassion' but our approachable and unprejudiced nature, which precisely does *not* 'suffer with'[154] but, on the contrary, delights in a hundred things at which one used to suffer (was outraged or affected, or cast a cold and hostile glance –). Suffering in all its nuances is now interesting for us: this has certainly *not* made us the more compassionate, even if the sight of suffering shakes us through and through and we shed tears – this simply doesn't make us feel more willing to help.

In this *voluntary* wish to gaze on all kinds of distress and transgressions, we've become stronger and more vigorous than the eighteenth century was; it's a proof of the growth in our force (– we have *come closer* to the seventeenth and sixteenth centuries...). But it is a profound misunderstanding to take our 'Romanticism' as proof of a 'beautified soul'...

We want *strong* sensations, just as all the *coarser* eras and classes do... This must be clearly distinguished from the needs of those with weak nerves and the décadents: in their case, there's a need for spice, even for cruelty...

We *all* seek states in which bourgeois morality *no longer has any say*, even less so priestly morality (– every book with a lingering odour of the pastor

---

[153] See note to 10[45].   [154] See note to 36[7].

and theologian about it gives us the impression of pitiable niaiserie[155] and impoverishment...). 'Good society' is that where at bottom nothing is found interesting except what's *forbidden* in bourgeois society and what ruins one's reputation: the same applies to books, music, politics, the appreciation of women

10[124]

Thinking on the most general things always lags behind: the final 'desirabilities' with respect to man, e.g., have really never been taken as a problem by philosophers. They all naively posit the 'improvement' of man, as if some intuition or other had raised us above the question of *why*, exactly, 'improve'? To what extent is it *desirable* for man to become *more virtuous*? or *more prudent*? or *happier*? If one doesn't already *know* the 'Why?' of man, there's no point in any such intention; and if one wants one of these, who knows – perhaps one cannot want the other as well?... Is an increase in virtuousness compatible with a simultaneous increase in prudence and understanding? Dubito:[156] I'll have only too much opportunity to prove the opposite. Has virtuousness as a goal in the rigorous sense not, in fact, hitherto stood in contradiction to becoming happy? Does it not, on the contrary, require unhappiness, privation and maltreatment of self as its necessary means? And if *highest understanding* were the goal, would that not precisely mean having to reject the increase of happiness? and choosing danger, adventure, suspicion, seduction as the path to understanding?...

And if one wants *happiness*, well, perhaps one has to go and join the 'poor in spirit'.

10[125]

The benevolent, helpful, kindly dispositions have absolutely *not* been honoured for the sake of their usefulness, but because they are states of *rich souls* which can afford to give and which carry their value as a feeling of life's plenitude. Look at the eyes of a benefactor! That's the antitype of self-negation, of hatred for the 'moi', of 'Pascalism'.[157] –

---

[155] Silliness.   [156] I doubt it.

[157] Allusion to Pascal's phrase, often cited by Nietzsche: 'Le moi est toujours haïssable', the I is always detestable (*Pensées*, ed. Lafuma, No. 373, 597).

10[126]

Whatever comes out of weakness, out of doubt of the self and sickliness of the soul, is good for nothing – even if it finds expression in the greatest casting away of goods and chattels. For it poisons life through its *example*...The gaze of a priest, his pale aloofness, has produced more damage to life than all the benefits produced by his devotion: such aloofness *slanders* life...

10[127]

Preoccupation with oneself and one's 'eternal salvation' is *not* the expression of a rich and self-assured nature: a nature like that doesn't give a damn about whether it will achieve bliss – it has no such interest in happiness in any form whatsoever, it is force, deed, desire – it imposes itself upon things, it *lays violent hands* on them...Christianity is a romantic hypochondria of those unsteady on their feet. – Wherever the *hedonistic* perspective takes the fore, one can conclude that there's suffering and a certain *malformation*.

10[128]

How, under the pressure of the ascetic *morality of self-negation*, precisely the affects of love, kindness, compassion, even of justice, magnanimity, heroism, were bound to be *misunderstood*: **main chapter.**

It is *wealth of personality*, plenitude in oneself, overflowing and giving away, instinctive well-being and saying Yes to oneself which enables great sacrifices and great love: what these affects grow from is strong and divine *selfness*, as surely as do the desire to master, the invading, the inner assurance of having a right to everything. What common opinion considers *opposite* dispositions are, instead, a *single* disposition; and without standing steady and secure in oneself, one can have nothing to give, no hand to stretch out, no protection to offer...

How could these instincts be *reinterpreted* in such a way that man finds valuable what runs counter to his own self? abandoning his self to another self!

Oh, the psychological contemptibility and lying which have ruled the roost up to now in the church and in a philosophy infected with the church!

If man is sinful, through and through, then he may only hate himself. At bottom his feelings towards his fellow men ought to be no different from those towards himself; love of mankind requires a justification – which lies in *God's having commanded it*. – It follows from this that all man's natural instincts (to love, etc.) appear to him to be prohibited in themselves, and can regain their rights only once they've been *denied*, on the basis of obedience to God ... Pascal, Christianity's admirable *logician*, went as far as that! Consider his relationship to his sister, p. 162:[158] '*not* making oneself loved' seemed Christian to him.

10[134]

That stupid parochialism, that stay-at-home cloddishness of moral evaluation and its 'useful' and 'harmful' does make sense: it's the necessary perspective of society, which, *as regards the consequences*, can see only what's near and nearest. – The state and the politician need a way of thinking that is, rather, *above morality*: because they have much larger complexes of effects to calculate. Likewise, there might be a world economy which had such distant perspectives that all its individual demands would at that moment seem unjust and arbitrary.

10[135]

Christianity is possible as the *most private* form of existence; it presupposes a narrow, secluded, entirely apolitical society – its place is in the conventicle. A 'Christian state', in contrast, a 'Christian politics' – these are simply words from a prayer of thanks by those who have *reasons* to mouth prayers of thanks. That they also speak of a 'God of Hosts' as a chief of staff: this doesn't fool anyone. In the end the Christian prince, too, practises the politics of Machiavelli: assuming, that is, he doesn't practise bad politics.

10[137]

Necessity of an objective *positing of values*

In relation to the tremendous and manifold mutual collaboration and counteraction which is the total life of every organism, that organism's

---

[158] See *La Vie de Monsieur Pascal, écrite par Madame Périer, sa soeur*, in Pascal, *Oeuvres Complètes*, ed. Louis Lafuma, Paris: Seuil, 1963, p. 29.

conscious world of feelings, intentions, valuations is just a small segment. We have no right whatsoever to posit this bit of consciousness as an end, as a Why? for that total phenomenon of life: obviously, becoming conscious is only one more means in life's unfolding and the expansion of its power. It is therefore naive to posit pleasure or intellectuality or morality or any other detail of the sphere of consciousness as being the supreme value – perhaps even to justify 'the world' out of them. – That is my *fundamental objection* to every philosophical-moral cosmodicy[159] and theodicy, to every *Why* and *supreme value* in philosophy and philosophy of religion up to now. *A kind of means has been misunderstood as an end: conversely, life and the enhancement of its power have been* demoted to a *means*.

If we wanted to posit an end adequate to life, it would have to avoid coinciding with any category of conscious life; it would, instead, have to *explain* them all as means to itself...

the 'negation of life' as goal of life, goal of development, existence as a great stupidity: such a *crazed interpretation* is merely the outgrowth of a *measuring* of life by factors of *consciousness* (pleasure and unpleasure, good and evil). Here the means are upheld against the end; the 'unholy', absurd, above all *disagreeable* means – how can it be a good end that makes use of such means! But the mistake lies in our presupposing from the outset an end that precisely *excludes* such means, instead of *looking for* the end that would explain the *necessity* of such means. That is to say, we take something that's desirable in respect to certain means (agreeable, rational, virtuous ones) and make it a *norm*, according to which we now posit what *overall end* is *desirable*...

The *fundamental mistake* always lies in our positing consciousness not as a tool and detail in the whole of life, but as a yardstick, as the highest value state of life: in short, the erroneous perspective of the 'a parte ad totum'.[160] Which is why the instinctive aim of all philosophers is to imagine a total consciousness, a conscious living and willing with everything that happens, a 'spirit', 'God'. However, they must be told that it's *precisely this* which makes *existence* a *monstrosity*; that a 'God' and total sensorium[161] would indeed be something on account of which existence would have to be *condemned*... Precisely that we have *eliminated* total consciousness as a

---

[159] Analogous to theodicy (see note to 10[21]): a justification of the cosmos.
[160] Inferring from a part to the whole.   [161] See note to 7[62].

positer of ends and means: that is our *great relief* – it means we no longer
have to be pessimists... *Our* greatest *reproach* against existence was the
existence of God...

10[138]

The only possibility of maintaining a meaning for the concept of 'God'
would be: God *not* as driving force but as *maximal state*, as an *epoch*...
One point in the development of the *will to power*, out of which both the
subsequent development and what went before, the up-to-that-point, was
explicable...

– in terms of mechanicist theory, the energy of the totality of becoming
remains constant; in terms of economics, it rises to its highest point then
falls again in an eternal cycle; this 'will to power' expresses itself in the
interpretation, in the *way* that *force is consumed* – the goal thus appears as
the transformation of energy into life and life in its highest potency. The
same quantum of energy means different things at the different stages of
development:

– what characterises growth in life is the ever thriftier and further-
calculating economy that achieves more and more while expending
less and less force... The principle of the lowest expenditure as an
ideal...

– that the world does *not* aim for a state of permanence is the only thing
which has been demonstrated. Consequently one *must* think of its highest
point in such a way that it is not a state of equilibrium...

– the absolute necessity of the same things happening in one course of
the world as in all others throughout eternity: *not* a determinism above
what happens but merely the expression of the fact that the impossible is not possible... that one particular force just cannot be anything
other than precisely that particular force; that it does not discharge itself
against a quantum of resisting force in any other way than according to its
strength – 'what happens' and 'what necessarily happens' is a *tautology*.

10[145]

Viewpoints for *my* values: whether out of plenitude or hunger... whether
one observes or intervenes... or looks away, moves aside... whether ani-
mated, stimulated 'spontaneously' out of the build-up of force or merely

reactively... whether *simply*, out of the fewness of the elements, *or* out of overwhelming mastery over many, so that it takes them into service when it needs them... whether one is *problem* or *solution*... whether *perfect* in the smallness of the task or *imperfect* in the extraordinariness of a goal... whether one is *genuine* or just an *actor*, whether one is genuine as an actor or just an imitation of an actor, whether one is a 'representative' or the represented itself – whether 'person' or merely a rendezvous of persons... whether *sick* out of sickness or out of a *superfluity* of health... whether one goes on ahead as shepherd or as 'exception' (third species: as runaway)... whether one has need of *dignity* – or to be the buffoon? Whether one seeks resistance or avoids it? Whether one is imperfect as 'too early' or as 'too late'... Whether by nature one says Yes or No or is a peacock fan of motley things? Whether one is proud enough not to be ashamed even of one's vanity? Whether one is still capable of feeling the bites of conscience (this species is becoming rare: in the past the conscience had too much to bite on; now, apparently, it has too few teeth left)? Whether one is still capable of 'duty'? (– there are those who would lose the last remnants of their lust for life if they were to let themselves be *robbed* of 'duty'... especially the womanly ones, the ones born subservient...)

10[154]

My intention to show the absolute homogeneity in all that happens and the application of the moral distinction as only *perspectivally conditioned*; to show how everything that is morally praised is the same in essence as everything immoral and how, like every development of morality, it was only made possible by immoral means and for immoral ends...; how, conversely, everything defamed as immoral is, viewed in economic terms, the higher and more essential and how development towards a greater fullness of life necessarily also implies the *progress of immorality*... 'truth' the degree to which we *permit* ourselves to understand *this* fact...

10[165]

What has been *spoiled* by the church's misuse of it:

1. *ascesis*: one no longer really dares to point out the natural usefulness of ascesis, its indispensability in the service of *educating the will*. Our absurd world of educators (which has in mind the 'efficient servant of the state' as a regulating model) believes it can make do with 'instruction',

with dressage of the brain; it lacks even the concept that something else must come *first* – education of the *will-power*. Examinations are sat in everything except the main issue: whether one is capable of *willing*, entitled to *promise*: the young man *finishes* his education without having so much as a question, a curiosity about this highest value problem of his nature

2. *fasting*: in every sense, including as a means of maintaining the fine capacity to enjoy all good things (e.g., not reading for a time; not listening to music; not being amiable; one must also hold fast days abstaining from virtue)

3. the '*cloister*', temporary isolation with strict refusal of, e.g., letters; a kind of deepest recollection and rediscovery of oneself which aims to shun not 'temptations' but 'duties': stepping out of the set dance of milieu, stepping out of the tyranny of pernicious little habits and rules; struggling against the squandering of our forces in mere reactions; attempting to give our force time to accumulate, to regain *spontaneity*. Take a close look at our scholars: they now think only *reactively*, i.e., they have to read before they can think

4. *festivals*. Only the coarsest can fail to experience the presence of Christians and Christian values as an *oppression* under which every truly festive mood goes to the devil. The festival includes: pride, exuberance, unruliness; foolishness; mockery of all kinds of earnest stuffiness; a divine Yes to oneself out of animal plenitude and perfection – all states to which the Christian may not honestly say Yes.

The festival is paganism par excellence.

5. *lack of courage*[162] *in the face of one's own* **nature:** *dressing oneself up as 'moral'* –

that one has no need of *moral formulas* to *welcome* an affect in oneself

the measure is how far a man can say Yes to nature in himself, how much or little he has to resort to morality . . .

6. *death*

10[167]

Aesthetica

On the genesis of the *beautiful* and the *ugly*. What is instinctively *repugnant* to us, aesthetically, is what the very longest experience has demonstrated

---

[162] While this list begins with things spoiled by the church but not originally bad, here Nietzsche shifts to something originally bad that the church promotes.

to be harmful, dangerous, suspect to man: the aesthetic instinct which suddenly raises its voice (e.g., when we feel disgust) contains a *judgement*. To this extent, the *beautiful* belongs within the general category of the biological values of the useful, beneficent, life-intensifying: but in such a way that many stimuli which very distantly remind us of and are associated with useful things and states arouse in us the feeling of the beautiful, i.e., of growth in the feeling of power (– thus not just things, but also the feelings that accompany such things, or their symbols).

With this, we have recognised that the beautiful and the ugly are *conditional*; conditioned by our most fundamental *values of preservation*. It's pointless to want to posit a beautiful and an ugly aside from that. *The* beautiful exists as little as does *the* good, *the* true. Each separate case is again a matter of the *conditions of preservation* for a particular kind of man: thus the *value feeling of the beautiful* will be aroused by different things for the *man of the herd* and for the *exceptional* and super-man.

It is the *perspective of the foreground*, considering only the *most immediate consequences*, which gives rise to the value of the beautiful (also of the good, also of the true)

All the judgements of instinct are *short-sighted* with regard to the chain of consequences: they counsel on what's to be done *first*. The intellect is essentially an *apparatus for inhibiting* the immediate reaction to the judgement of instinct: it reins in, it considers, it sees the chain of consequences for longer and further.

Judgements of beauty and *ugliness* are *short-sighted* – they always have the intellect *against* them – but in the *highest degree persuasive*; they appeal to our instincts at the point where these decide most rapidly and say their Yes or No *before* the intellect has had a chance to speak . . .

Our most habituated affirmations of beauty *excite and stimulate each other*; once the aesthetic drive has started to work, a whole abundance of other perfections, originating elsewhere, crystallise around 'the particular beauty'. It's not possible to remain *objective*, or to uncouple the fabricating force that interprets, supplements and fills out (the force which is itself that concatenation of the affirmations of beauty). The sight of a 'beautiful woman' . . .

Thus: (1) the judgement of beauty is *short-sighted*, it only sees the most immediate consequences

(2) it *heaps* upon the object stimulating it a *magic* conditioned by the association of many different judgements of beauty – but which is *quite alien to the nature of that object.*

To experience a thing as beautiful necessarily means experiencing it wrongly . . . (– which, by the way, is why marriage for love is socially the most unreasonable kind of marriage –)

10[175]

Hatred of mediocrity is unworthy of a philosopher: it is almost a question mark over his *right* to 'philosophy'. Precisely because he is the exception, he must take the rule under his wing, must help everything average to keep up its faith in itself

10[176]

In society today there's a great deal of considerateness, of tact and forbearance, of good-natured pause before the rights of others, even before the claims of others; more than that, there's a certain benevolent instinct of human value in general, which reveals itself in trust and credit of every kind; *respect* for men, and by no means just for the virtuous ones – is perhaps the element which separates us most sharply from a Christian valuation. We feel a good measure of irony if we so much as hear morality being preached nowadays; preaching morality lowers a man in our eyes and makes him comical.

This *moralist liberality* is among the best signs of our era. If we find cases where it's clearly lacking, this strikes us as a sickness (the case of Carlyle in England, of Ibsen in Norway, of Schopenhauerian pessimism throughout Europe). If anything reconciles us to our era, then the large amount of *immorality* it permits itself without therefore thinking less of itself. On the contrary! – So what constitutes the superiority of culture over unculture? of, e.g., the Renaissance over the Middle Ages? – Always one thing alone: the large amount of *admitted* immorality. It follows from this, necessarily, how all the *heights* of human development must appear to the eye of the moral fanatic: as the non plus ultra of corruption (– think of Plato's judgement of Periclean Athens, Savonarola's judgement of

Florence, Luther's judgement of Rome, Rousseau's judgement of Voltaire's society, the judgement of the Germans *against* Goethe).

10[181]

The reality upon which Christianity could build itself was the small *Jewish family* of the Diaspora, with its warmth and tenderness, with its readiness to help and to stand up for each other, unprecedented and perhaps uncomprehended in the whole of the Roman Empire, with its pride, hidden and disguised as humility, of the 'chosen ones', with its unenvious saying No, deep within, to everything which has the upper hand and possesses power and magnificence. *To have recognised this as power*, to have recognised this *psychological* state as communicative, seductive, infectious for heathens too – that is the *genius* of Paul: to exploit the treasure of latent energy, of prudent happiness to create a 'Jewish church of freer confession', the whole of Jewish experience and skill in the *self-preservation of the community* under alien rule, also Jewish propaganda – he sensed this was his task. What he found was precisely that absolutely apolitical and excluded kind of *little people*: their art of asserting themselves and getting their way, cultivated in a number of virtues which expressed the sole meaning of virtue (as a 'means of preserving and enhancing a particular kind of man')

The principle of *love* originates in the small Jewish community: it is a *more passionate* soul which here glows beneath the ashes of humility and impoverishment; thus it was neither Greek nor Indian, certainly not Germanic. The hymn to love that Paul composed is not something Christian, but a Jewish flaring of the eternal flame, which is a Semitic one. If Christianity did anything essential in a psychological respect, it was to *raise the temperature of the soul* in the colder and nobler races who then had the upper hand; it was to discover that the most wretched life can become rich and inestimable when its temperature is raised...

It goes without saying that *no* such transfer was possible with regard to the ruling orders: the Jews and Christians were set at a disadvantage by their bad manners – and when combined with bad manners, strength and passion of the soul are repulsive and almost nauseating. (– I can *see* those bad manners when I read the New Testament). To sense the attraction, one had to be related by lowliness and hardship to the type of lowly people speaking here . . . How one stands on the New Testament is a test of whether one has any *classical taste* in one's body (cf. Tacitus): anyone who isn't revolted by it, who doesn't honestly and profoundly feel something of *foeda* superstitio,[163] something from which the hand is snatched away to avoid dirtying it, does not know what is classical. One must feel the 'cross' as Goethe did –

10[191]

I regard Christianity as the most disastrous lie of seduction there has ever been, as the great *unholy lie*: I draw its aftergrowth and tendrils of ideal out from under all other disguises, I resist all half and three-quarter positions towards it – there must be war against it.

The *morality of little people* as the measure of things: that is the most disgusting degeneration culture has so far exhibited. And *this kind of ideal* still hanging over the heads of mankind, as 'God'!!

10[192]

On the plan

Radical nihilism is the conviction of an absolute untenability of existence when it comes to the highest values that are acknowledged; added to this, the *realisation* that we have not the slightest right to posit a beyond or an in-itself of things which would be 'divine', which would be morality incarnate.

This realisation is a consequence of 'truthfulness' cultivated to the full; thus is itself a consequence of the belief in morality.

This is the antinomy: to the extent that we believe in morality, we *condemn* existence.

The logic of pessimism up to the furthest point of **nihilism***: what is the driving force here?* – Notion of *valuelessness, meaninglessness*: how far moral valuations lie behind all other high values.

– Result: *moral value judgements are condemnations, negations; morality means turning one's back on the will to existence* . . .

Problem: *but what is* **morality***?*

[163] Repugnant superstition.

10[194]

'*Morality for morality's sake*' – an important stage in its denaturalisation: it appears as the ultimate value itself. In this phase it has permeated religion: e.g., in Judaism. There is also a phase when it *severs itself from religion* again, and no God is 'moral' enough for it: then it prefers the impersonal ideal . . . That is the case today.

'*Art for art's sake*' – this is an equally dangerous principle: it brings a false opposition into things – it amounts to slandering reality ('idealisation' *into the ugly*). When one separates an ideal from what's real, one casts down the real, impoverishes it, slanders it. '*Beauty for beauty's sake*', '*Truth for truth's sake*', '*Good for good's sake*' – for the real, these are three forms of the *evil eye*.

– *Art, knowledge, morality* are *means*: instead of recognising in them the intention to enhance life, one has associated them with an *opposite of life*, with '*God*' – as revelations, so to speak, of a higher world that peeps through this one here and there . . .

'*beautiful* and *ugly*', '*true* and *false*', '*good* and *evil*' – these *divisions* and *antagonisms* betray conditions of existence and enhancement not of man in general but of various fixed and lasting complexes which sever their adversaries from themselves. The *war* thus produced is what's essential: as a means of *setting apart* that *increases* the isolation . . .

10[202]

The 'thing-in-itself' absurd. If I think away all the relationships, all the 'qualities', all the 'activities' of a thing, then the thing does *not* remain behind: because thingness was only a *fiction added* by us, out of the needs of logic, thus for the purpose of designation, communication, *not* – – – (to bind together that multiplicity of relationships, qualities, activities)

Notebook 11, November 1887 – March 1888

11[3]

The price of being an artist is that one feels what all non-artists call 'form' to be *content*, to be 'the matter itself'. Certainly, this places one in a *world turned upside down*: for now content becomes something merely formal – including our life.

11[29]

The cause of there *being* development at all cannot be found by studying development; one shouldn't try to understand it as 'becoming', and even less as having become . . .
   the 'will to power' cannot have become

11[30]

To attain a height and bird's-eye view where one understands how every-thing actually runs *as it should run*: how every kind of 'imperfection' and the suffering that results are also part of the *highest desirability* . . .

11[31]

Overall view of the European of the future: as the most intelligent slave animal, very industrious, at bottom very modest, inquisitive to excess, multifarious, coddled, weak-willed – a cosmopolitan chaos of affects and intelligences. How might a *stronger* species arise out of this? One with *classical* taste? Classical taste: that is the will to simplify, to strengthen, to the visibility of happiness, to dreadfulness, the courage for psychological *nakedness* (– simplification is a consequence of the will to strengthen; allowing happiness and likewise nakedness to become visible is a consequence of the will to dreadfulness . . .). To fight one's way up out of this chaos towards *giving form* – that requires *compulsion*: one must have to choose between either perishing or *asserting oneself*. A masterful race can only grow up out of dreadful and violent beginnings. Problem: where are the *barbarians* of the twentieth century? Clearly, only after tremendous socialist crises will they become visible and consolidate themselves – they'll be the elements that are capable of the *greatest harshness towards themselves* and that can guarantee the *longest-lived will* . . .

11[35]

Sexuality, lust for power, pleasure in illusion and in deceiving, the great joyful gratitude for life and its typical states – this is what, in the pagan cult, is essential and has good conscience on its side. – In classical Greece *unnature* as morality, dialectic, already battles against the pagan.

Nice, 15th December 1887

11[36]

What decides rank is the quantum of power that you are; the rest is cowardice.

11[37]

Anyone whose instinct aims for an order of rank hates intermediate forms and intermediate makers: everything *middling* is his enemy.

11[38]

Out of the pressure of plenitude, out of the tension of forces that constantly grow within us and don't yet know how to discharge themselves, a state arises like that preceding a storm: nature, which we are, *darkens*. That too is pessimism … A doctrine which puts an end to such a state by *commanding* something, a revaluation of values by means of which the accumulated forces are shown a path, a direction, so that they explode in lightning and deeds – certainly doesn't have to be a doctrine of happiness: by releasing force which had been cramped and dammed to the point of agony, *it brings happiness.*

11[44]

Hazarding one's life, one's health, one's honour, is the consequence of exuberance and an overflowing, spendthrift will: not out of love for mankind but because every great danger challenges our curiosity about the measure of our force, of our courage.

11[50]

The 'true world', however it has been conceived of up to now – it was always the apparent world *once again.*

11[51]

One must have some courage in one's body to permit oneself a base action: most are too cowardly for it.

11[55]

One should never forgive Christianity for having destroyed men like Pascal. One should never cease fighting against this in Christianity: that it has the will to shatter precisely the strongest and most noble souls. One should never be pacified until this one thing has been utterly eradicated: the ideal of man invented by Christianity. The whole absurd residue of Christian fable, its spinning of conceptual gossamer and its theology, does not concern us; it could be a thousand times more absurd and we wouldn't lift a finger against it. But we do fight that ideal which, with its diseased beauty and its feminine seductiveness, its secret, slanderous eloquence, addresses its persuasion to all the cowardices and vanities of wearied souls (and even the strongest have weary moments), as if everything that in those states may seem most useful and desirable – trust, guilelessness, modesty, patience, love of one's peers, resignation, devotion to God, a kind of unharnessing and abdication of one's whole self – were also the most useful and desirable as such; as if the little, modest abortion of a soul, man the virtuous, average animal and herded sheep, not only ranked above the stronger, greedier, more evil, refractory, prodigal and for those very reasons a hundred times more imperilled kind of man, but constituted nothing less than the ideal, the goal, the measure, the highest desirability for man in general. *This* setting up of an ideal was the most sinister temptation man has yet been exposed to: for it meant the exceptions who had turned out stronger, the strokes of luck among men, in whom the will to power and to growth of the whole human type took a step forward, were threatened with ruin; the values of that ideal were designed to attack at its very root the growth of those men of increase who, for the sake of their higher claims and tasks, voluntarily took on the risks of a more dangerous life (in economic terms: an increase in both the entrepreneur's costs and the unlikelihood of success). What are we fighting against in Christianity? That it wants to shatter the strong, that it wants to discourage their courage, exploit their bad moments and weariness, transform their proud assurance into unease and qualms of conscience; that it knows how to make the noble instincts poisonous and sick, until their force, their will to power turns back, turns against itself – until the strong are destroyed by orgies of despising and maltreating themselves: that horrifying kind of destruction whose most famous example is Pascal.

11[71]

Unpleasure and pleasure are the stupidest possible *means of expression* of judgements: which does not, of course, mean the judgements that make themselves heard this way are necessarily stupid. The leaving aside of all reasoning and logic, a Yes or No as reduced to a passionate wanting-to-have or pushing-away, an imperative abbreviation whose usefulness is unmistakable: that is pleasure and unpleasure. Its origin is in the central sphere of the intellect; its precondition an infinitely accelerated perceiving, ordering, subsuming, calculating, inferring: pleasure and unpleasure are always final phenomena, not 'causes'...

The decision on what excites pleasure and unpleasure depends on the degree of power: the same thing that, in the case of a small quantum of power, appears as a danger and as having to be repulsed immediately, with a greater consciousness of the plenitude of power can result in a voluptuous stimulation, a feeling of pleasure.

All feelings of pleasure and unpleasure presuppose a *measuring in terms of overall usefulness, overall harmfulness*: thus, a sphere where a goal (a state) is willed and the means to it selected. Pleasure and unpleasure are never 'original facts'

feelings of pleasure and unpleasure are *reactions of the will* (*affects*) in which the intellectual centre sets the value of certain changes that have occurred as a total value, simultaneously as the initiation of counter-actions.

11[72]

If the world process were directed towards a final state, that state would have been reached by now. The sole fundamental fact is, however, that it is *not* directed towards a final state, and every philosophy or scientific hypothesis (e.g., mechanicist theory) which requires such a state is *refuted* by that single fact... I am looking for a conception of the world which does justice to *this* fact: becoming must be explained without taking refuge in such intentions directed towards an end: at every moment, becoming must appear justified (or *unevaluable*, which amounts to the same thing); the present must absolutely not be justified by reference to a future, or the past by reference to the present. 'Necessity' not in the shape of an overarching, dominating total power, or of a prime mover; even less as necessary to condition something valuable. For this, we have to deny a total consciousness of becoming, a 'God', so as to avoid drawing what happens into the perspective of a being that feels with what happens and knows with it, yet *wills* nothing: 'God' is useless if he doesn't will something; and on the other hand this means a *summation of unpleasure and unlogic* is posited which would reduce the total value of 'becoming'. Luckily, what's missing is precisely such a summating power (– a suffering and all-seeing God, a 'total sensorium'[164] and 'universal spirit', would be the *greatest objection to being*).

---

[164] See note to 7[62].

More strictly: one *must not allow of anything at all that has being* – because then becoming loses its value and appears downright meaningless and superfluous.

Consequently it must be asked how the illusion of being was able (was bound) to arise

Likewise: how all value judgements are devaluated which rest on the hypothesis that anything has being.

with that, however, one realises that this *hypothesis of being* is the source of all *slandering of the world*:

'the better world, the true world, the world "beyond", the thing-in-itself'

1. becoming does *not* aim for a *final state*, does not flow into 'being'.
2. becoming is *not an illusory state*; the world of *being* may be an illusion.
3. becoming has equal value at every moment: the sum of its value remains the same: *in other words, it has no value at all*, for there is nothing against which it could be measured and in relation to which the word 'value' would have meaning.

The *total value of the world is unevaluable*, consequently philosophical pessimism is among the comical things

11[73]

The viewpoint of 'value' is the viewpoint of *conditions of preservation and enhancement* in regard to complex structures that have relatively lasting life within becoming:

– : there are no lasting, final units, no atoms, no monads: here too the 'being' of things has been *inserted* by us (for practical, useful, perspectival reasons)

– 'formations of rule'; the sphere of what rules continually growing or else periodically waxing and waning; or, under favourable or unfavourable circumstances (nourishment –)

– 'value' is essentially the standpoint for the waxing or waning of these ruling centres ('multiplicities', at any rate, but there's no such thing as 'unity' in the nature of becoming)

– *a quantum of power*, a becoming, inasmuch as nothing in it has the character of 'being'; inasmuch as

– the means of expression that language offers are of no use to express becoming: it's part of our *inescapable need for preservation* that we constantly posit a cruder world of the permanent, of 'things', etc. In relative terms, we may speak of atoms and monads: and it's certain that the *smallest world is, as regards permanence, the most permanent*...

there is no will: there are points of will constantly augmenting or losing their power

11[74]

– that in the '*process of the whole*' *the work of mankind is of no account*, because there is no total process (conceived of as a system –) at all:

– that there is no 'whole', that *no evaluation of human existence*, of human goals can be made with a view to something which doesn't exist...

– that necessity, causality, purposiveness are useful *illusions*

– that the goal is *not* the increase of consciousness but the enhancement of power, an enhancement in which the usefulness of consciousness is included, with pleasure as much as with unpleasure

– that one does not take *means* as the highest measure of value (thus not states of consciousness, such as pleasure and pain, if consciousness is itself a means –)

– that the world is not at all an organism, but chaos: that the development of 'mental life' is a means for the organisation to gain relative permanence...

– that all 'desirability' is meaningless with respect to the total character of being.

11[75]

the satisfaction of the will is *not* the cause of pleasure: I particularly want to combat this most superficial of theories. The absurd psychological counterfeiting of the nearest things...

instead, that the will wants to move forwards, and again and again becomes master of what stands in its way: the feeling of pleasure lies precisely in the unsatisfaction of the will, in the way it is not yet satiated unless it has boundaries and resistances...

'The happy man': herd ideal

11[76]

The normal *unsatisfaction* of our drives, e.g., of hunger, the sexual drive, the drive to move, does not in itself imply something dispiriting; instead, it has a piquing effect on the feeling of life, just as every rhythm of small painful stimuli *strengthens* that feeling, whatever the pessimists would have us believe. This unsatisfaction, far from blighting life, is life's great *stimulus*.

– Perhaps one could even describe pleasure in general as a rhythm of small unpleasurable stimuli...

11[77]

The greater the resistances a force seeks out in order to master them, the greater is the magnitude of the failure and misfortune thus provoked: and as every force can only expend itself on what resists, every action necessarily contains an *ingredient of unpleasure*. But the effect of that unpleasure is to stimulate life – and to strengthen the *will to power*!

11[82]

At every moment the meaning of becoming must be fulfilled, achieved, completed.

11[83]

What's called a good action is just a misunderstanding; such actions are not possible.

'Egoism', like 'selflessness', is a fiction for the common people; likewise the individual, the soul.

In the tremendous multiplicity of what happens within an organism, the part we become conscious of is merely a little corner: and the rest of the totality of what happens gives the lie to the little scrap of 'virtue', 'selflessness' and similar fictions in a perfectly radical way. We do well to study our organism in its perfect immorality...

The animal functions are, after all, in principle a million times more important than all beautiful states and heights of consciousness: these are a surplus, except where they have to be tools for the animal functions.

The whole of *conscious* life, the mind including the soul, including the heart, including goodness, including virtue: in whose service does it work? In that of the greatest possible perfection of the means (means of nourishment, of enhancement) of the basic animal functions: above all, of the *enhancement of life.*

What has been called 'body' and 'flesh' is unutterably more important: the remainder is just a minor accessory. The task of weaving onwards the whole rope of life, and in such a way *that the thread becomes stronger and stronger* – that is the task. But now see how heart, soul, virtue, mind quite conspire to *turn* this fundamental task *upside down*: as if *they* were the goals instead... The degeneration of life is essentially conditioned by consciousness's extraordinary capacity for error: consciousness is kept under control by instincts least of all, and thus *errs* longest and most thoroughly.

Using the *agreeable or disagreeable feelings of this consciousness* as a measure of whether existence has value: can a crazier extravagance of vanity be imagined? For consciousness is just a means: and agreeable or disagreeable feelings are just means as well! – What is the objective yardstick of *value*? Only the quantum of *enhanced* and *organised power*, only what happens in everything that happens, a will to more...

11[87]

All the beauty and sublimity we've lent to real and imagined things I want to demand back, as the property and product of man: as his most splendid vindication. Man as poet, as thinker, as God, as love, as power – oh, the kingly prodigality with which he has given gifts to things, only to *impoverish* himself and *himself* feel miserable! That has been man's greatest selflessness so far, that he admired and worshipped and knew how to conceal from himself the fact that it was *he* who created what he admired. –

11[89]

Humans have always misunderstood love: they think that in loving they are selfless because they want another being's advantage, often to their own disadvantage: but on the other hand they want to *possess* that being... In other cases love is a subtler parasitism, one soul's dangerous and unscrupulous nesting in another soul – or occasionally in the flesh . . . oh! at what cost to the 'host'!

How much advantage man sacrifices, how little 'self-interested' he is! All his affects and passions want to be given their due – and how far affect is from the prudent interest of self-interestedness!

One does not want one's 'happiness'; only an Englishman can believe that man always seeks his own advantage; our desires want to commit violence on things in a long passion – their dammed-up force seeks resistances

11[94]

That emperor[165] constantly kept in mind the transience of all things so as not to take them *too seriously* and to remain calm among them. To me, conversely, it seems that everything is far too valuable to be so fleeting: I seek an eternity for everything – ought one to pour the costliest balms and wines into the sea? – and my consolation is that everything which has been is eternal: the sea washes it up again

11[95]

As is well known, Voltaire was pestered in his very last moments: 'Do you believe in the divinity of Christ?' his curé asked him; and, not satisfied with Voltaire indicating he wanted to be left in peace, repeated his question. Upon this the dying man was overcome by his final rage: he rebuffed the impertinent questioner angrily: 'Au nom du dieu!' he shouted at him, 'ne me parlez pas de cet-homme-là!'[166] – immortal last words encapsulating everything this bravest of spirits had fought against. –

Voltaire judged that 'there is nothing divine about this Jew of Nazareth'; thus, *classical taste* judged through him.

Classical taste and Christian taste posit the concept 'divine' in fundamentally different ways; and anyone who has any classical taste in his body cannot but feel Christianity to be a foeda superstitio[167] and the Christian ideal a caricature and degradation of the divine.

---

[165] Marcus Aurelius (121–180), Roman emperor.
[166] 'In God's name, don't talk to me about that man!'   [167] See note to 10[181].

11[96]

That one takes the *doer* back into doing, after having conceptually extracted it and thus emptied doing;

that one takes the doing-*something*, 'the goal', the 'intention', the 'purpose' back into doing, after having artificially extracted it and thus emptied doing;

that all 'purposes', 'goals', 'meanings' are only modes of expression and metamorphoses of the single will that inheres in all that happens, the will to power; that having purposes, goals, intentions, *willing* in general, amounts to willing more strength, willing growth, and also willing the *means to this*;

that the most general and basic instinct in all doing and willing has remained the least known and most hidden precisely because in practice we always follow its commandment – because we *are* that commandment... All valuations are only consequences and narrower perspectives *in the service of this one will*: valuation itself is only this will to power; to criticise being from the standpoint of one of these values is absurd and misleading; even supposing it ushers in a process of decline, it's a process which still stands *in the service of that will*...

To appraise being itself: but the act of appraising is itself still this being – and by saying No we still do what we *are*...One must understand the *absurdity* of this gesture of passing sentence on existence; and then also try to divine *what* is really happening here. It is symptomatic.

11[99]

Critique of nihilism –

I

Nihilism as a *psychological state* will have to come about *firstly* when we have sought in everything that happens a 'meaning' it doesn't contain, so that in the end the searcher loses courage. Nihilism is then the becoming conscious of the long *squandering* of our strength, the torment of the 'In vain', the uncertainty, the lack of opportunity somehow to recuperate, to calm oneself about something – being ashamed towards oneself as if one had *deceived* oneself for far too long...That '*meaning*' might have been: the 'fulfilment' of a highest canon of morality in all that happens, the moral order of the world; or increasing love and harmony in the interaction of beings; or coming closer to a general state of happiness; or even setting off on the path to a general state of nothingness – any goal is still a meaning. What all these kinds of ideas share is that the process aims to *achieve* something: – and now it is realised that becoming aims for *nothing*, achieves *nothing*... Hence, disappointment about a supposed *purpose of becoming* as a cause of nihilism: whether in regard to a particular purpose or, more generally, realising the inadequacy of all those hypotheses of purpose which have concerned the whole of 'evolution' (– man *no longer* a collaborator in, let alone the centre of, becoming).

Nihilism as a psychological state comes about *secondly* when a *wholeness*, a *systematisation*, even an *organisation* has been posited within and below everything that happens: so that the soul, hungering to admire and revere, now feasts on the total idea of a supreme form of dominion and administration (– in the case of a logician's soul, absolute consistency and objective dialectic alone are enough to reconcile it to everything...). Some kind of unity, any form of 'monism': and as a result of this belief, man feels deeply connected with and dependent on a whole that is infinitely superior to him, feels he is a mode of the deity... 'The well-being of the whole demands the sacrifice of the individual'... but behold, there *is* no such whole! At bottom, man loses his belief in his own value if he ceases to be the vehicle for an infinitely valuable whole: i.e., he conceived of such a whole *in order to be able to believe in his own value*.

Nihilism as a psychological state has a *third* and *last* form. Given these two *insights*, that becoming does not aim to achieve anything and that all becoming is not governed by a great unity in which the individual could submerge himself as in an element of supreme value – given these, there remains an *escape*: to condemn this whole world of becoming as a deception, and to invent a world that lies beyond it as the *true* world. But as soon as man realises how that other world is merely assembled out of psychological needs and how he has absolutely no right to it, the last form of nihilism arises, one which includes *disbelief in any metaphysical world* – which forbids itself belief in a *true* world. Having arrived at this standpoint, one admits that the reality of becoming is the *only* reality, forbids oneself every kind of secret route to worlds beyond and false divinities – but *cannot endure this world which one yet does not want to deny*...

– What, at bottom, has happened? The feeling of *valuelessness* was reached on understanding that neither the concept of '*purpose*', nor the concept of '*unity*', nor the concept of '*truth*' may be used to interpret the total character of existence. Nothing is aimed for and achieved with it; there is no overarching unity in the diversity of events; the character of existence is not 'true', is *false*..., one simply no longer has any reason to talk oneself into there being a *true* world...

In short: the categories 'purpose', 'unity', 'being', by means of which we put a value into the world, we now *extract* again – and now the world *looks valueless*...

2

Assuming we have recognised how the world may no longer be *interpreted* with these *three* categories and that upon this recognition the world begins to be without value for us: then we must ask *where* our belief in these three categories came from – let us see if it isn't possible to cancel our belief in *them*. Once we have *devaluated* these three categories, demonstrating that they can't be applied to the universe *ceases to be a reason to devaluate the universe*.

* * *

Result: *belief in the categories of reason* is the cause of nihilism – we have measured the value of the world against categories *that refer to a purely invented world*.

* * *

Final result: all the values by means of which up to now we first tried to make the world estimable to us and with which, once they proved inapplicable, we then *devaluated* it – all these values are, calculated psychologically, the results of particular perspectives of usefulness for the preservation and enhancement of human formations of rule, and only falsely *projected* into the essence of things. It's still the *hyperbolic naivety* of man, positing himself as the meaning of things and the measure of their value...

11[100]

The highest values in whose service man *was supposed to* live, especially when they governed him with difficulty and at great cost: these *social values* have been built up above man as 'reality', 'true' world, as hope and *future* world for the purpose of *amplifying* their volume, as if they were God's commands. Now that the shabby origin of these values is becoming clear, this seems to us to devalue the universe, make it 'meaningless'... but this is just an *intermediate state*.

11[103]

One should at last put human values nicely back in the corner where alone they have any right to be: as personal little values. Many species of animal have already disappeared; if man disappeared as well, nothing would be lacking in the world. One must be enough of a philosopher to admire even *this* nothingness (– nil admirari[168] –)

11[104]

If one is clear about the 'Why?' of one's life, one gives little weight to its 'How?' When the value of pleasure and unpleasure comes to the fore and hedonistic-pessimist teachings find a hearing, this is itself a sign of disbelief in the Why?, in purpose and meaning, is a *lack of will*; and renunciation, resignation, virtue, 'objectivity' *may* at least be signs that there is beginning to be a lack of the chief thing.

That one is able to give oneself a goal – – –

11[108]

A philosopher finds recreation differently and in different things: he finds recreation, for example, in nihilism. The belief that truth does not exist, the nihilists' belief, is a great stretching of the limbs for someone who, as a warrior of knowledge, is constantly at struggle with so many ugly truths. For the truth is ugly

11[111]

How is it that psychology's fundamental articles of faith are all a pack of the worst distortions and shams? '*Man strives for happiness*', for example –

---

[168] Admire nothing. Horace, Epistles I, 6, 1.

what's true about that! To understand what life is, what kind of striving and tension life is, the formula must be applicable to trees and plants as well as to animals. 'What does the plant strive for?' – but here we've already fabricated a false unity that does not exist: the fact of a millionfold growth, with initiatives of its own and half its own, is hidden and denied if we begin by positing a crude unity 'plant'. That the last, smallest 'individuals' can *not* be understood in the sense of a 'metaphysical individual' and atom, that their sphere of power continually shifts – this is the very first thing to become clear: but is every one of them, when it transforms itself like this, striving *for* '*happiness*'? – But all expanding, incorporating, growing is a striving against what resists, motion is essentially something connected with states of unpleasure: at any rate, what's driving here must will something else, if it wills unpleasure and continually seeks it out like this. – What do the trees in a jungle fight each other for? For 'happiness'? – For *power*...

Man, having become master of the forces of nature, master of his own wildness and licentiousness: the desires have learned to obey, to be useful

Man, compared to a pre-man, represents a tremendous quantum of *power* – *not* an increment in 'happiness': how can one assert that he has *striven* for happiness?...

11[113]

On psychology and theory of knowledge

I maintain that the *inner* world is phenomenal as well: everything *we become conscious of* has first been thoroughly trimmed, simplified, schematised, interpreted – the *real* process of inner 'perception', the *causal association* between thoughts, feelings, desires is absolutely hidden from us, like that between subject and object – and may be just a figment of our imagination. This 'apparent *inner* world' is managed with quite the same forms and procedures as the 'outer' world. We never encounter 'facts': pleasure and unpleasure are late and derivative phenomena of the intellect...

'Causality' escapes us; to assume an immediate, causal bond between thoughts, as logic does, is the consequence of the crudest and clumsiest observation. *Between* two thoughts there are, in addition, *all sorts of affects* at play: but they move so fast that we *mistake* them, we *deny* them...

'Thinking', as posited by the theorists of knowledge, simply doesn't occur: it is a quite arbitrary fiction achieved by selecting one element from the process and subtracting all the others, an artificial trimming for the purpose of intelligibility...

The 'mind', *something that thinks*: maybe even 'the mind absolute, pure, unmixed' – this conception is a derivative, second consequence of the false self-observation that believes in 'thinking': here *first* an act is imagined that doesn't occur, 'thinking', and *secondly* a subject-substratum is imagined in which every act of this thinking, and nothing else, originates; i.e., *both doing and doer are fictions*

11[114]

'willing' is *not* 'desiring', striving, wanting: it distinguishes itself from these by the *affect of the command*

there is no '*willing*', but only a *willing-something*: one must not uncouple the goal from the state, as the theorists of knowledge do. 'Willing' in the way they understand it occurs just as little as 'thinking'; is pure fiction.

that *something is commanded* is part of willing (this does not, of course, mean that the will is 'executed'...)

That general *state of tension* by means of which a force strives to discharge itself – is not 'willing'

11[115]

In a world that is essentially false, truthfulness would be an *anti-natural tendency*, and such a tendency could only make sense as a means to a special, *higher potency of falseness*: for a world of the true, of being, to be fabricated, the truthful man first had to be created (which includes such a man believing himself 'truthful').

Simple, transparent, free of contradiction with himself, lasting, remaining the same, without fold or volte, cloak or form: a man of this kind conceives a world of being as '*God*' in his own image.

For truthfulness to be possible, the whole sphere of man must be very clean, small and respectable: *advantage* in every sense must be on the side of the truthful man. – Lies, malice, pretence must arouse surprise...

Hatred of lies and pretence out of *pride*, out of a sensitive notion of honour; but such hatred can also come from cowardice: because lying is forbidden. – For *another* kind of man, all moralising ('Thou shalt not lie') is useless against the instinct which constantly needs lies: witness the *New Testament*.

11[116]

There are those who go looking for immorality; when they judge: 'That is wrong', they believe it ought to be abolished and changed. I, on the contrary, have no peace anywhere until I have understood a matter's *immorality*. Once I've found that, my equanimity is restored.

11[118]

we Hyperboreans[169]

My conclusion is that *real* man represents a far higher value than the 'desirable' man of any ideal hitherto; that all 'desirabilities' in respect to man are absurd and dangerous dissipations with which a single type of man tried to set up the conditions of *its* survival and growth as a law above mankind as a whole; that up to now, every 'desirability' originating this way that has achieved dominion has *forced down* the value of man, his strength, his certainty of the future; that man's paltriness and petty intellectuality reveal themselves most clearly, even today, when he *wishes*; that up to now, man's capacity to posit values has not been well enough developed to account for the actual, not merely 'desirable', *values of man*; that the ideal up to now has been the core of the force that slandered world and man, the breath of poison on reality, the great *seduction to nothingness* . . .

11[120]

The idea that there is a kind of adequate relation between subject and object, that the object is something which *seen from the inside* would be a subject, is an amiable invention which, I think, has had its day. After all, the amount we become conscious of depends entirely on the crude usefulness of that becoming-conscious: how could this petty perspective of

---

[169] Pindar, in Pyth. 10, speaks of this mythical people living in the far north.

consciousness allow us to make any statements whatsoever about 'subject' and 'object' that even grazed reality! –

11[121]

one cannot derive the lowest and most primordial activity in protoplasm from a will to self-preservation, for the protoplasm takes into itself an absurdly greater amount than it would need for preservation: and, above all, the point is that it does *not* thereby 'preserve itself', but *disintegrates...* The drive that governs here must explain precisely this *not* wanting to preserve itself: 'hunger' is already an interpretation, based on incomparably more complex organisms (– hunger is a specialised and later form of the drive, an expression of the division of labour, in the service of a higher, governing drive).

11[122]

– what isolates *us* is not that we don't *find* any God, either in history, or in nature, or behind nature – but that we feel what was revered as God to be not 'divine' but a hideous holy grimace, a sheep-like, absurd and pitiful inanity, a principle of slander against man and the world: in short, that we deny God as God. It is the pinnacle of man's psychological mendacity to think up a being as a beginning and 'in-itself', according to the very particular yardstick of what he happens to find good, wise, powerful, valuable at that moment – and thereby to think away the *whole causality* by means of which any goodness, any wisdom, any power at all exists and has value. In short, to posit elements that arose most recently and most conditionally not as having originated at all but as 'in-themselves', or even as the cause of all origination in general... If we proceed from experience, from every case where a man has risen significantly above the measure of the human, then we see that every high degree of power involves freedom from good and evil as well as from 'true' and 'false', and cannot take account of what goodness wants. We grasp the same thing again for every high degree of wisdom – in it, goodness has no place, neither do truthfulness, justice, virtue and other capricious valuations of the common people. Finally, every high degree of goodness itself: is it not obvious that this presupposes an intellectual myopia and lack of refinement? Likewise an incapacity to distinguish at a distance between true and false, between useful and harmful? Quite apart from the fact that a high degree of power in the hands of the highest goodness would entail the most disastrous consequences ('the abolition of evil')? – Indeed, one need only consider what tendencies the 'God of Love' puts into the heads of his believers: they ruin mankind for the benefit of the 'good'. – In practice that same God has, in view of the real nature of the world, proved to be the *God of the greatest short-sightedness, devilry* and *powerlessness*: which tells us how much value the idea of him has.

Knowledge and wisdom have no value as such; nor does goodness: one must always first have a goal that confers value or disvalue on these qualities – there *could be a goal* that gave extreme knowledge a high disvalue (for example if extreme deception were one of the preconditions for the enhancement of life; likewise if goodness were capable of paralysing and disheartening the springs that drive great desire...

Our human life being as it is, all 'truth', all 'goodness', all 'holiness', all 'divinity' in the Christian style has hitherto proved to be a great danger – even now, mankind is in danger of perishing through an ideality hostile to life

11[123]

The rise of *nihilism*

Nihilism is not just a contemplation of the 'In vain!', and not just the belief that everything deserves to perish: one puts one's hand to it, one *makes it perish*... That is, perhaps, *illogical*: but the nihilist doesn't believe in the compulsion to be logical... Nihilism is the state of strong spirits and wills: and for these it's not possible to stop at the No 'of judgement' – the *No of the deed* springs from their nature. An-nihil-ation by the judgement is seconded by annihilation by the hand.[170]

11[127]

NB. against *justice*... Against J. Stuart Mill: I abhor that vulgarity of his which says: 'What's sauce for the goose is sauce for the gander; do as you would be done by, etc., etc.'; which wants to base the whole of human intercourse on *mutuality of services rendered*, so that every action

---

[170] *Ver-Nichtsung, Ver-Nichtung*: in *Ver-Nichtung* Nietzsche highlights the composition of the common German word *Vernichtung*, destruction or, literally, 'making not'; *Ver-Nichtsung* is formed by analogy, and literally means 'making into nothing'.

appears as a kind of payment for something that's been done for us. Here the *presupposition* is **ignoble** in the lowest sense: here an *equivalence in the value of an action* in my case and in yours is presupposed; here the *most personal* value of an action is simply annulled (that which can't be settled up or paid for with anything –). 'Reciprocity' is a great piece of vulgarity; precisely that something *I* do *could not* be, and *ought not* to be, done by someone else, that there must be *no settling up* – except in the *choicest sphere* of 'my equals', inter pares;[171] that in a deeper sense one never pays anything back, because one *is something unique* and only *does unique things* – this fundamental conviction contains the cause of *aristocratic separation from the crowd*, because the crowd believes in 'equality' and *consequently* in 'reciprocity' and the possibility of settling up.

11[132]

– a man as he *ought to* be: that sounds as preposterous to us as: 'A tree as it ought to be'

11[138]

The origins of the ideal. Examination of the soil on which it grows.

A. To proceed from the 'aesthetic' states where the world is *seen* as fuller, rounder, *more perfect* –
   the *pagan* ideal: in this, self-affirmation prevailing from the buffo[172] onwards
   – the highest type: the *classical* ideal – as an expression of *all* the chief instincts having turned out well
   – in this, once again the highest style: *the grand style* as an expression of the 'will to power' itself (the most feared instinct *dares to unmask itself*)
   – *one gives away* –

B. To proceed from states where the world is *seen* as more empty, pale, diluted, where 'intellectualisation' and unsensuality take on the rank of perfection; where the brutal, the animal and direct, what's closest are most avoided: the 'sage', the 'angel' (priestly = virginal = unknowing) physiological characteristics of such 'idealists' . . .

---

[171] See note to 2[12].   [172] Comic actor in Italian opera, often a socially inferior figure.

226

the *anaemic* ideal: in some circumstances this may be the ideal of the natures who *instantiate* the first, pagan one (thus, Goethe finds his 'saint' in Spinoza)

– *one subtracts, one selects* –

C. To proceed from states where we experience the world as too absurd, base, poor, deceptive for us to suppose or wish to find in it the ideal: the projection of the ideal into the anti-natural, anti-factual, anti-logical. The state of the man who judges like this (– the 'impoverishment' of the world as a consequence of suffering: one *takes, one no longer gives* –)

: the *anti-natural ideal*

– *one negates,* one *annihilates* –

(The *Christian ideal* is an *intermediate structure* between the second and the third, where sometimes the former, sometimes the latter form prevails.)

the three ideals

A.	Either a *strengthening* (pagan)	⎫
B.	or a *diluting* (anaemic)	⎬ of life
C.	or a *denial* (anti-natural)	⎭
'deification' felt	in the highest plenitude	
	in the most delicate selection	
	in the destruction and scorning of life.	

11[141]

if you want to do away with strong oppositions and differences of rank, you will also be doing away with strong love, noble disposition, the feeling of self.

11[142]

On the *real* psychology of the society of freedom and equality:

what is diminishing? The will to *one's own responsibility* – sign of the decline of autonomy *fitness to defend oneself* and *bear arms*, in the most intellectual matters as well – the force to command

the sense of *reverence*, of subordination, of being able to keep silent.

great passion, the great task, tragedy, serenity

11[145]

Role of 'consciousness'

It's essential that one makes no mistake about the role of 'consciousness': *what developed it* is our *relationship with the 'external world'*. In contrast, the *administration*, or the care and protection accorded the coordination of the bodily functions, does *not* enter our consciousness; just as little as does the mental *sorting and storing*. There can be no doubt that a highest authority exists for these processes: a kind of managing committee where the various *chief desires* assert their votes and power. 'Pleasure', 'unpleasure' are hints from that sphere... likewise the act of *will*. Likewise *ideas*

In sum: what becomes conscious is subject to causal relations entirely concealed from us – the succession of thoughts, feelings, ideas in consciousness tells us nothing about whether this succession is a causal one: but it gives the *illusion* of being so, in the highest degree. Upon this *illusion we have founded our whole notion of mind, reason, logic*, etc. (none of these exist: they are fictitious syntheses and unities)... And these, in turn, we have projected *into* things, *behind* things!

Usually one takes *consciousness* itself to be the total sensorium[173] and highest authority: yet it is only a *means for communicability*: it has developed in the course of interaction and with respect to the interests of interaction... 'interaction' here also understood from the point of view of the influences of the external world and the reactions they require of us, as well as of our influences *on* the external world. Consciousness is *not* the management but an *organ of the management* –

11[146]

The means by which a stronger species preserves itself.

Granting oneself a right to exceptional actions; as an attempt at self-overcoming and freedom

[173] See note to 7[62].

Entering into states where it is not permitted *not* to be a barbarian

Obtaining for oneself, through every kind of asceticism, an ascendancy and certainty in respect to one's strength of will.

Not communicating; silence; taking care not to be charming.

Learning to obey, in such a way that it provides a test of how far one can uphold one's self. Casuistry of the point of honour, taken to extremes of subtlety.

Never inferring 'What's sauce for the goose is sauce for the gander' – but the opposite!

Treating retaliation, or the *permission to* give as good as one gets, as a privilege, conceding it as a distinction –

Not making an ambition of *another man's* virtue.

11[148]

The time is coming when we have to *pay* for having been *Christians* for two thousand years: the *weight* that allowed us to live is gone – for a while we don't know which way to turn. We rush headlong into the *opposite* valuations, with the same degree of energy with which we used to be Christians – with which the nonsensical exaggeration of Christian – – –

1. the 'immortal soul'; the eternal value of the 'person' –
2. the solution, direction, valuation in the 'beyond' –
3. moral value as the highest value, the 'salvation of the soul' as the cardinal interest –
4. 'sin', 'earthly', 'flesh', 'pleasures' – stigmatised as 'world'.

Now everything is thoroughly false, 'word', confused, weak or over-wrought

a. one attempts a kind of *earthly solution*, yet in the same sense – that of the *final triumph* of truth, love, justice: socialism: 'equality of persons'
b. one likewise attempts to hold on to the *moral ideal* (giving precedence to the unegoistic, self-denial, the negation of the will)
c. one even tries to hold on to the 'beyond', if only as some anti-logical x: but one immediately elaborates it in such a way that it can yield a kind of metaphysical consolation in the old style
d. one tries to read out of what happens a *divine guidance in the old style*, the rewarding, punishing, educating, *improving* order of things

e. one continues to believe in good and evil: in such a way that one feels the victory of good and the annihilation of evil to be a *task* (– this is English; a typical case is that shallow-headed John Stuart Mill)

f. contempt for 'naturalness', for desire, for the ego: attempt to regard even the highest intellectuality and art as a consequence of depersonalisation and as désintéressement[174]

g. one allows the *church* to continue intruding into all the essential experiences and most important points of an individual life and give them *consecration*, *higher meaning*: we certainly have a 'Christian state', Christian 'marriage' –

11[152]

my 'future'

a robust polytechnical education
military service: so that on average every man of the higher classes is an officer, whatever else he is

11[153]

The *dissolute* and *licentious*: their depressing influence on the *value of the desires*. It was the atrocious barbarism of morals that, particularly in the Middle Ages, necessitated a real 'league of virtue' – alongside equally atrocious exaggerations about what constitutes the *value* of man. Combative 'civilisation' (*taming*) needs all sorts of irons and tortures to maintain itself against dreadfulness and the nature of the beast of prey.

Here a confusion is quite natural, though terrible in its effects: what *men of power and will* can demand of themselves also provides a standard for what they may allow themselves. Such natures are the opposite of the dissolute and the licentious: although they might do things for which a lesser man would be convicted of vice and intemperance.

Here the concept of 'the *equal value* of men *before God*' is extraordinarily harmful: one forbade actions and dispositions that as such were among the prerogatives of the strong – as if they were, in themselves, unworthy of man. The whole tendency of the strong was brought into disrepute by

---

[174] Disinterestedness.

setting up as a value norm the protective measures of the weakest (weakest towards themselves, as well).

The confusion goes so far that precisely the great *virtuosi* of life (whose self-sovereignty provides the sharpest contrast to the dissolute and 'licentious') were branded with the most insulting names. Even now, it's believed necessary to disapprove of a Cesare Borgia:[175] that is simply laughable. The church excommunicated German emperors because of their vices: as if a monk or a priest were entitled to talk about what a Frederick II[176] might demand of himself. A man like Don Juan is sent to hell: that is very naive. Has anyone noticed that in heaven, all the interesting men are missing?...Just a hint for the ladies about where they might best find their salvation...If one thinks in the least consistently, and with deeper insight into what a 'great man' is, no doubt remains that the church sends all 'great men' to hell – it fights *against* every 'greatness of man'...

11[154]

The 'concept of honour': based on the belief in 'good society', in the central qualities of chivalry, in the obligation constantly to present oneself to be seen. Essential: that one doesn't take one's life seriously; that one always attaches importance to the most respectful manners on the part of everybody one encounters (at least, everybody who isn't one of '*us*'); that one is neither familiar, nor good-natured, nor merry, nor modest, except inter pares;[177] that one *always presents oneself to be seen*...

11[156]

One speaks of the 'deep injustice' of the social pact: as if the fact that one man was born under favourable, another under unfavourable circumstances were an injustice; or even that one man was born with these, another with different qualities...This absolutely must be fought against. The false concept of the 'individual' is what leads to this nonsense. To

---

[175] Cesare Borgia, duc de Valentinois (*c.* 1475–1507), famous for the unscrupulousness with which he is said to have pursued his aims, political or otherwise.

[176] Frederick II of Hohenstaufen (1194–1250), German King and Holy Roman Emperor, highly independent and modern in his views, who fiercely opposed the papacy.

[177] See note to 2[12].

separate a man from the circumstances out of which he grows and, so to speak, simply put or drop him *into* them like a 'soul monad': this is a consequence of that miserable metaphysics of soul. No one *gave* him qualities, neither God *nor* his parents; no one is responsible for his *being*, for his being thus and thus, for his being under these circumstances... The thread of life he now represents cannot be disentangled from everything that was and that must be: since he isn't the result of a long-term intention, of any will at all to an 'ideal of man' or an 'ideal of happiness' or an 'ideal of morality', it's absurd to want to 'shift the blame' anywhere else: as if somewhere there were a *responsibility.*

The *revolt* of the man who 'suffers', against
> God
> society
> nature
> forebears
> education, etc.,

imagines *responsibilities* and *forms of will* that do not exist. One must not speak of a *wrong* in cases where there are no *preconditions* at all *for right and wrong.* That *one* soul is in itself just like *every* soul, or *ought to* be: that is the worst kind of optimistic enthusiasm. The reverse is what's desirable: the greatest possible *dissimilarity* and consequently friction, struggle, contradiction – and, fortunately, what's desirable is what's *really* the case!

11[157]

To aim for *equal rights* and ultimately *equal needs*, an almost inevitable consequence of our kind of civilisation of commerce and the equal value of votes in politics, brings with it the exclusion and slow extinction of the higher, more dangerous, stranger and, in short, *newer* men: *experimentation* ceases, so to speak, and a certain stasis is achieved.

11[226]

1

The idea that mankind has a total task to fulfil, that as a whole it is moving towards some kind of goal, this very obscure and arbitrary idea is still very young. Perhaps we'll rid ourselves of it before it becomes an 'idée fixe'... It's not a whole, this mankind: it is an indissoluble multiplicity of ascending and declining processes of life – it doesn't have youth, and then maturity, and finally old age. For the layers are juxtaposed and inter-mixed – and some thousands of years from now there may still be younger types of man than those we can find today. Décadence, on the other hand, belongs to all human epochs: everywhere there is waste, decayed matter; the excretion of the products of decline and decay is itself a life process.

2

Under the rule of Christian prejudice *this question did not even exist*: meaning lay in saving the individual soul; a longer or shorter lifespan for mankind was of no account. The best Christians wished it would come to an end as soon as possible – and as for what the individual needed, *there was no doubt*... The task now arose for every individual, as it would in any future for a future one: the value, meaning, horizons of values were fixed, unconditional, eternal, one with God... What deviated from this eternal type was sinful, devilish, condemned...

For each soul the focus of value lay in itself: salvation or damnation! The salvation of the *eternal* soul! Most extreme form of *setting up a self*... For each soul there was just one perfecting; just one ideal; just one path to redemption... Most extreme form of *equal rights*, tied to an optical magnification of one's own importance to the point of absurdity... Nothing but absurdly important souls, circling about themselves with terrible anxiety...

3

Now nobody believes in this ridiculous self-importance any more: and we have sifted our wisdom through a sieve of contempt. Even so, the *optical habit* remains unshaken of seeking a value for man in his approximation to an *ideal man*: basically, one still upholds both the *perspective of self* and *equal rights before the ideal*. In sum: *one believes one knows* what the *final desirability* is in respect of the ideal man...

However, this belief is only the consequence of a tremendous *pampering* by the Christian ideal: an ideal which immediately re-emerges as soon as the 'ideal type' is carefully examined. One believes, *firstly*, one knows that the approximation to a single type is desirable; one believes *secondly* one knows what that type is like; thirdly that every deviation from the type is a retrogression, an inhibition, a loss of force and power for man... To dream of conditions where this *perfect man* is supported by the overwhelming majority: even our socialists, even our dear Utilitarians, haven't reached higher peaks than this. – With that, a *goal* seems to enter the development of mankind: at least, belief in *progress towards the ideal* is the only form in which a kind of *goal* in human history is conceived of today. In sum: one has shifted the arrival of the '*kingdom of God*' into the future, onto the earth, into the human – while basically still clinging to belief in the *old* ideal...

11[227]

To understand:
That all kinds of decay and sickening have continually contributed to overall value judgements: that in the value judgements which have come to dominate, décadence has even gained ascendancy: that we not only have to struggle against the states resulting from all the present misery of degeneration, but that *all* the previous décadence has remained as a residue, i.e., *alive*. Such an aberration of the whole of mankind from its fundamental instincts, such a décadence of the whole of value judgement, is the question mark par excellence, the real riddle the animal called 'man' sets the philosopher –

11[251]

Not for a single hour of my life have I been a Christian: I regard everything I have seen as Christianity, as a *contemptible ambiguity of words*, a real *cowardice* towards all the powers that otherwise rule...

Christians of general military conscription, of parliamentary suffrage, of newspaper culture and, in the middle of all that, talking about 'sin', 'redemption', 'the beyond', death on the cross – how can one endure such a mess!

11[285]

To feel stronger – or put another way: joy – always presupposes a comparing (*not* necessarily with others but with oneself, in the midst of a state of growth, without yet *knowing* the extent to which one compares –)

– *artificial* strengthening: whether through stimulating chemicals or stimulating errors ('delusions'):

e.g., the feeling of *security* like the Christian's. He may trust, he may be patient and composed: this is where his strength lies. He owes this artificial strengthening to the delusion of being shielded by a God

e.g., the feeling of *superiority*, e.g., when the caliph of Morocco is only given globes that show his three united kingdoms taking up four fifths of the earth's surface

e.g., the feeling of *uniqueness*, e.g., when the European imagines that the course of culture is played out in Europe, and strikes himself as being a kind of summarised world process; or when the Christian has all existence revolve around the 'salvation of man' –

It depends on where one feels the pressure, the unfreedom: according to that, different feelings of *being stronger* are generated. A philosopher, e.g., in the midst of the coldest, most outlandish gymnastics of abstraction feels like a fish entering its water: while colours and sounds weigh on him, not to mention the dumb desires – what the others call 'the ideal'.

11[300]

'Objectivity' in the philosopher: moral indifferentism towards oneself, blindness to good and bad consequences: lack of scruples in using dangerous means; perversity and multiplicity of character detected as advantages and exploited –

My deep indifference to myself: I want no advantage from what I know, neither do I evade the disadvantages it involves – including what one might call *corruption* of the character; this is an external perspective. I manage my character but it doesn't occur to me either to understand it or to change it – the personal calculus of virtue hasn't entered my head for a moment. It seems to me that one closes the gates of knowledge to oneself immediately one becomes interested in one's own personal case – or worse, in the 'salvation' of one's soul!...One must not take one's morality too seriously and must insist on keeping a modest claim to its opposite...

Perhaps a kind of *inherited wealth of morality* is assumed here: one senses that plenty of it can be squandered, thrown out of the window, without one's becoming particularly poor. Never to feel tempted to admire 'beautiful souls'. Always to know oneself superior to them. To meet the monsters of virtue with inward mockery; déniaiser la vertu[178] – secret enjoyment.

To revolve about oneself; no wish to become 'better' or even just 'different'; too interested not to cast out tentacles and nets of every morality towards things –

11[310]

The whole view of the rank of the *passions*: as if the right and normal thing were to be guided by *reason* – while the passions were the abnormal, dangerous, semi-animal, and additionally, in terms of their goal, nothing other than *desires for pleasure*...

Passion is degraded (1) as if its being the moving force were only something *un*seemly, instead of something necessary and constant, (2) when it is directed at something that has no high value, an amusement...

The mistaking of passion and *reason*, as if the latter were an entity of its own rather than a state of relations between different passions and desires; and as if every passion did not have within itself its quantum of reason...

11[374]

Our pre-eminence: we live in the age of *comparison*, we can check the calculation as never before: we are the self-consciousness of history in general...

We enjoy differently, we suffer differently: comparing an unprecedented multiplicity is our most instinctive activity...

We understand everything, we live everything, we have no hostile feelings left...Even if it's to our own disadvantage, our eager and almost loving curiosity undauntedly goes off to meet the most dangerous things...

'Everything is good' – we find it difficult to negate...

We suffer when we become unintelligent enough to take sides against something...

At bottom, we scholars are the ones who best fulfil the teachings of Christ today – –

[178] Rob virtue of its innocence.

11[375]

On the critique of Greek philosophy

The appearance of the Greek philosophers from Socrates on is a symptom of décadence; the anti-Hellenic instincts gain the upper hand...

Still fully Hellenic is the 'Sophist' – including Anaxagoras, Democritus, the great Ionians –

but as a transitional form: the polis[179] loses its belief in its uniqueness of culture, in its right to rule over every other polis...

culture, i.e., 'the gods', are exchanged – so that one loses belief in the sole privilege of the deus autochthonus[180]...

good and evil of different lineages intermingle: the boundary between good and evil *blurs*...

That is the 'Sophist' –

The 'philosopher', in contrast, is the *reaction*: he wants the *old* virtue...

– he sees the reason for decay in the decay of institutions, he wants old institutions

– he sees decay in the decay of authority: he looks for new authorities (travelling to foreign countries, to foreign literatures, to exotic religions)

– he wants the *ideal polis*, after the concept 'polis' has had its day (more or less as the Jews sustained themselves as a 'people' after they had fallen into servitude)

: they are interested in all tyrants: they want to restore virtue by force majeure[181] –

– bit by bit, everything that's *genuinely Hellenic* is made responsible for *decay* (and Plato is just as ungrateful towards Homer, tragedy, rhetoric, Pericles, as the prophets were towards David and Saul)

– *the decline of Greece* is interpreted as *an objection to the foundations of Hellenic* culture: *fundamental error of the philosophers* –

Conclusion: the Greek world perishes. *Cause*: Homer, myth, ancient morality, etc.

---

[179] See note to 34[92].   [180] A god belonging to the particular land.
[181] Action by a superior or irresistible force.

The *anti*-Hellenic development of the philosophers' value judgement:
: the Egyptian ('life after death' as a court of justice...)
: the Semitic (the 'dignity of the sage', the 'sheikh' –
: the Pythagoreans, the subterranean cults, silence, the beyond as a tool of fear; *mathematics*: religious valuation, a kind of commerce with the whole of the cosmos
: the priestly, ascetic, transcendent –
: *dialectic* – isn't there an abominable and pedantic conceptual quibbling already in Plato?

Decline of intellectual good taste: one has already ceased to notice the ugliness and prattle in all direct dialectics.

The *two* décadence movements and the two extremes run in parallel:

a. the sumptuous, charmingly malicious décadence that loves art and splendour,

b. and the gathering gloom of the religious-moral pathos,[182] the Stoic self-hardening, the Platonic slandering of the senses, the preparation of the ground for Christianity...

11[407]

The *state*, or organised *immorality*...
inward: as police, criminal law, classes, commerce, family
outward: as will to power, to war, to conquest, to revenge
how is it achieved that a *great mass* does things the *individual* would never consent to do?
– by the division of responsibility
– of commanding and carrying out commands
– by *intercalating* the virtues of obedience, of duty, of the love of prince and fatherland
upholding pride, severity, strength, hatred, revenge, in short all the traits that *contradict* the herd type...

The *sleights of hand* to make possible actions, measures, affects which, from the individual's point of view, are no longer 'acceptable' – and are also no longer 'palatable' –

they are 'made palatable to us' by the *art* that lets us enter such 'alienated' worlds

---

[182] See note to 35[24].

the *historian* shows the kind of right and reason they have; travels; exoticism; psychology; penal law; the madhouse; criminals; sociology

'impersonality': so that as *means* of a collective being we permit ourselves these affects and actions (judiciaries, jury, citizen, soldier, minister, prince, society, 'critic')...and feel as if we were *making a sacrifice*...

The *upholding of the military state* is the ultimate means to either adopt or keep hold of the *great tradition* respecting the *highest* human *type*, the *strong type*. And all *concepts* that immortalise the enmity of states and the distance in rank between them may seem sanctioned by this...

e.g., nationalism, protective tariffs, – – –

the *strong type* is upheld as *determining value*...

Notebook 14, spring 1888

14[4]

Psychologica

Desire, agreeable if one believes oneself strong enough to reach its objects
as an idea of what would augment our feeling of power: the first beginning of enjoyment
otherwise *disagreeable*; and soon turning one against *it*. *Desire becomes
a state of distress: as with Schopenhauer.*

14[5]

Religion. Décadence

The dangerousness of Christianity

Even though Christianity brought the doctrine of unselfishness and love
to the fore, its real historical effect remains the *intensification of egoism*, of
individual egoism, to the furthest extreme – that extreme is the belief in
individual immortality. The individual had become so important that he
could no longer be *sacrificed*: before God, 'souls' were equal. That, though,
meant casting doubt on the life of the species in the most dangerous way: it
favoured a practice directly contrary to the species interest. The altruism
of Christianity is a *mortally dangerous* conception: it equates everyone with
everyone else . . .

But with that, the natural course of evolution...and all natural *values* are overturned. If the sick man is to have as much value as the healthy one (or even more value, according to Pascal[183])

This general *philanthropy*, in practice the preference given to all who suffer, who have come off badly, who are sick,

has indeed weakened the power *to sacrifice men*: it has wanted to reduce responsibility to sacrificing oneself – but precisely this absurd *personal* altruism has, from the viewpoint of breeding, *no value at all*. Anyone waiting to see how many sacrifice themselves for the preservation of the species would be *sorely fooled*...

all the great movements, wars, etc., drive men to sacrifice themselves: it's the *strong* whose numbers continually *decline* this way...

in contrast, the *weak* have a horrible instinct to *be careful with* themselves, to preserve themselves, to uphold *each other*...

this 'mutuality of preservation' *is supposed to be* almost virtue and certainly philanthropy!...*typical*: they want to be *protected* by the state, they think this is 'its highest duty!'

behind the general praise for 'altruism' is the instinct that the individual will be best safeguarded if everyone looks after each other...it's the *egoism of the weak* that created the praise, the exclusive praise for altruism...

The dangerous anti-natural character of Christianity:

– it thwarts *natural selection* –

1. it invents an *imaginary* value of the person, so exaggerated and weighty that just about everyone is worth the same
2. it regards the *protective drive for self-preservation of the weak among themselves* as the highest measure of value, it fights most against the way *nature* deals with the weak and badly off: damaging, exploiting, destroying...
3. it won't admit that the highest type of man is the one who has turned out well, the happy one...it is the slander, the poisoning, the chipping away of all natural valuation

---

[183] See *La Vie de Monsieur Pascal, écrite par Madame Périer, sa soeur*, in Pascal, *Oeuvres Complètes*, ed. Louis Lafuma, Paris: Seuil, 1963, p. 32.

14[11]

The *Yes-saying* affects

Pride
joy
health
the love of the sexes
enmity and war
reverence
beautiful gestures, manners, objects
strong will
the discipline of high intellectuality
will to power
gratitude towards earth and life

   : everything that's rich and wants to give away, and bestows gifts on life and gilds and immortalises and deifies it – the whole power of *transfiguring* virtues . . . everything that calls good, says Yes, does Yes –

14[29]

Origin of moral values

Egoism is worth as much as the physiological value of the man who has it.

   Each individual is also the whole line of development (and not just, as morality thinks, something that begins at birth). If he represents the ascent of the human line, then his value is indeed extraordinary; and extreme care may be taken to preserve and promote his growth. (It's care for the future promised in him which gives the well-constituted individual such an extraordinary right to egoism.) If he represents the descending line, decay, chronic sickening, then his value is small: and it's of prime fairness that he take as little space, force and sunshine as possible away from the well-constituted. In this case, society's task is to *suppress egoism* (– which occasionally expresses itself as absurd, pathological, seditious): whether this applies to individuals or to whole decaying, withered classes of the population. Within such classes a doctrine and religion of 'love', of the *suppression* of self-affirmation, of tolerating, bearing, helping, of reciprocity in word and deed, may be of the highest value, even in the eyes of the rulers: for it keeps down the feelings of rivalry, ressentiment,[184] envy, the all too natural feelings of those who have come off badly – it even, under the ideal of humility and obedience, deifies for them their being slaves, ruled, poor, sick, their being underdogs. From this it follows why the ruling classes or races and individuals of every era have upheld the cult of selflessness, the gospel of the lowly, the 'God on the cross'.

The ascendancy of an altruistic way of valuating is the consequence of an instinct of being ill-constituted. The value judgement on the most basic level says: 'I am not worth much' – a purely physiological value judgement, or more clearly still: the feeling of powerlessness, the absence of the great affirming feelings of power (in the muscles, nerves, centres of motion). Depending on the culture of these classes, the value judgement translates itself into a moral or religious judgement (– the predominance of religious and moral judgements is always a sign of lower culture –): this judgement tries to support itself by referring to the spheres from which such classes draw their familiarity with the concept of 'value' in the first place. The interpretation with which the Christian sinner believes he understands himself is an attempt to find his lack of power and self-assurance *justified*: he would rather find himself guilty than feel bad for no reason: in itself, it's a symptom of decay to need interpretations of this kind at all. In other cases, the man who has come off badly seeks the reason not in his 'guilt' (like the Christian) but in society: feeling his existence to be something for which someone is *to blame*, the socialist, the anarchist, the nihilist is thus still the closest relative of the Christian, who also believes his feeling bad and his ill-constitution will be easier to bear if he can find someone to make *responsible* for it. The instinct of *revenge* and *ressentiment* is present in both cases, appearing here as a means of enduring, as an instinct of self-preservation; just as the preference for *altruistic* theory and practice. *Hating egoism*, whether one's own, like the Christian, or another's, like the socialist, thus proves to be a value judgement ruled by revenge; and on the other hand a prudence of the self-preservation of those who suffer, increasing their feelings of reciprocity and solidarity . . . Finally, as already hinted, that discharge of ressentiment through judging, repudiating, punishing egoism (one's own or another's) is also an instinct of self-preservation among those who have come off badly. In sum: the

[184] See note to 2[171].

cult of altruism is a specific form of egoism, which appears regularly under particular physiological conditions.

14[31]

Value…

The concept of a 'reprehensible action' causes us difficulties: in itself, there cannot be anything reprehensible. Of everything that happens, nothing can be reprehensible in itself: *for one must not want to be rid of it* – for any one thing is so connected to everything that wanting to reject anything at all means rejecting everything. A reprehensible action means a reprehended world in general…

And even then: in a reprehended world even reprehending would be reprehensible… And the consequence of a theory that reprehends everything would be a practice which affirms everything… If becoming is a great ring, then each thing is equally valuable, eternal, necessary…

In all the correlations of Yes and No, of preferring and refusing, loving and hating, all that's expressed is a perspective, an interest of particular types of life: in itself, everything which is says Yes.

14[37]

On *modernity*

What does us honour

If anything at all does us honour, it's this: we have placed *seriousness* somewhere else: we take seriously the *low* things despised and left aside by all eras – while we sell 'beautiful feelings' off cheap…

Can one go more dangerously wrong than by despising the body? As if that contempt did not condemn all intellectuality to sickliness, to the fits of the vapours that are 'idealism'!

Nothing thought up by Christians and idealists has rhyme or reason: we are more radical. We have discovered the 'smallest world' to be what everywhere decides: we are dangerously to the – – –

We have understood in their value well-paved roads, fresh air in one's room, clean lodgings, food; we take seriously all the *necessities* of existence and *despise* all this business of 'beautiful souls' as a kind of 'levity and frivolity'.

What was previously most despised has now come to the fore.

I'll add immorality to that: morality is only a form of immorality which, in regard to the profit a particular species can draw from it, – – –

14[64]

Question: is it *depersonalisation* by a truth when one submerges oneself in a thought?

...Herzen[185] claims this is so: in his opinion it's quite usual to forget one's 'moi'[186] and let it go –

Question: whether this too is not mere *illusion*; whether the thing which finds a question interesting is not our whole, manifold *I*...

14[76]

In the past one said of every morality: 'By its fruits shall ye know it'; I say of every morality: it is a fruit by which I know the *soil* from which it grew.

14[79]

Will to power

Philosophy

Quanta of power. *Critique of mechanistic theory*

let us here remove the two popular concepts 'necessity' and 'law': the first puts a false compulsion, the second a false freedom into the world. 'Things' do not behave regularly, not according to a *rule*: there are no things (– they are our fiction), and nor do they behave under the compulsion of necessity. Here there is no obeying: for *that something is as it is*, as strong or as weak, is not the consequence of an obeying or of a rule or of a compulsion...

The degree of resistance and the degree of superior strength – this is the point in everything that happens: if, for our day-to-day habits of calculation, *we* are able to express it in formulas of 'laws', all the better for

---

[185] Alexander Herzen (1812–1870), Russian social philosopher whose memoirs Nietzsche had read.
[186] Ego.

us! But feigning the world as obedient doesn't mean we have put 'morality' into it –

There is no law: every power at every moment draws its ultimate conclusion. It is precisely on the lack of a mezzo termine[187] that calculability rests.

A quantum of power is characterised by the effect it exerts and the effect it resists. There is no adiaphoria,[188] though in itself this would be conceivable. The quantum of power is essentially a will to violate and to defend oneself against being violated. Not self-preservation: every atom's effect spreads out into the whole of being – if one thinks away this radiation of power-will, the atom itself is thought away. That's why I call it a quantum of '*will to power*': this expresses the character that cannot *be* thought away from the mechanical order without thinking away that order itself.

A translation of this world of effect into a *visible* world – a world for the eyes – is the concept of 'motion'. Here the implication is always that *something* is moved, and whether in the fiction of a lump atom or even of its abstraction, the dynamic atom, we still conceive of a thing which effects – that is, we haven't left behind the habit that senses and language seduce us to. Subject, object, a doer for every doing, the doing separated from what does it: let's not forget that this is mere semiotics and does not refer to something real. Mechanics as a theory of *motion* is itself already a translation into the sensual language of man.

We need unities in order to be able to count: we should not therefore assume that such unities exist. We have borrowed the concept of unity from our concept of 'I' – our oldest article of faith. If we didn't consider ourselves to be unities, we would never have created the concept of 'thing'. Now, rather late in the day, we have become quite convinced that our concept of 'I' guarantees nothing in the way of a real unity. Thus, in order to sustain the mechanistic theory of the world, we always have to include a proviso about the use we are making of two fictions: the concept of motion (taken from the language of our senses) and the concept of the atom $=$ unity (originating in our psychological 'experience'). Its prerequisites are a *sensual prejudice* and a *psychological prejudice*.

The *mechanistic* world is imagined the only way that eye and fingertips can imagine a world (as 'being moved')

---

[187] Half-way.   [188] State of indifference, originally with respect to good and evil.

in such a way that it can be calculated – that unities are invented,

in such a way that causal unities are invented, 'things' (atoms) whose effect remains constant (– the false concept of subject is transferred to the concept of the atom)

Concept of number.

Concept of thing (concept of subject

Concept of activity (separation of 'being a cause' and 'effecting')

Motion (eye and fingertips)

: that all effect is *motion*

: that where there is motion, *something* is being moved

Phenomenal, then, is this: mixing in the concept of number, the concept of subject, the concept of motion: we still have our *eyes*, our *psychology* in the world.

If we eliminate these ingredients, what remains are not things but dynamic quanta in a relationship of tension with all other dynamic quanta, whose essence consists in their relation to all other quanta, in their 'effects' on these – the will to power not a being, not a becoming, but a *pathos*,[189] is the most elementary fact, and becoming, effecting, is only a result of this . . .

mechanics also formulates resulting phenomena in semiotic terms, using sensual and psychological means of expression; it does not touch upon the causal force . . .

14[80]

If the innermost essence of being is will to power, if pleasure is all growth of power, unpleasure all feeling unable to resist and master: may we not, then, posit pleasure and unpleasure as cardinal facts? Is will possible without these two oscillations of Yes and No? But *who* feels pleasure? . . . But *who* wills power? . . . Absurd question, if the essence is itself will to power and thus feeling pleasure and unpleasure. Nevertheless, there must be oppositions, resistances, and thus, relatively, *overarching unities* . . . Localised – – –

if A exerts an effect on B, then only as localised is A separated from B

---

[189] See note to 35[24].

14[82]

Can we assume a *striving for power* without a sensation of pleasure and unpleasure, i.e., without a feeling of the increase and diminution of power?

mechanistic language is just a sign language for the *internal* factual world of quanta of will that struggle and overcome each other?

all the presuppositions of mechanistic language – matter, atom, pressure and impact, gravity – are not 'facts-in-themselves' but interpretations aided by *psychological* fictions.

life, as the form of being that is best known to us, is specifically a will to the accumulation of force

: this is the lever of all the processes of life

: nothing wants to preserve itself, everything is to be added up and accumulated

Life, as an individual case: hypothesis starting from here and extending to the total nature of existence

: strives for a *maximum feeling of power*

: is essentially a striving for more power

: striving is nothing other than striving for power

: the most basic and innermost thing remains this will: mechanics is a mere semiotics of the consequences.

14[86]

On the concept of 'décadence' –

1. scepticism is a consequence of décadence, as is the libertinage of the mind.
2. the corruption of morals is a consequence of décadence: weakness of will, need for strong stimulants...
3. therapeutic methods, the psychological, moral ones, don't change the course of décadence, they do not halt it, they are physiologically *null*
   : insight into the *great nullity* of these arrogant 'reactions'
   : they are forms of narcotisation against certain pernicious consequences, they don't get rid of the morbid element
   : they are often heroic attempts to annul the man of décadence, to minimise his *harmful effect*.

4. nihilism is not a cause, but just the logic of décadence
5. the 'good' and the 'bad' man are just two types of décadence: they remain together in all fundamental phenomena.
6. *the social question* is a consequence of décadence
7. sicknesses, especially the sicknesses of the head and nerves, are signs that the *defensive* force of the strong nature is absent; irritability is evidence of the same, so that *pleasure* and *unpleasure* become the most significant problems.

14[89]

Counter-movement: religion

The two types:
Dionysos and the *Crucified One.*

To remember: the typical *religious* man – whether a form of décadence?
 The great innovators are, every one of them, pathological and epileptic
 : but are we not omitting one type of the religious man, the *pagan*? Is the pagan cult not a form of thanking and affirming life? Ought not its highest representative to be a vindication and deification of life?
 Type of a completely well-formed and ecstatically overflowing spirit...
 Type of a man[190] taking into himself and *redeeming* the contradictions and doubtfulness of existence?
 – This is where I set the *Dionysos* of the Greeks:
 the religious affirmation of life, of life as a whole, not denied and halved
 typical: that the sexual act awakens depth, mystery, awe
 Dionysos versus the 'Crucified One': there you have the opposition. It's *not* a distinction regarding their martyrdom – just that this martyrdom has a different meaning. Life itself, its eternal fruitfulness and recurrence, conditions torment, destruction, the will to annihilation...
 in the other case suffering, 'the Crucified as the innocent', counts as an objection to this life, a formula to condemn it.
 One divines that the problem here is that of the meaning of suffering: whether a Christian meaning, a tragic meaning... In the former case it's

---

[190] Clearly a slip in the manuscript, where Nietzsche writes, translated literally: 'type of a type'.

held to be the path to a blissful existence; in the latter, *existence* is held to be *blissful enough* to justify even monstrous suffering

The tragic man says Yes to even the bitterest suffering: he is strong, full, deifying enough to do so

The Christian says No to even the happiest earthly lot: he is weak, poor, disinherited enough to suffer from life in whatever form . . .

'the God on the cross' is a curse on life, a hint to deliver oneself from it

Dionysos cut to pieces is a *promise* to life: it will eternally be reborn and come home out of destruction

14[93]

Will to power as knowledge

Critique of the concept 'true and illusory world'

of these, the first is a mere fiction, formed exclusively out of invented things

'illusoriness' itself belongs to reality: it is a form of reality's being, i.e.

in a world where there is no being, a certain calculable world of *identical* cases must first be created by *illusion*: a tempo in which observation and comparison are possible, etc.

'illusoriness' is a trimmed and simplified world on which our *practical* instincts have worked. It suits *us* perfectly: we *live* in it, we can live in it – *proof* of its truth for us . . .

: the world apart from our condition of living in it, the world we have not reduced to our being, our logic and psychological prejudices

does *not* exist as a world 'in-itself'

it is essentially a world of relationships: it could have a *different face* when looked at from each different point: its being is essentially different at every point: it presses on every point, every point resists it – and these summations are in every case entirely *incongruent*.

The *measure of power* determines which *being* has the other measure of power: under which form, rule, constraint it effects or resists

Our individual case is interesting enough: we have made a conception in order to live in a world, in order to perceive just enough to still be able to *endure* it . . .

14[98]

Will to power in principle

Critique of the concept of 'cause'

I need the *starting point* 'will to power' as the origin of motion. Consequently, motion must not be conditioned from outside – not *caused* . . .

I need beginnings and centres of motion, starting from which the will reaches out . . .

We have absolutely no experience of a *cause*
: calculated psychologically, we get the whole concept from the subjective conviction that *we* are a cause, namely, that the arm moves . . . *But that is an error*
: we distinguish ourselves, the doers, from the doing, and make use of this schema everywhere – we seek a doer for everything that happens . . .
: what does that mean? It means we've *misunderstood* as a cause what is a feeling of force, tension, resistance, a feeling in the muscles that's already the beginning of the action
: or understood the will to do this or that as a cause, because the action follows upon it – cause, i.e. – – –
'cause' does not occur: in several cases where it seemed to be given and starting from which we projected it out as a way of *understanding what happens*, we've been shown to have deceived ourselves.

Our 'understanding of something that happens' has consisted in our inventing a subject which was made responsible for something having happened and how it happened.

We have summarised our feeling of will, our 'feeling of freedom', our feeling of responsibility and our intention to do something into the concept of 'cause':
: in their basic conception, causa efficiens and finalis[191] are one.

We thought an effect was explained once we had found a state in which that effect already inhered

In fact we invent all causes according to the schema of the effect, the effect being familiar to us . . . Conversely, we are unable to predict of anything what it will 'effect'.

---

[191] See note to 34[53].

Thing, subject, will, intention – all inhere in the conception of 'cause'.

We look for things so as to explain why something has changed. Even the *atom* is such a 'thing' and 'primitive subject' added on in thought...

Finally we grasp that things, and thus also atoms, do not effect at all: *because they do not exist at all*... that the concept of causality is completely unusable – A necessary sequence of states does *not* imply a causal relationship between them (– that would mean making their *capacity to effect* jump from 1 to 2, to 3, to 4, to 5)

The causality interpretation is a deception...

motion is a word, motion is not a cause –

a 'thing' is a sum of its effects, synthetically bound together by a concept, an image...

There are neither causes nor effects.

Linguistically we don't know how to free ourselves from them. But that doesn't matter. If I conceive of the *muscle* as separated from its 'effects', then I have negated it...

In sum: *something that happens neither is effected nor itself effects*

Causa is a *capacity to effect*, invented onto what happens...

there isn't what Kant thinks: *no* sense of causality

one is surprised, one is unsettled, one wants something familiar to hold on to...

as soon as we are shown something old in the new, we are reassured.

The supposed instinct for causality is only the *fear of what one isn't used to* and the attempt to discover something *familiar* in it

a search not for causes but for what is familiar...

Man is immediately reassured when for something new he – – – he does *not* take pains to understand how the match causes the fire

In fact, science has emptied the concept of causality of its content and kept it on as a metaphorical formula where it has basically become irrelevant which side is cause and which effect. It is asserted that in two complex states (constellations of force), the quanta of force remain equal.

The *calculability of something that happens* does not lie in a rule being followed

or in a necessity being obeyed

or in a law of causality having been projected by us into everything that happens:

it lies in the *recurrence of identical cases*

14[101]

décadence *in general*

If *pleasure* and *unpleasure* relate to the feeling of power, life ought to be a growth of power, so that the difference 'more' entered consciousness... Having fixed a level of power, pleasure would only have to measure itself against reductions of the level, against states of unpleasure – *not* against states of pleasure... The will to more is of the very essence of pleasure: that power grows, that the difference enters consciousness...

From a certain point on, in décadence the *reverse difference* enters consciousness: reduction; the memory of the strong moments of the past depresses the present feelings of pleasure – comparison now *weakens* pleasure...

14[105]

Our knowledge has become scientific to the degree that it can apply number and measure...

One could try the experiment whether a scientific ordering of values couldn't be constructed simply on a *number and measure scale of force*...

– all other '*values*' are prejudices, naiveties, misunderstandings...

– everywhere they are *reducible* to this number and measure scale of force

– the *upwards* direction on the scale means every *growth in value*:

– the *downwards* direction on the scale means *diminution in value*

Here appearances and prejudice are ranged against one.

a morality, a way of living tried out, *proved* through long experience and testing, finally comes to consciousness as a law, as *dominating*...

and with that, the whole group of related values and states enters it: it becomes venerable, inviolable, holy, truthful

that this morality's origins are *forgotten* is part of its development... It's a sign that it has become master...

* * *

Just the same thing might have happened with the *categories of reason*: these might, with much tentative feeling and reaching around, have proved their worth through relative usefulness... A point came where they were synthesised, brought to consciousness as a whole – and where one *commanded* them... i.e., where they exerted their effect as *commanding*...

From then on they counted as a priori... as beyond experience, as not to be denied...

And yet perhaps they express nothing but the particular expediency of a race and species – their 'truth' is merely their usefulness –

On the origin of *reason* –
A.
Up to now the highest values have been the moral ones.
B.
Critique of these values.
C.
– – –

14[111]

Philosophy as *décadence*

The great reason in all education to morality has always been that one tried to achieve the *sureness of an instinct*: so that neither the good intention nor the good means even entered consciousness. Just as the soldier drills, so the man was to learn to act. And indeed, this unconsciousness is part of every kind of perfection: even the mathematician's combinations are done unconsciously...

Now, what should one make of the *reaction* of Socrates, who recommended dialectic as the path to virtue and mocked morality's inability to justify itself with logic?... Yet precisely that is part of its *goodness*... without it, morality *is useless*!... Arousing *shame* was a necessary attribute of the perfect!...

Making *demonstrability* a prerequisite of personal excellence in virtue meant precisely the *dissolution* of the *Greek instincts*. They are themselves types of dissolution, all these great 'virtuous ones' and phrasemakers...

In practice it means that moral judgements are torn out of the conditionality they grew from and within which alone they make sense, out of their Greek and Greek-political soil, and, under the semblance of *subli-mation*, are *denaturalised*. The great concepts 'good', 'just' are severed from the preconditions they belong to, and as 'ideas' *set free* they become the objects of dialectic. One seeks a truth behind them, one takes them as entities or as signs of entities: one *fabricates* a world where they're at home, where they originate...

In sum: the mischief already reached its peak with Plato... And it was now found necessary to invent the *abstract, perfect* man in addition

good, just, wise, dialectician – in short, the scarecrow of the ancient philosopher,

a plant uprooted from every soil; a humanity without any definite regulating instincts; a virtue that 'demonstrates' itself with reasons.

the perfectly *absurd* 'individual' in itself! *unnature* of the highest rank...

In short, the denaturalisation of moral values resulted in the creation of a degenerating *type of man* – 'the good man', 'the happy man', 'the wise man'

Socrates is a moment of the *deepest perversity* in the history of men

14[120]

Love

Is the most astonishing proof wanted of how far the transfigurative force of intoxication can go? 'Love' is that proof, what's called love in all the languages and mutenesses of the world. Intoxication here gets the better of reality in such a way that, in the consciousness of the lover, the cause seems obliterated and something else located in its place – a quivering and a sudden gleam of all the magic mirrors of Circe[192]... Here man or animal makes no difference; even less do spirit, goodness, probity... One is made a fine fool of if one is fine, a gross fool of if one is gross; but love, and even love of God, the saintly love of 'saved souls', at root remains one thing: a fever that has reasons to transfigure itself, an intoxication that does well to lie about itself... And anyway, when one loves one is a good liar, to oneself and about oneself: one strikes oneself as transfigured, stronger, richer, more perfect, one *is* more perfect... Here we find *art* as an organic function: we find it embedded in life's most angelic instinct:

---

[192] See note to 2[203].

we find it as life's greatest stimulus – art, thus, sublimely expedient even in its lying... But it would be a mistake to stop at love's power to lie: it does more than just imagine, and actually alters the ranking of values. And not only does it change the feeling of values... The lover is more valuable, is stronger. With the animals, this state produces new substances, pigments, colours and forms: especially new movements, new rhythms, new calls and seductions. With man it's no different. The economy of a man is richer than ever, more powerful, *more whole* than the non-lover's. The lover becomes a spendthrift: he's rich enough for it. He now dares, becomes an adventurer, becomes a donkey of generosity and innocence; he believes in God again, he believes in virtue because he believes in love. On the other hand this idiot of happiness grows wings and new capacities, and even the doors of art open up to him. Discount from poetry in sounds and words the suggestion of that intestinal fever – and what remains of poetry and music?... L'art pour l'art,[193] perhaps: the virtuoso croaking of abandoned frogs despairing in their swamp... All the *rest* was created by love...

14[121]

Will to power psychologically

Psychology's concept of unity

We are used to keeping the elaboration of a tremendous abundance of forms compatible with an origin in unity.

That the will to power is the primitive form of affect, that all other affects are just elaborations of it:

That there is considerable enlightenment to be gained by positing power in place of the individual 'happiness' each living thing is supposed to be striving for: 'It strives for power, for an augmentation of power' – pleasure is only a symptom of the feeling of power achieved, a consciousness of difference –

– it doesn't strive for pleasure; rather, pleasure occurs when what was striven for has been achieved: pleasure accompanies, it doesn't set in motion...

That all driving force is will to power, that there is no physical, dynamic or psychological force apart from this...

[193] Art for art's sake.

– in our science, where the concept of cause and effect is reduced to the relationship of an equation, with the ambition of proving there's the same quantum of force on either side, the *driving force* is *lacking*: we only consider results, we posit them as being equal in respect to the force they contain, we let ourselves off the question of how a change is *caused* . . .

it's simply a matter of experience that change *does not cease*: we don't really have the slightest reason to find it comprehensible that one change must be followed by another. On the contrary: a *state achieved* would seem bound to preserve itself if there weren't a capacity in it precisely *not* to want to preserve itself . . .

Spinoza's principle of self-preservation ought really to put a stop to change: but the principle is false, the *opposite* is true. Everything that lives is exactly what shows most clearly that it does everything possible *not* to preserve itself but to become *more* . . .

is 'will to power' a kind of 'will' or identical with the concept 'will'? Does it amount to desiring? or commanding?

is it that 'will' of which Schopenhauer says it is the 'in-themselves of things'?

: my proposition is that *will* in psychology up to now has been an unjustified generalisation, that this will *does not exist*, that instead of grasping the elaboration of a single, *determinate* will into many forms, one has *struck out* the character of will by *sub*tracting from it its content, its 'Where to?'

: this applies to *Schopenhauer* in the highest degree: what he calls 'will' is nothing but an empty word. Still less is it a 'will *to life*': for life is simply an *individual case* of the will to power – it's quite arbitrary to claim that everything strives to move across into this form of the will to power

14[122]

On epistemology: merely empirical:

There is neither 'mind', nor reason, nor thinking, nor consciousness, nor soul, nor will, nor truth: all fictions, and unusable ones. It's not a matter of 'subject and object' but of a particular animal species which only thrives under a certain relative *rightness*, above all *regularity*, of its perceptions (so it can capitalise on experience) . . .

Knowledge works as a *tool* of power. It's obvious, therefore, that it grows with every growth in power . . .

Meaning of 'knowledge': here, as with 'good' or 'beautiful', the concept is to be taken in a strict and narrowly anthropocentric and biological sense. For a particular species to survive – and grow in power – its conception of reality must be able to encompass enough of what's calculable and constant to construct on this basis a schema for its behaviour. *Usefulness for preservation*, and *not* some abstract theoretical need not to be deceived, is what motivates the development of the organs of knowledge... they develop in such a way that their capacity to observe suffices for our preservation. In other words: the *measure* of the will to know depends on the measure of the growth in the species' *will to power*: a species seizes that much reality *in order to become master of it, to take it into service.*

the mechanistic concept of *motion* is itself a translation of the original occurrence into the *sign-language of eye and fingertip.*

the concept of 'atom', the distinction between a 'seat of the driving force and the driving force itself', is a *sign-language originating in our logical-psychological world.*

We are not free to change our means of expression at our own discretion: it is possible to understand the extent to which it's mere semiotics.

The demand for an *adequate mode of expression* is *nonsensical*: it's of the essence of a language, of a means of expression, to express only a relation... The concept of 'truth' is *absurd*... the whole realm of 'true', 'false' refers only to relations between entities, not to the 'in-itself'... *Nonsense*: there is no 'entity-in-itself', it's only relations that constitute entities, and neither can there be a 'knowledge-in-itself'...

14[123]

Counter-movement

Anti-Darwin

What surprises me most when surveying the great destinies of man is always seeing before me the opposite of what Darwin and his school see or *want to* see today: selection in favour of the stronger, in favour of those who have come off better, the progress of the species. The very opposite is quite palpably the case: the elimination of the strokes of luck, the uselessness of the better-constituted types, the inevitable domination achieved by the average, even *below-average* types. Assuming we aren't given any reason why man should be the exception among creatures, I incline to the prejudice that the school of Darwin has everywhere deceived itself. That will to power in which I recognise the ultimate grounds and character of all change supplies the means of understanding why selection in favour of the exceptions and strokes of luck is precisely what doesn't happen: the strongest and happiest men are weak when the organised herd instincts, the timidity of the weak, of the majority, are ranged against them. My overall view of the world of values shows that in the highest values hanging above mankind today, it is *not* the strokes of luck, the selection types who have the upper hand, but rather the types of décadence – perhaps there's nothing more interesting in the world than this *unwelcome* spectacle...

Strange as it sounds: one has always to arm the strong against the weak; the fortunate against the failures; the healthy against those decaying and with a hereditary taint. If one wants to formulate reality as *morality*, then this morality runs as follows: the average are worth more than the exceptions, the products of decadence more than the average, the will to nothingness has the upper hand over the will to life – and the overall goal is

now, put in Christian, Buddhist, Schopenhauerian terms:

better *not* to be than to be

Against the formulation of reality as morality I *revolt*: that is why I abhor Christianity with a deadly hatred, because it created the sublime words and gestures to wrap a horrible reality in the cloak of right, of virtue, of divinity...

I see all philosophers, I see science on their knees before the reality of a struggle for existence the *reverse* of that taught by the school of Darwin – namely, everywhere those who compromise life, the value of life, are the ones on top, the ones who survive. – The error of the Darwinist school has become a problem for me: how can one be so blind as to fail to see clearly *here?* ... That the *species* represent progress is the most unreasonable assertion in the world: for the time being they represent a level reached, –

so far not a single case has testified to the evolution of the higher organisms from the lower ones –

I see that the lower ones predominate through numbers, through prudence, through cunning – I do not see how a chance variation produces an advantage, at least not for such a long time; which would be another, new way of explaining why a chance variation has become so very strong –

– I find the much-discussed 'cruelty of nature' somewhere else: nature is cruel towards its favourites, it spares and protects and loves les humbles[194] – just as – – –

* * *

In sum: the growth of the *power* of a species is perhaps guaranteed less by the preponderance of its favourites, its strongest members, than by the preponderance of the average and lower types... In the latter is the great fruitfulness, duration; with the former comes growing danger, rapid devastation, speedy reduction in numbers.

* * *

14[124]

Counter-movement

On the origin of religion

In the same way as even now the uneducated man believes anger is the cause of his being angry, that the mind is the cause of his thinking, the soul of his feeling; in short, just as even now a mass of psychological entities are unhesitatingly posited which are supposed to be causes: in that same way man at an even naiver stage explained these phenomena with the aid of psychological personal entities. The states which struck him as alien, transporting, overwhelming he explained to himself as obsession and enchantment under the power of a person. Thus the Christian, the most naive and backward kind of man today, attributes hope, ease, the feeling of 'salvation' to a psychological inspiration by God: for him, as an essentially suffering and uneasy type, it's only to be expected that feelings of happiness, exaltation and ease appear as the *alien*, as what needs explanation. Among intelligent, strong and vigorous races, it's been the epileptic who most aroused the conviction that an *alien power* is at work; but every related unfreedom, e.g., that of the enthusiast, the poet, of the great criminal, of passions like love and revenge, also plays its part in the invention of extra-human powers. One gives concrete form to a state as a person, then asserts that the state, when it occurs in us, is the effect of that person. In other words: in the psychological

---

[194] Nietzsche borrows the expression from Ernst Renan (1823–1892), who characterised the message of Jesus as the 'gospel of the humble'. Cf. TI Skirmishes 2.

formation of God, a state is personified as a cause in order to be an effect.

The psychological logic is this: the *feeling of power*, when it suddenly and overwhelmingly overruns a man – and this is the case in all great affects – makes him doubt his own person: he doesn't dare think of himself as the cause of this astonishing feeling – and so he posits a *stronger* person, a divinity, to explain it.

In sum: the origin of religion lies in the extreme feelings of power which take man by surprise as *alien*: and like the sick man who feels his limbs are heavy and strange and concludes that someone else is lying on top of him, the naive homo religiosus[195] dissects himself into *several persons*. Religion is a case of 'altération de la personnalité'.[196] A kind of *feeling of dread* and *terror* before oneself . . .

But equally an extraordinary *feeling of happiness and exaltation* . . .

among the sick, the *feeling of health* is enough to make them believe in God, in God's proximity

14[148]

Parmenides said: 'One does not think that which is not'[197] – we are at the other extreme and say: 'What can be thought must certainly be a fiction'. Thinking has no grip on the real, but only on – – –

14[157]

Morality as décadence

décadence

'Senses', 'passions'

Fear of the senses, of the desires, of the passions, if it goes far enough to *dissuade us from* them, is already a symptom of *weakness*: extreme measures always characterise abnormal states. What's lacking here, or is *crumbling at the edges*, is the strength to *inhibit* an impulse: if one has the instinct of having to give way, i.e., *having to* react, then one is well-advised to steer clear of opportunities ('seductions').

---

[195] Religious man.   [196] Deformation of the personality.   [197] Parmenides fr. 2, v. 7.

A 'stimulation of the senses' is only a *seduction* for those beings whose system is too easily moved, too easily determined: in the opposite case, where the system is very rigid and slow-moving, strong stimuli are needed to set the functions in motion...

We have no objection to dissipation except in the case of the man who has no right to it; and almost all passions have come into disrepute because of those who aren't strong enough to turn them *to their advantage* –

One must be clear that the same objection can be made to *passion* as to *sickness*: and yet – we couldn't do without sickness and even less without the passions...

We *need* the abnormal, we give life a tremendous shock with these great sicknesses...

$$* * *$$

In detail, one must distinguish between

1. the *dominating passion*, which even brings with it the highest form of health there is: here the coordination of the inner systems and their work towards a single end have been most successfully accomplished – but that's almost the definition of health!

2. the antagonism of the passions, the twoness, threeness, manifoldness of the 'souls within one breast':[198] very unhealthy, inner ruin, disintegration, revealing and intensifying an inner schism and anarchy – unless one passion finally becomes master. *Return of health* –

3. coexistence *without* being against or for one other: often periodic, and then, as soon as it has found some order, also healthy...The most interesting men belong in this category: the chameleons. They are not in contradiction with themselves, they are happy and assured, but they don't develop – their states coexist, however much they are separated. They change over, they don't *become*...

14[173]

The will to power as life

Psychology of the will to power.

pleasure unpleasure

---

[198] Reference to Faust's complaint: 'Two souls reside, alas, within my breast', Goethe, *Faust I*, 1112.

Pain is something different from pleasure – I mean to say, it is *not* its opposite. If the essence of pleasure has been accurately described as a feeling of *more power* (thus as a feeling of differentiation that presupposes comparison), this doesn't mean the essence of unpleasure has thus been defined. The false oppositions believed in by the common people and *consequently* by language have always been dangerous shackles for the course of truth. There are even cases where a kind of pleasure is conditioned by a certain *rhythmic succession* of small unpleasurable stimuli: this leads to a very rapid growth of the feeling of power, the feeling of pleasure. This is the case, e.g., in tickling, including the sexual tickling in the act of coitus: here we see unpleasure working as an ingredient in pleasure. It seems a little resistance is overcome and is immediately followed by another little resistance, which in turn is overcome – this play of resistance and victory most strongly stimulates that overall feeling of surplus, excessive power, that feeling which amounts to the essence of pleasure. – The reverse, an augmentation of the feeling of pain through little interpolated pleasurable stimuli, doesn't exist: pleasure and pain are, precisely, not the reverse of one another. – Pain is an intellectual process in which a judgement makes itself unmistakeably heard – the judgement 'harmful', into which long experience has accumulated. In itself there is no pain. It is *not* the wound that hurts; it is the experience of what grave consequences a wound can have for the organism as a whole that speaks in the shape of that deep agitation called unpleasure (in the case of harmful influences unknown to earlier men, e.g., from new combinations of toxic chemicals, pain bears no witness – and we are undone...). In pain, the really specific thing is always the long agitation, the after-trembling of a terrifying shock in the cerebral focus of the nervous system: one's suffering is *not* actually due to the cause of the pain (some injury, for example) but to the long-lasting upset of equilibrium proceeding from that shock. Pain is a sickness of the cerebral nerve centres – whereas pleasure is by no means a sickness...– That pain is the cause of counter-movements may be supported by appearances and even by the prejudice of philosophers; but in sudden cases, if one looks closely, the counter-movement manifestly arrives earlier than the feeling of pain. I'd be in a sorry plight if, having stumbled, I had to wait until the fact struck the bell of consciousness and a hint of what to do was telegraphed back... Instead, I distinguish as clearly as possible that the counter-movement of the foot happens first, to prevent a fall, and then, after a measurable passage of time, a kind of painful wave suddenly makes itself felt in the front of my head. One does *not*, thus, react to the pain. Pain is afterwards projected into the injured place – but the essence of this local pain is, nevertheless, not the expression of the type of local injury: it's merely a place-sign, appropriate to the injury in strength and tone, that the nerve centres have received from it. If the organism's muscular strength drops measurably as a consequence of the shock, this by no means indicates that the *essence* of pain should be sought in a lessening of the feeling of power... To repeat, one does *not* react to pain: unpleasure is not a 'cause' of actions, pain itself is a reaction, the counter-movement is another and *earlier* reaction – the two things originate in different places. –

14[174]

The will to power as *life*

Man does *not* seek pleasure and does *not* avoid unpleasure: it will be clear which famous prejudice I am contradicting here. Pleasure and unpleasure are mere consequences, mere accompanying phenomena – what man wants, what every smallest part of a living organism wants, is an increment of power. Striving for this gives rise to both pleasure and unpleasure; out of that will man seeks resistance, needs something to oppose him. Unpleasure, as an inhibition of his will to power, is thus a normal fact, the normal ingredient of everything that happens in the organic world, and man does not avoid it but instead has constant need of it: every conquest, every pleasurable feeling, everything that happens presupposes a resistance overcome.

Let us take the simplest case, that of primitive feeding: protoplasm stretches out pseudopodia to seek something that resists it – not out of hunger but out of a will to power. Then it tries to overcome what it has found, to appropriate it, incorporate it – what is called 'feeding' is merely a subsequent phenomenon, a practical application of that original will to become *stronger*

Hunger cannot be taken as the primum mobile,[199] nor can self-preservation: hunger, understood as a consequence of undernourishment, means hunger as a consequence of a will to power that is *no longer achieving mastery*

---

[199] See note to 9[102].

duality as a consequence of unity being too weak

it is by no means a matter of restoring something lost – only at a late stage, in the wake of the division of labour, after the will to power learns to take quite other paths to its satisfaction, is the organism's need to appropriate *reduced* to hunger, to the need to replace what has been lost.

Thus, unpleasure does not necessarily result in a *diminution of our feeling of power* – so little so that, in the average case, it actually stimulates this feeling of power: the resistance is the *stimulus* of this will to power.

Unpleasure has been confused with a particular kind of unpleasure, that of exhaustion, which does indeed represent a profound diminution and abatement of the will to power, a measurable loss of force. In other words: there is unpleasure as a stimulant to strengthen power, and unpleasure following a squandering of power; in the former case a stimulus, in the latter the result of overstimulation... An incapacity for resistance marks the latter type of unpleasure; the former is characterised by the challenge to what resists... The only pleasure still experienced in a state of exhaustion is falling asleep; the pleasure in the other case is conquest...

The psychologists' great confusion has lain in their failure to distinguish those two *types of pleasure*, that of *falling asleep* and that of *conquest*

the exhausted want rest, to stretch out their limbs, they want peace, quiet –

that is the *happiness* of the nihilistic religions and philosophies

the rich and vital want conquest, defeated opponents, want an overflowing of their feeling of power into wider domains than before:

all the healthy functions of the organism have this need – and the whole organism, until the age of puberty, is one such complex of systems struggling for the growth of feelings of power – – –

14[193]

In ancient criminal law a *religious* concept held sway: that of the expiatory force of punishment. Punishment cleansed: in the modern world it besmirches. Punishment is a paying off: one really rids oneself of what one *wanted* to suffer so much for. Supposing one believes in this power of punishment, then afterwards there's a feeling of *relief, breathing freely again*, that really approaches a new health, a restoration. Not only has one made one's peace with society, one has also become worthy of respect again in one's own eyes – 'cleansed'... Today punishment leads to isolation even more than crime does; the *fate* attached to a crime has grown so much that it has become irredeemable. One emerges from punishment as an *enemy* of society... From now on there's one enemy more...

The lex talionis[200] *may* be dictated by the spirit of retaliation (i.e., by a kind of moderation of the instinct for revenge); but in the case of *Manu*,[201] for example, it's the need to have an equivalent, so as to *expiate*, to be 'free' again in a religious sense

14[205]

One thing is least easily forgiven: respecting yourself. A being who does this is simply abominable: after all, he brings to light what's really involved in tolerance, the only virtue of the rest and of everyone...

I wish men would begin by *respecting* themselves: everything else follows from that. Certainly, with just *that* one is finished for the others: it's the last thing they can forgive. What? A man who respects himself?

This is something different from the blind drive to *love* oneself: nothing is more common, both in the love of the sexes and in that duality named 'I', than *contempt* for what one loves, fatalism in love –

14[219]

Weakness of the will: this is a metaphor which can be misleading. For there is no will, and hence neither a strong will nor a weak one. Multiplicity and disaggregation of the impulses, lack of system among them, results as 'weak will'; their coordination under the dominance of a single one results as 'strong will' – in the first case it is oscillation and the lack of a centre of gravity; in the second precision and clarity of direction

---

[200] The principle that the punishment for a crime should reflect literally the injuries or damage caused by the criminal.
[201] The legendary author of a Sanskrit legal code.

14[226]

what creates a morality or a law-book, the deep instinct for the fact that only *automatism* can enable perfection in living and creating…

But now we have reached the opposite point, indeed we have *wanted* to reach it – conscious to the most extreme degree, man and history seeing through themselves…

– in practical terms this makes us furthest from perfection in being, doing and willing: our desire, our will even to knowledge is a symptom of a tremendous décadence… We strive for the opposite of what is willed by *strong races, strong natures*

– understanding is an *ending*…

That science is possible in this sense, as it's practised today, proves that all life's elementary instincts, instincts of *self-defence* and *protection*, have ceased to function –

we are no longer accumulating, we are squandering the capital of our forebears, even in our way of *knowing* –

Notebook 15, spring 1888

15[8]

Progress

Let's not deceive ourselves! Time moves forwards – we would like to believe that everything in it moves forwards too... that development is a forwards development... This is the appearance that seduces even the most circumspect: yet the nineteenth century does not represent progress over the sixteenth, and the German spirit of 1888 represents regression from the German spirit of 1788... 'Mankind' does not advance – it doesn't even exist... The overall aspect is that of a tremendous experimental workshop where some things, scattered throughout the eras, work out and unutterably much goes wrong, where all order, logic, connection and binding force is absent... How could we fail to see that the rise of Christianity is a movement of décadence?... That the German Reformation is a recrudescence of Christian barbarism?... That the revolution destroyed the instinct for great organisation, the possibility of a society?... Man does not represent progress over the animal: the milksop of culture is a deformity compared with the Arab and the Corsican; the Chinese is a type that has turned out well, namely more lasting than the European...

15[51]

It is not the victory of science that distinguishes our nineteenth century, but the victory of scientific method over science

15[60]

If anything signifies our *humanisation*, a true and actual *progress*, then the fact that we no longer need any excessive oppositions, any oppositions at all...

we may love the senses, we have intellectualised them and made them artistic in every degree

we have a right to all the things that up to now have been most *vilified*

15[63]

Judging on the whole, in mankind today a tremendous quantum of *humaneness* has been achieved. That this is generally not felt to be so is itself a proof: we've become so sensitive to *small distresses* that we unfairly overlook what has been achieved.

: here one must make allowances for the fact that there is much décadence, and that viewed through such eyes, our world *is bound to look* bad and wretched. But those eyes have seen the same thing in every era...

1. a certain overstimulation even of moral feeling
2. the quantum of embitterment and darkening that pessimism brings with it into judgement

: together, these two have helped to its ascendancy the *opposite* notion: that our morality is *in a bad way*.

The fact of credit, of the whole of world trade, of the means of transport – in all this, a tremendous, mild *trust* in man finds expression...

Also contributing to it is
3. the separation of science from moral and religious intentions: a very good sign which, however, is mostly misunderstood.

In my way, I attempt a justification of history

15[70]

We somewhat mistrust all those enraptured and extreme states in which one fancies one 'grasps the truth in one's hands' –

15[73]

Man imprisoned in an iron cage of errors, become a caricature of man, sick, stunted, malevolent towards himself, full of hatred for the impulses of life, full of mistrust for everything in life that's beautiful and happy, a walking misery: that artificial, arbitrary, *belated* abortion the priests have drawn out of their soil, the 'sinner': how will we manage, despite it all, to *justify* this phenomenon?

15[74]

The only means of refuting priests and religions is always this: showing that their errors have ceased to be *beneficial* – that they rather do harm; in short, that their own 'proof of their force' no longer holds...

15[79]

NB. NB. *The values of the weak* have the upper hand because the strong have taken them over to *lead* with them...

15[90]

The phenomenalism of the 'inner world'

chronological inversion, so that the cause enters consciousness later than the effect.

we have learnt that pain is projected to a part of the body without having its seat there

we have learnt that the sense impression naively posited as conditioned by the outer world is actually conditioned by the inner world: that every real action of the outer world always takes its course unconsciously... The bit of outer world we become conscious of is born only after the effect exerted on us from outside, and is retrospectively projected as its 'cause'...

In the phenomenalism of the 'inner world' we invert the chronology of cause and effect.

The fundamental fact of 'inner experience' is that the cause is imagined after the effect has taken place...

The same applies to the succession of thoughts... we look for the reason for a thought before we've even become conscious of it: and then first the reason, then its consequence, enters our consciousness...

The whole of our dreaming is the interpretation of total feelings with a view to possible causes, and in such a way that we only become conscious of a state when the chain of causality we've invented for it has entered our consciousness...

the whole of 'inner experience' rests on a cause being sought and imagined for a stimulation of the nerve centres – and that it's only the cause we've found which enters our *consciousness*: this cause is simply not adequate to the real cause – it is a feeling one's way on the basis of previous 'inner experiences' – i.e., on the basis of memory. Memory, however, also preserves the habits of the old interpretation, i.e., its erroneous causalities... so that the 'inner experience' has to carry within it the consequences of all previous, false fictions of causality

our 'outer world', as we project it at every moment, is suffused and indissolubly bound up with the old error of the underlying reason: we interpret the outer world with the schematism of the 'thing'

just as an individual case of pain doesn't represent merely the individual case but, instead, long experience about the consequences of certain injuries, including errors in the appraisal of these consequences

The 'inner experience' only enters our consciousness after it's found a language that the individual *understands*... i.e., a translation of a state into states *more familiar* to the individual –

in naive terms, 'understanding' just means: being able to express something new in the language of something old, familiar

e.g., 'I am unwell' – a judgement like this presupposes a *great and late-attained neutrality on the part of the observer*: the naive man always says 'This or that makes me unwell' – his being unwell only becomes clear to him once he sees a reason for being unwell...

This I call the *lack of philology*: being able to read off a text as text, without mixing in an interpretation, is the last-attained form of 'inner experience' – perhaps one that's barely possible...

15[91]

The causes of error lie just as much in the *good will* of man as in his ill will: in a thousand cases he hides reality from himself, he falsifies it so as not to suffer in his good will

E.g., God as the one who guides man's destiny: or the interpretation of his little fate as if everything had been sent and contrived with a view to the salvation of the soul – this lack of 'philology', which a subtler mind is bound to consider sloppiness and counterfeiting, is on average inspired by *good will* . . .

As far as their means are concerned, good will, 'noble feelings', 'exalted states' are just as much counterfeiters and swindlers as the affects that are morally repudiated and called egoistic, like love, hatred, revenge.

* * *

Errors are what mankind has to pay for most dearly: and, judged on the whole, it's the errors of 'good will' which have harmed mankind most deeply. The delusion that brings happiness is more pernicious than the one with immediate ill-consequences: the latter makes one sharper, suspicious, cleanses reason – the former lulls it to sleep . . .

in physiological terms, beautiful feelings, 'sublime agitations', are among the narcotic substances: their abuse has quite the same result as the abuse of another opium – *neurasthenia* . . .

15[117]

On the asceticism of the strong

The task of this asceticism, which is only a transitional training and not a goal: to free oneself from the old emotional impulses of traditional values. To learn, step by step, how to follow one's path to the 'beyond good and evil'.

First stage: to endure atrocities
                    to commit atrocities

Second, *more difficult*, stage: to endure basenesses
                    to commit basenesses: including, as a
                    preliminary exercise: to become
                    ludicrous, make oneself ludicrous.

– To provoke contempt and nevertheless sustain distance by means of an (*unfathomable*) smile from above

– to take upon oneself a number of degrading crimes, e.g., stealing money, so as to test one's sense of balance

– for a while not to do, speak, strive for anything that doesn't arouse fear or contempt, that doesn't force the decent and virtuous into war – that doesn't *shut* one *out* . . .

to represent the opposite of what one is (better still, not the exact opposite but simply something different: this is more difficult)

– to walk every tightrope, to dance on every possibility: to get one's genius into one's *feet*

– for stretches of time, to deny – even slander – one's ends with one's means

– once and for all to represent a character which hides the fact that one has five or six others

– not to be afraid of the five bad things: cowardice, ill repute, vice, lying, woman –

Notebook 16, spring – summer 1888

16[12]

Life itself is not a means to something; it is merely a growth-form of power.

16[16]

We few or many who dare to live again in a world *emptied of morality*, we who are pagan by belief: we are probably also the first to understand what a pagan belief is: having to imagine *higher beings* than man, but these as beyond good and evil; having to appraise all being-higher as also being-immoral. We believe in Olympus – and *not* in the 'Crucified One'...

16[29]

In music we lack an aesthetics capable of imposing laws on the musicians and which would create a conscience; as a consequence, we lack a real struggle over 'principles' – for as musicians we laugh at Herbart's[202] caprices in this domain as much as at Schopenhauer's. In fact a great difficulty arises from this: we no longer know how to *justify* the concepts 'model', 'mastery', 'perfection' – we grope blindly around the realm of values with the instinct of old love and admiration, we almost believe that 'what's good is what pleases *us*'... It arouses my suspicion when Beethoven is everywhere quite innocently called a 'classic': I would strictly

[202] Johann Friedrich Herbart (1776–1841), German philosopher of education.

274

maintain the point that in the other arts it's the opposite of Beethoven's type which is regarded as the classic. But when Wagner's complete and immediately striking dissolution of style, his so-called dramatic style, is taught and revered as 'exemplary', 'mastery', 'progress', my impatience reaches its peak. The dramatic style in music, as Wagner understands it, is the renunciation of style in general on the assumption that something else is a hundred times more important than music, namely drama. Wagner can paint, he uses music for something other than music, he intensifies poses, he is a poet; finally, he has appealed to 'beautiful feelings' and 'heaving bosoms' like all artists of the theatre – with all this he won over women and even those in need of education: but what does music concern women and those in need of education! That type has no conscience for art; they don't suffer when all the prime and most indispensable virtues of an art are trampled underfoot and made ridiculous for the benefit of peripheral objectives, as an ancilla dramaturgica.[203] – What's the point of expanding the means of expression if what expresses, art itself, has lost the law to rule itself? The painterly magnificence and power of tone, the symbolism of sound, rhythm, colours of harmony and disharmony, the suggestive significance of music in respect to other arts, the whole *sensuality* of music that Wagner brought to domination – Wagner recognised all this in music, drew it out, developed it. Victor Hugo did something similar for language: but in Hugo's case the French are already asking whether it was not to language's debasement... whether increasing the sensuality of language did not depress the reason, intellectuality, profound lawfulness of language? That the writers in France have become sculptors, the musicians in Germany actors and cultural daubers – are these not signs of *décadence*?

With the help of music Wagner does all sorts of things which are not music: he suggests swellings, virtues, passions.

For him, music is a means

Has it not lost all the more intellectual beauty, the high, exuberant perfection which in its daring still embraces grace, the enchanting leap and dance of logic, the – – –

203 Handmaiden of drama.

Notebook 18, July – August 1888

18[11]

Sickness is a powerful stimulant – but one has to be healthy enough for it.

Index of names

Index of subjects

Cambridge texts in the history of philosophy

Titles published in the series thus far